Beneath the Dust of Time

*A History
of the Names of
Peoples and Places*

Jacques R. Pauwels

2010

London (UK) & Colombo (Sri Lanka)
www.battlebridge.com
info@battlebridge.com

Copyright

Jacques R. Pauwels 2009
<jackpauwels@yahoo.ca>

Cataloguing data

Title: Beneath the Dust of Time
Subtitle: A History of the Names of Peoples and Places
Author: Jacques R. Pauwels
Includes bibliography, index, and more than 100 illustrations

ISBN(10)   1453766081
ISBN(13) 9781453766088

1. History
2. Names: Ethnonyms, Toponyms

Cover design

Philip Baker & Jeehoon Kim

Cover picture

The Tower of Babel, by Pieter Bruegel the Elder, 1563.
This picture is currently in the Kunsthistorisches Museum, Vienna
(source: Wikimedia Commons).

CONTENTS

Foreword: Before the coming of the Indo-Europeans   1

1. Neolithic and early civilizations
    From the Sahara to Sumer   15
    When Egypt was known as Kemit   20
    Berbers from Libya to Iberia   25
    Semites, Hittites, and Aryans   30
    Into, and out of, India   40

2. Phoenicians in the land of rabbits
    Between Mesopotamia and Egypt   47
    The Minerals of Hispania   49
    Hercules visits Tartessos   53
    A Phoenician base in the dusty land   59

3. Between Ashiwa and Atlas: the *Oikoumene* of the Greeks
    Land of the Rising Sun, Land of the Setting Sun   65
    The Golden Fleece and the Apples of the Hesperides   75
    Etruscans and other Pelasgians   81
    Magna Graecia   91
    Hellas or Greece?   95

4. The *Imperium Romanum* and its Neighbors
    How Italy became Roman   103
    Transalpine Gaul   106
    The Far Side of the Rhine   115
    Primeval Hydronyms   119
    Land surrounded by water   125
    The End of the World   128
    Margins of Empire   134

5. Barbarian invasions and Dark Ages
    Huns and other Vandals   139
    Deutsch versus Welsch   146
    Magyars and Slavs   149

6. In the name of Allah
The Desert between Petra and Arabia Felix 153
An Arab Far West 158
In the footsteps of Alexander the Great 167
The mountains, deserts, and oases of Central Asia 171
Beyond the World of Islam: China and its neighbors 174

7. The saga of the Vikings:
The Emigrants 181
Distant Vinland 185
In the land of the Rus 186
Varangians in the Imperial City 190
Between Baghdad and Baltic 194

Conclusion: Archaic Usko-Mediterranean and Indo-European names 197

Bibliography 207

Index 213

FOREWORD

Before the coming of the Indo-Europeans

It is rather well known that America does not bear the name of the alleged discoverer of the New World, Christopher Columbus, but of another Italian explorer, Amerigo Vespucci. However, only relatively few people appear to know the origin and meaning of the name of their own country. The Germans, for example, call their fatherland *Deutschland*, but very few of them know what *deutsch* means. Somewhat more understandably, they also have no clue why the British and Americans call their country "Germany", or why the French call it *l'Allemagne*. Speaking of France, how many Parisians would be able to tell us why, about 1,500 years ago, their country exchanged its fine original name, Gaul, for the admittedly equally concise and elegant "France"? And how many proud Spaniards are aware that the name of their country means 'land of rabbits', and that this name was concocted almost 3,000 years ago by the Phoenicians, a people from the opposite end of the Mediterranean, an area now known as the Middle East? Probably only a handful. Finally, what percentage of Greeks would be able to tell us why we call them "Greeks" while they refer to themselves as "Hellenes"?

Why are most people so poorly informed about the meaning and origin of the names of their own countries and, less surprisingly, of the names of other countries and peoples? One of the most important reasons is that in their history lessons our primary and secondary schoolchildren are bombarded with the names of kings and presidents, generals and popes, but hardly ever hear their teachers say anything about the name of the supposedly beloved father- or motherland. At our universities, the situation is hardly better, as the professors of these institutions typically find it below their dignity to deal with such banalities. Beyond the walls of our schools and universities, the situation is no better. Even in the most voluminous works about the history of a people or the geography of a country, this theme is almost always ignored. Take, for example, *L'identité de la France,* a brilliant work by Fernand Braudel (1986), the most celebrated French historian of the twentieth century: three volumes and more than a thousand pages about this "Great Nation", but not a single word about the origins of its name. As for those who travel abroad and would like to know where the name of the country they visit originated and what it means, they will find the answer only very rarely in the Fodors, Frommers, or other tourist guides. Local tour guides all too often reveal themselves to be equally reticent on this subject; even those who are able to tell a thousand-and-one anecdotes about the history and geography of their country tend to dismiss questions about this topic with the pseudo-answer: "It is merely a name".

What follows is an attempt to fill this void. This book investigates the names of peoples (ethnonyms), countries, regions, and cities (toponyms), mountains (oronyms), and even seas, lakes, and rivers (hydronyms). Linguists call this kind of work etymology, the study (*logos* in Greek) of the meaning (*etymos*) of words; when dealing with the etymology of proper names, they speak of onomastics, a term that contains the Greek word *onoma*, "name"; in the case of the etymology of place names, the conventional term is toponomastics.

The names of countries and peoples did not fall out of the sky; they have their origins in words that have meaning. Any attempt to discover this meaning involves etymology, but while a generous dose of etymology and (top)onomastics is woven into this study, it is important to point out that it was not written by an expert in linguistics, nor is it intended as an exercise in etymological research, but rather as a *history*. Countries and peoples were not given their names by gods or mythical heroes, as the ancient Greeks believed. The peoples of the world have given names to themselves, to their countries, to other peoples and countries, and to striking features of their environment such as mountains and rivers. The names that are the subject of this book made their appearance at a given time in the epic of humanity. They emerged over the course of important historical developments such as the original settlement of land, migrations, political and social conflicts, wars and revolutions, and discoveries and colonizations. Inquiring about the name of a country or a people involves not only finding out the meaning of the name, i.e., its etymology, but also investigating the historical circumstances of its emergence and therefore the history of the country and the people involved. The latter constitutes the real focus of this book, which is therefore a historical study, albeit one larded with a generous dose of etymology and (top)onomastics.

Many countries, peoples, mountain ranges, and rivers of Africa, Asia, and Europe received their names thousands of years ago. This book concentrates on the so-called "Old World", and on the distant past in which these names originated. We start with a gigantic leap backward into the Stone Age, usually ignored by historians because it is considered "prehistory", a mere prelude to "real" history.[1] We are not so much interested in the Paleolithic, those tens of thousands of years when humans were hunters and gatherers, but rather in the Neolithic, the last (and relatively short) stage of the Stone Age, when a new, sedentary lifestyle emerged, based on agriculture and animal husbandry. We are also interested in the Bronze Age and in the very first

---

[1] The reason usually given for neglecting the history of an era that covered approximately 99% of the history of mankind is that no written sources are available for it; for a comment on the untenability of this argument, see Whitelam (1997: 65-66).

great civilizations, namely those of Mesopotamia and Ancient Egypt. (After all, do we not all want to know the meaning of the hydronym "Nile" and the reason why we speak of "Egypt", when the name of the Pharaohs' empire was actually "Kemit"?). Then we cross the Mediterranean Sea and arrive in "Classical" Antiquity, where we meet not only the familiar darlings of the historians of that era, the "Aryan" Greeks and Romans, but also all sorts of non-Indo-Europeans such as the Etruscans, Iberians, and Illyrians; we will learn that many ethnonyms and toponyms have been assumed all-too-readily to be of Greco-Roman origin.

The implosion of the Western Roman Empire was the starting point of five centuries that are usually denigrated by our history textbooks as the "Dark Ages". However, for our purposes even that era proves to be extremely important. Indeed, it was then that the map of the Old World was redrawn from top to bottom on account of massive migrations by barbarian peoples, and that new names were distributed with great generosity by the Franks and other Germanic tribes, as well as Arabs, Vikings, and Magyars.

Our story finishes in the year 1000 CE. The legendary Silk Road between Baghdad, the brilliant city of the Abbasid Caliphs, and Changan (now Xian), the great metropolis of China, functioned at that time as the axis between the two poles of the Old World. The inhabitants of comparatively primitive Europe, also known as Christendom, meanwhile, cowered in fear that the end of the world was near. However, it was precisely there that an economic development was getting underway which in the not-so-very-long run would radically alter power relations within the Old World, and even make it possible for Europe to dominate the entire *orbis terrarum* and to rename peoples and countries accordingly. But that is a story that will be dealt with later, in a sequel to this study.

Along the Silk Road
(Location and source not identified)

This book differs in a number of important ways from the conventional treatments of Prehistory, Antiquity, and the early Middle Ages. First, as already mentioned, its *leitmotif* is the origin and meaning of the names of countries and peoples, a theme to which mainstream historiography hardly ever pays any attention. Second, this study is informed by a recent, bold, even revolutionary new theory that views the "deep history" of the Old World through an entirely new lens. This theory is the "Sahara Hypothesis", outlined briefly in books such as Brian Griffith's *The Gardens of Their Dreams* (2001), but developed mainly in the impressive opus of two Spanish scholars, the geneticist Antonio Arnáiz-Villena and the historian Jorge Alonso. According to the Sahara Hypothesis, one of the first Neolithic cultures emerged in the center of North Africa more-or-less ten thousand years ago, i.e. during the era known as the "Neolithic Subpluvial" or "Wet Phase" of the Holocene, the geological epoch that began approximately 8000 BCE. This part of the world was not yet a desert but a relatively fertile region, crisscrossed by rivers and dotted with lakes big and small – and inhabited not only by all sorts of animals but also by humans. The local population grew and reportedly made the transition from hunters, fishers, and gatherers to nomadic cattle herders, though apparently not to sedentary cereal farmers, since the savannah-like environment "still provided sufficient wild-growing grains, fruits, and tubers". In spite of this difference with the traditional model of Neolithization, that of the Middle East, which did of course involve cereal farming, the transition from the Paleolithic way of life to "a productive economy" in what is now the Sahara, based on the world's first domestication of cattle, amounted to a kind of "Neolithic revolution" (Kuper & Kröpelin 2006: 806).[2]

Rupestrian representation of a bull in the Libyan desert
(Photo: J Pauwels, 2004)

---

[2] See also Nantet (1998 89, 92-93, 96-97). Guilaine (2000: 256-57) acknowledges the merits of "the hypothesis of a Saharan agriculture in the early Holocene", i.e., during the 8th millennium BCE. On the Neolithic Subpluvial, see: *http://en.wikipedia.org/wiki/Neolithic_Subpluvial*. In Briggs (2006: 2), Rudolph Kuper decribes the "change of lifestyle from the life of hunters and gatherers to that of cattle herders" as "an important step in the history of mankind, which was taken for the first time in the African Sahara".

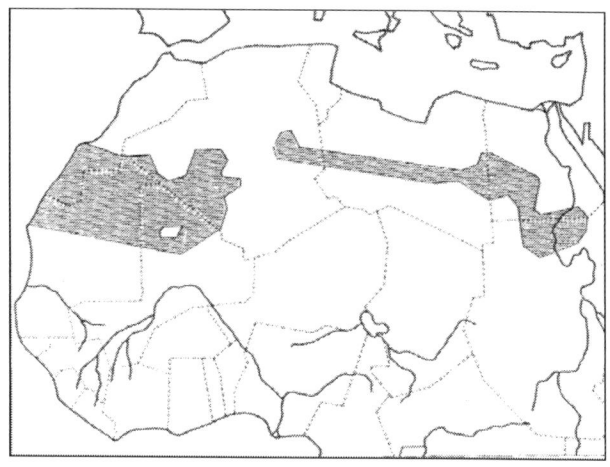

Deserts in North Africa, 6.000 - 5,000 BCE
(Source: Unesco 1986: 11)

The desertification of the Sahara began with the end of the last Ice Age, took thousands of years, and forced the "Saharans" to emigrate in all directions. Some of their descendants eventually reached the river valleys of Mesopotamia, Egypt, and India, where they developed the first great civilizations, while others migrated to the valleys of the distant Caucasus, and to islands of the Mediterranean Sea such as Crete where, after their arrival, the Minoan civilization blossomed. Fleeing their increasingly hot, arid North African homeland, successive waves of Saharans also headed for Europe. They appear to have taken a direct route, via the Strait of Gibraltar and the islands of the Mediterranean, in addition to a detour via the Middle East and the Balkan Peninsula. In Europe, the northward retreat of the glaciers happened to be making that continent's formerly frozen reaches available for human settlement, it made possible what has been called the "postglacial recolonization of Europe".[3] Thus there occurred a crucial event of human history, or rather prehistory, namely, the very first large-scale "colonization" of Europe. Previously Europe north of the Pyrenees had been inhabited mainly by Neanderthals – definitely no ancestors of ours![4] – and by relatively small numbers of *homo sapiens* such as the Cro-Magnons and Magdalenians; the cave paintings at Lascaux in France and Altamira in Spain bear artistic witness to this early human presence in Europe, or at least in certain "refugia" in southern Europe. Thus already thousands of years BCE, people of Saharan origin, that is, people of the same ethnic background and speaking varieties of essentially the same language, settled in Europe as far north as Finland, and also in the British Isles.[5]

---

[3] Terminology used in *http://dienekes.blogspot.com/search/label/Basques*
[4] See S Wells (2002: 125).
[5] Already in 1919, H G Wells, a distinguished historian of his times although remembered today mainly for his science fiction works such as *The War of the Worlds,* anticipated this part of the Sahara Hypothesis. In his book *The Outline of History*, he described "[a] darkish, fine-featured people …, the first comers of a race, the Mediterranean, dark-white or Iberian race, which is still the prevailing race in southern Europe…whose communities extended northward…some

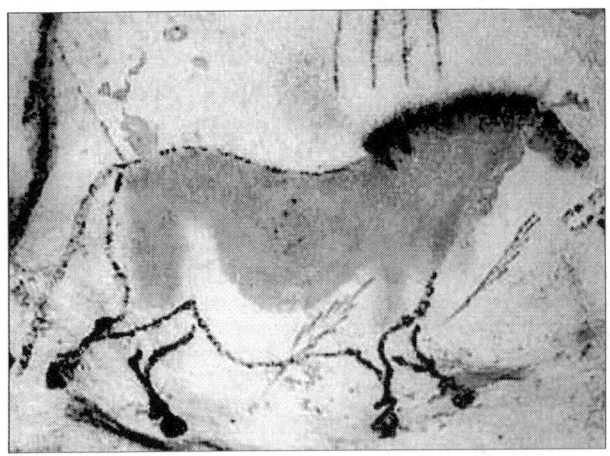

Image of a horse, painted in the Lascaux caves ca. 16,000 years ago
(Source: Wikimedia Commons)

The Saharan migrants probably made a contribution, and perhaps an important one, to the introduction into Europe of agriculture and animal husbandry. (That phenomenon is traditionally attributed exclusively to a slow "diffusion" – far from uniform, and either purely cultural or "demic", i.e. involving migrations - from a cradle in the Middle East, but it remains the subject of much controversy among archaeologists, geneticists, linguists etc., with the demic model recently losing ground.[6]) The Saharan settlers were very likely the builders of the famous menhirs, dolmens, and similar megalithic monuments that can still be admired on the island of Malta, at Stonehenge in England,[7] and in the village of Carnac in Brittany. Last, but not least, they gave names to the regions they settled and to the mountains and rivers they found there.[8] Of these names, surprisingly many have survived in some form or another until the present time, for example "Iberia", "Alps", and "Rhine".

The great megalithic monument of Stonehenge, probably created by Saharan settlers
(Photo by Matthew Brennan, 2007; source Wikimedia Commons)

10,000 or 12,000 years ago", adding that "hitherto men in Europe had never gone farther north than the Baltic Sea or the British Isles, but now the Scandinavian Peninsula and perhaps Great Russia were becoming possible regions for human occupation" (H G Wells 1919: 83-86).

[6] See e.g. Jobling, Hurles, & Tyler-Smith (2004: 309-24); also S Wells (2002: 152ff).

[7] This monument rises to a height of almost five metres above the ground, equivalent to the height of three adults of average size.

[8] See e.g. Vennemann (2003: 517ff).

The Saharans and their descendants were not Indo-Europeans. They spoke a language termed "Usko-Mediterranean" by Arnáiz-Villena & Alonso (2000), and "Old-Mediterranean" or "Old-European" by others.[9] However, instead of speaking of an Usko-Mediterranean language in the singular, it is of course more appropriate to use the plural, because the successive waves of Saharan migrants departed in many different directions and were therefore predestined to develop an increasing linguistic and cultural diversity over the centuries. (They also developed a remarkable physiological diversity; their adjustment to the local climate led – obviously only in the long run – to a lighter skin color in northern regions and a darker skin color in southern, warmer areas, as the well-known American anthropologist Marvin Harris has pointed out in some of his fascinating studies.[10])

Migrants whose ancestors had been forced to leave their homeland in what is now the Sahara not only settled in the Middle East and colonized all of Europe, but also penetrated into the depths of Asia, into Siberia and China, and even reached the Americas via the Bering land bridge. This particular part of the Sahara Hypothesis is not only supported by genetic evidence (S Wells 2003: 137-43), but also by a kind of linguistics trail of that historic migration. Basque and a number of Caucasian tongues – Usko-Mediterranean languages from our point of view – have been classified, together with Chinese and the languages of certain Amerindian nations such as the Apaches and the Navajos, as members of one large family of languages, called Dené-Caucasian or Dené-Sino-Caucasian, which is said to have dispersed some 11,000 years ago (Ruhlen 1994: 74; Bengtson 1994: 207).[11]

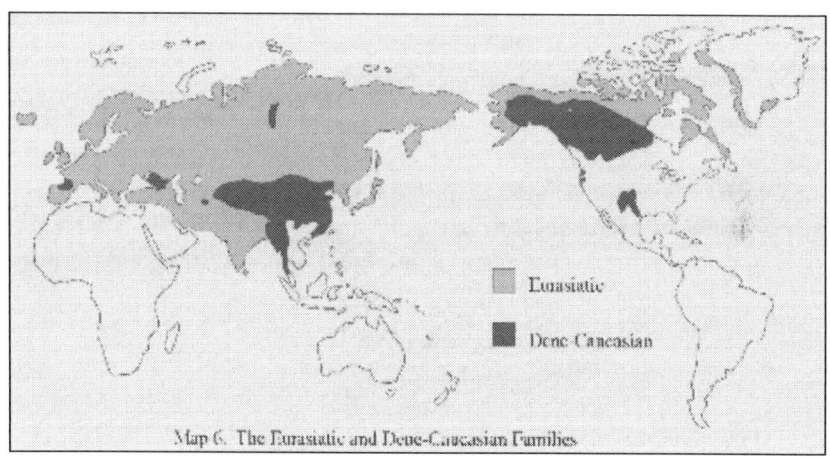

Map 6. The Eurasiatic and Dene-Caucasian Families

(Reproduced by courtesy of Merritt Ruhlen)

---

[9] None of these names is really satisfactory, since that language, or at least offshoots of it, would proliferate to regions far removed from the Mediterranean and from Europe, as we shall soon see.

[10] See also Jobling, Hurles, & Tyler-Smith (2004: 407-14), about "adaptation to climate: The evolutionary genetics of pigmentation".

[11] The theory of the Dené-Caucasian language family was developed in the 1980s by linguists such as Sergei Starostin and Sergei L Nikolayev in Russia and John Bengtson and Merritt Ruhlen in the USA.

The Dené-Caucasian proposal, like similar proposals in the past, has failed to win much support due to the alleged inadequacy of linguistic evidence. However, in defense of such theories, it might be argued that, in seeking to establish historical links between languages which separated thousands of years ago, it is unreasonable to expect to find etymological evidence of the same quality as can be found for languages which separated only a few hundred years ago. In any event, onomastics appears to provide a modest measure of support for the Dené-(Sino)-Caucasian theory, for we will see that even in far eastern Asia and in the Americas, toponyms and ethnonyms such as Siberia, Han, Ainu, and Dené itself appear to be of Usko-Mediterranean origin.

In the course of the second millennium BCE, a counter-migration ensued. From their hypothetical *Urheimat* somewhere in the north or the east – Russia, according to some, Anatolia according to others – Indo-European peoples or, to put it more accurately, speakers of Indo-European languages, appeared on the scene in the Middle East and in Europe, for example the Persians and the ancestors of the Greeks and the Romans. However, it is unclear whether this involved gargantuan "waves" of armed conquerors or a gradual, quantitatively modest, and peaceful "infiltration" (Finley 2002: 7). Primarily in Europe, but also in parts of the Middle East, these migrants submerged the Usko-Mediterranean linguistic "substrate", described in the Greek contexts as "Pelasgian". The allegedly warlike Indo-Europeans proceeded to dominate the Usko-Mediterraneans, foist their language and religion onto them, and assimilate them. However, insofar as the coming of the Indo-Europeans may have amounted to no more than a series of so-called "elite invasions" – invasions by small groups of warriors – it might be more accurate to say that the newcomers were gradually absorbed - or "phagocytized" - by the indigenous population, as would also be the case with the Franks who invaded Gaul at the time of the fall of the Roman Empire. (This is the kind of scenario that is suggested by the results of genetic tests that reveal, for example, that the great majority of the inhabitants of Turkey are descendants of the original Anatolian population and not of the Turkic conquerors who invaded this part of the Middle East from Central Asia during the Middle Ages.) Here and there, furthermore, peoples, languages, and civilizations appear to have emerged in this historical context as a result of a kind of "fusion of ethnic and cultural identities", to use the words of the French-Greek historian Maria Daraki (1994:190), involving Indo-Europeans and the Usko-Mediterranean substrate. As an example one may cite the Celts, a mysterious and highly romanticized people whose arrival in Europe has never been convincingly dated, and whose language, while Indo-European in some ways, also reflects a strong Usko-Mediterranean influence, as we shall see. The peoples and languages we refer to as Semitic are probably the result of a similar fusion, but in the context of the Middle East. And even the Ancient Greeks cannot be said to have been a "pure" Indo-European race, but were rather a fusion of Indo-European elements and the Usko-Mediterranean or Pelasgian substrate. The historian M I Finley, for example, describes "the historical people we call the Greeks" as the "end-product" of a kind of "biological fusion" (2002: 7-8); and in

Antiquity certain Hellenic cities and regions – for example Athens and Arcadia – had a reputation of being more "Pelasgian" than others.

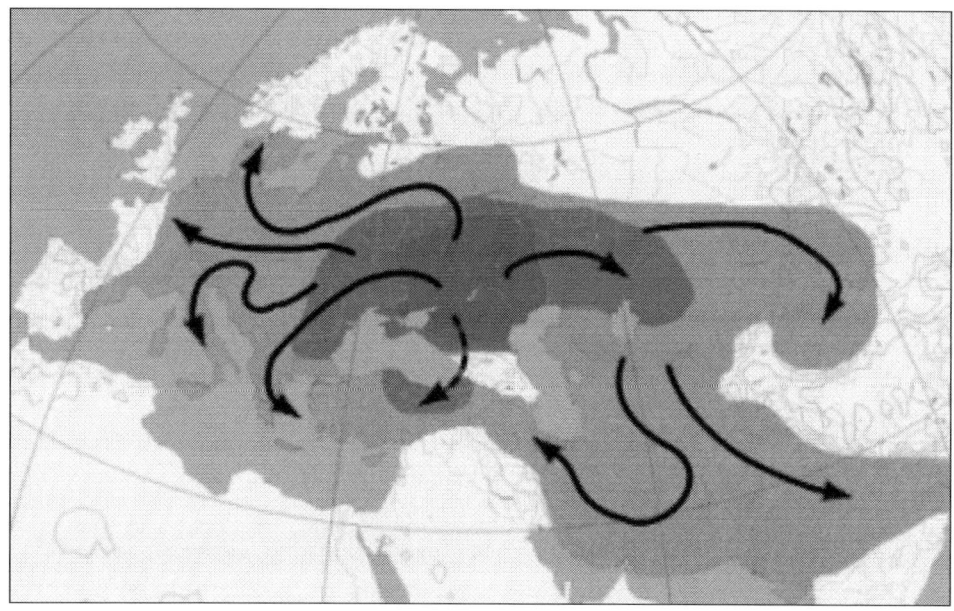

Indo-European expansion, 4000 - 1000 BCE, according to the Kurgan hypothesis
(Dbachmann, 2005; source: Wikimedia Commons)

In any case, in their religions and cultures, the Indo-European newcomers unquestionably integrated countless Usko-Mediterranean elements, for example the cult of fertility goddesses. Similarly, at least in their vocabularies and possibly also in their syntax and grammar, the Indo-European languages inherited a great deal from the older Usko-Mediterranean tongues. According to the authors of a new etymological dictionary of the Dutch language, for example, this close Germanic relative of English contains countless words that have their origin in the pre-Indo-European "substrate languages" (Philippa, Debrabandere, & Quak 2003, 2005). Such words include *appel* (apple), *haring* (herring), and *dief* (thief). Without exception, moreover, the Indo-European languages took over existing names of lands and peoples, mountains, seas, lakes and rivers, that is, names that had been given by the speakers of Usko-Mediterranean languages hundreds or even thousands of years before the coming of the Indo-Europeans. The onomastic legacy of Europe's Saharan settlers has thus been preserved until the present day. Moreover, we have ways to unveil its secrets.

As already mentioned, faced with the arrival of the Indo-Europeans, the Usko-Mediterranean element avoided total obliteration by contributing to new, hybrid cultures, of which that of the Celts may have been an example. In addition, in certain regions it survived more or less intact, for example in the case of the Basques and of some Caucasian peoples such as the Chechens. The Usko-Mediterranean language of the Basques consequently forms a kind of Rosetta Stone that helps us not only to translate ancient texts in dead Usko-Mediterranean languages such as Etruscan, but also – and this is of course crucial for our purposes – to find out the meaning of ancient Usko-Mediterranean ethno-, topo-, hydro-, and oronyms such as "Alps".[12] (It is worth mentioning here that the Basque language is called *euskara* by the Basques themselves, whose autethnonym is *Euzkadi,* meaning 'real'or 'pure' people; this name has inspired the "usko" in the term Usko-Mediterranean.) Finally, a huge tract of the Old World was simply never affected by Indo-European invasions large or small, namely, North Africa, including Egypt, and most of the Middle East. The living as well as the dead "Hamitic" and "Semitic" languages of that part of the world may therefore be said to be of Usko-Mediterranean origin. The Semitic tongues, however, probably also reflect the influence of languages spoken by the people who already inhabited the Middle East – the major corridor for migrations from the African homeland of *homo sapiens,* and occupied by representatives of that "modern" species of hominids around 45,000 years ago[13] – when the Saharans first arrived there. Until not so long ago, linguists used to differentiate neatly between Semitic languages such as Hebrew and Arabic, and Hamitic ones such as Ancient Egyptian and the language of the North African Berbers, but today they are all classified as members of the "Afro-Asiatic" family on account of their great similarities. These similarities are due to their common Usko-Mediterranean origin. Like Basque, then, living as well as dead Afro-Asiatic languages are eminently useful for the interpretation of ancient toponyms and ethnonyms. In this respect, impressive pioneering work has been performed by the recently deceased Nestor of (palaeo-) linguistics in Italy, Giovanni Semerano, long-time director of the National Library in Florence. In his remarkable studies, and primarily in his monumental two-volume *Le origini della cultura Europea* (1984, 1994), Semerano demonstrated that many ethno-, topo-, and hydronyms, not only in Greece and Italy but throughout Europe, may be interpreted with the help of Sumerian, Akkadian, Hebrew, and other ancient eastern languages. Although Semerano will be cited rather frequently in this study, it should be pointed out that he did not subscribe to the Sahara Hypothesis and may not even have been aware of its existence. While this hypothesis explains the linguistic similarities in the vast region between Europe and India in terms of a common North African, "Saharan" origin, Semerano was of the opinion that everything started with the very first civilizations in Mesopotamia, whose Semitic language and culture subsequently permeated not only in Asia, and notably in the subcontinent, but also into the depths of distant Europe. In addition, Semerano rejects in its entirety the conventional theory which holds that Indo-European peoples migrated from their hypothetical homeland to Europe, the Middle East, and India during the course of the second millennium BCE or at any other time. His verdict in this respect is merciless: "Indo-European, a linguistic entity with an absurd name, does not exist, and never existed" (2005: 84).[14] Semerano is of the opinion that in many ways, and certainly

---

[12] S Wells (2002: 190) refers to Basque as "the only remaining link back to the pre-Indo-European languages of Europe".
[13] See S Wells (2002: 98-99, 108-10).
[14] Here and throughout this book, quotations given in English from publications in other languages are my own translations.

with respect to their languages, the Europeans – and also the allegedly Indo-European Iranians and Indians – may be classified as "Semites" (2005: 84). One does not have to agree with this radical view in order to find Semerano's insights fascinating and extremely useful for the purpose of onomastic research. (However, Semerano is by no means the only scholar to reject the basic tenets of "Indo-Europeanism".[15])

Not everyone will find the charms of the Sahara Hypothesis irresistible, and there are scientific reasons for this. We are dealing with a hypothesis, a theoretical lens through which we are invited to re-examine the history of Antiquity. Research inspired by this hypothesis has started only recently, so it is much too early to know if the results will confirm the validity of the new theory. In the meantime, many scientists prefer to remain loyal to the conventional paradigm, and from a purely scientific viewpoint this is perfectly justifiable. However, there are also non-scientific reasons for rejecting the Sahara Hypothesis,[16] and it is worthwhile briefly examining those reasons. In the so-called "Western" world, historians, linguists, and other scholars already convinced themselves in the nineteenth century that the history of Europe boils down to the heroic epic of the Indo-Europeans, or "Aryans", as they used to say before that term lost favor on account of its association with Nazism. It is generally recognized that the very first civilizations originated far from Europe, namely in Mesopotamia, in the Nile Valley, and in India, and sometimes it is openly acknowledged that the bearers of these cultures were Semites or – as in the case of Egypt and India – dark-skinned people. But while it is freely admitted that the light dawned somewhere in the east, it is nevertheless the white, Indo-European Greeks who were, and continue to be, celebrated as the great heroes of Antiquity. With the Greeks, the focal point of world history shifted westward to the presumably correct locus, namely to Europe – in reality a little peninsula to the extreme west of the Asian land mass that claims to be a continent in its own right. In addition, we are asked to believe that those gifted Hellenes had learned little or nothing from their Semitic and other non-Indo-European neighbors in Asia and Africa: the so-called "Greek Miracle", to use a fitting metaphor, was supposedly born like the Greek goddess of wisdom, Athena, who emerged in complete adulthood from the brow of Zeus. Thus began the glorious history of "Western" culture, a culture that differs diametrically from – and is of course superior to – the cultures whose bearers were Semites or some other non-Indo-Europeans.

It is evident that we are dealing here with a "constructed history", whose prime function is to legitimate the present hierarchical world order, an order in which the "Western" First World dominates and exploits the rest of the world, the "Third World". The "West's" privileged place in the world hierarchy can thus be ascribed to the genius of its Indo-European inhabitants, a genius that supposedly first revealed itself with the arrival on the stage of history of the Hellenes. Conversely, this kind of

---

[15] See e.g. Danino (2006: 53-75).
[16] In his classic study, *The Structure of Scientific Revolutions*, Thomas Kuhn (1962) has demonstrated that the reasons for the acceptance or rejection of a new theory are frequently of a non-scientific nature.

view of history also suggests that the poverty of the Third World is not due to its conquest and exploitation by the "West" – as is believed by a small minority in the First World and by a majority in the Third World – but to the lack of genius, in other words, the inferiority, of the non-Indo-Europeans. (The problems of the Middle East, for example, can thus be ascribed to the so-called backwardness of the Arabs, a backwardness for which their religion, Islam, is usually blamed.) This view of history has been carefully constructed in the course of the last two centuries by "Western" scholars at "Western" universities. Conventional "Western" historiography, archeology, linguistics, and other fields continue to reflect this Eurocentric "Aryan Model", and the champions of this kind of orthodoxy are not amused when someone challenges their familiar scenario. They made clear their displeasure, for example, when some twenty years ago the historian Martin Bernal suggested in his book, *Black Athena*, that the Greeks owed a great intellectual debt to their non-Indo-European neighbors, specifically the Egyptians and the Phoenicians. (Since then this theory has actually gained a growing number of converts.[17]) Similarly, the Sahara Hypothesis will undoubtedly incur the wrath of mainstream historians and linguists. After all, it is a theory that holds that non-Indo-European peoples played an important role in Europe long before the arrival of the Indo-Europeans themselves. The Sahara Hypothesis goes even further by suggesting that a considerable part (and possibly the majority) of Europeans are *not* Indo-Europeans, but are descendants of Saharan immigrants, related to the Berbers of North Africa and the Semites of the Middle East, who at some point in history, and for reasons that remain unclear, started to speak Indo-European languages. It is generally known that the emergence of the Indo-European languages continues to be the object of much controversy among linguists as well as archaeologists and geneticists. This study will make a minor contribution to the debate by briefly exploring the possibility that Sanskrit, an ancient indigenous Indian language, was adopted by the Saharan migrants who founded India's first great civilization, the "Harappan" or "Indus Civilization"; that not some hypothetical "proto-Indo-European", but Sanskrit, was the "grandmother" of all Indo-European languages; and finally, that the Sanskrit-based "Indo-European" languages spread from India all the way to Europe, presumably through migrations, there to become the "superstrate languages" that submerged the Usko-Mediterranean linguistic "substrate".

This book was not written by an apostle of the Sahara Hypothesis hoping to use his theory to unveil the secrets of ancient names of countries and peoples; the opposite is actually the case. While investigating the meanings of names that are clearly very ancient, the relevance and above all the heuristic value of a new theory was revealed to an author who was previously totally unfamiliar with that theory. In other words, the practice of onomastic-historical research, of which this book is the result, demonstrated that this new theory made it possible to discover the meanings and origins of ancient names. The conventional paradigm, on the other hand, was all

---

[17] See for example the recent study by Walter Burkert (2004), *Babylon – Memphis – Persepolis: Eastern Contexts of Greek Culture.*

too often unable to offer a satisfactory solution to the riddle of ancient topo-, ethno-, and hydronyms. Furthermore, the Sahara Hypothesis revealed itself to be a key that unlocked the doors of the many anomalies of conventional historiography with respect to Antiquity. By "anomalies" we mean historical "mysteries", such as the sudden blossoming of the Pharaonic Civilization in the Nile Valley and the origin and identity not only of the Ancient Egyptians, but also of other important peoples and cultures of Antiquity, such as the Sumerians, the so-called Pelasgian indigenous inhabitants of Greece, the Etruscans, and the Celts. The Sahara Hypothesis has the advantage that in this respect it suggests plausible, interesting, consistent, and hopefully convincing answers, which have been woven into this study. For the purposes of this book, then, this new theory proved to be eminently useful and, reciprocally, this study demonstrates to a certain extent the value of the Sahara Hypothesis, which obviously does not yet mean that this hypothesis may therefore be considered to have been verified. In any event, the reader will find here not only an interpretation of the meaning and origin of numerous ancient names of countries and peoples, but also a new and heterodox interpretation of the history of Antiquity.

The sources that have been used for this study are extremely eclectic. As mentioned before, the origins and meanings of the names of countries and peoples are seldom mentioned in the history books. Fortunately, there are also exceptions to this rule, and the studies that constitute these exceptions obviously proved to be very useful for our purposes. In addition, some tour guides and guide books do provide interesting information about topo- and ethnonyms. The more recent editions of the Green Michelin guides, for example, pay attention to toponyms and ethnonyms. Etymological dictionaries also proved to be valuable sources of information, particularly when they focused on the names of countries and peoples. A number of toponomastic reference works deserve to be mentioned here: the excellent *Dictionnaire des noms de lieux* of Louis Deroy & Marianne Mulon (1992); the *Placenames of the World,* by Adrian Room (2006), Dietmar Urmes' voluminous *Handbuch der geographischen Namen* (2003); and Edgardo D Otero's recent *El origen de los nombres de los países del mundo* (2004). There is also a lot to be found on the internet; however, much of it appears to be nothing more than oft-repeated samples of "folk etymology" of very limited value for our purposes, although there are some distinguished exceptions.

This English version differs considerably from the first edition, published in Flemish, the Belgian variety of the Dutch language, and translated by the author. Additional research and constructive criticisms permitted expansions and revisions, particularly with respect to the emergence, in India, of the Indo-European languages. In addition, Wikimedia Commons' declared policy that "faithful reproductions of two-dimensional public domain works of art are public domain, and that claims to the contrary represent an assault on the very concept of a public domain" has helped to make it possible to enrich this English edition with a substantial number of attractive and highly relevant illustrations. Like its sister project, the Wikipedia online encyclopedia, Wikimedia Commons was set up by the non-profit Wikimedia Foundation.

I am grateful to all those who made a contribution, whether great or small, to the realization of this book. They are too numerous to be mentioned here and, should I try to do so, I would risk forgetting a number of them. However, four persons must be cited here. First, my son David, who helped with much of the research and edited the English manuscript; second, my Italian friend Silvio Calzavarini, who introduced me to the fascinating studies of the great linguist Giovanni Semerano; third, my friend Roger Buysse, who inspired me to write this book with his interest in the origin and meaning of the name of the Netherlands and of the "Netherlandic", i.e. Dutch, language; and fourth, Philip Baker of Battlebridge Publications, who generously provided much needed comment from a linguist's perspective. Finally, I also wish to emphatically extend my thanks to a collective, namely the numerous travelers whom I was privileged to accompany on tours all over the world, because it is they who have stimulated my interest in this topic with their questions and remarks, and who frequently helped me to find answers; it is to them that this book is dedicated.

The author at the Taj Mahal
(Source: *www.pauwelstours.com*)

1

Neolithic and early civilizations

From the Sahara to Sumer

Approximately 10,000 years ago, not only in Eurasia and in Africa but also in what would later be called the "New World", a revolution got underway that may be considered one of the most crucial developments in the history of mankind. Previously, humans had been "hunters and gatherers", subsisting through the hunting of wild animals and the collection of fruits, nuts, mushrooms, and other edibles found in the natural environment. With the end of the last Ice Age a new way of life emerged, one based on the cultivation of crops and the domestication of animals, in other words, agriculture and animal husbandry. This development is sometimes called the "Revolution of the Neolithic". The hunters of the Paleolithic had been constantly on the move, because they followed the herds of animals they hunted. With the Neolithic Revolution, nomadism would certainly not disappear, because animal husbandry would continue until the present time to involve moving around with flocks of sheep and goats and herds of cattle, but henceforth there existed an alternative, sedentary way of life. The new agriculturists were indeed inclined to settle permanently in regions blessed with a fertile soil, a climate that suited their crops, and sufficient supplies of water. Increasingly, these people started to identify with their territory, and thus gave names to the places they lived in, to neighboring territories, and to the mountains, rivers, and lakes of their familiar world. In addition, the development of agriculture and of a sedentary way of life led not only to the emergence of villages and cities, with their large communities of people, specialization in professions such as priestess and soldier, complex social systems, and religions, such as the cults that worshiped fertility goddesses, but also to the birth of the earliest great civilizations, and of the writing systems that made it possible for these names to survive until the present time.

It is quite likely that the hunters of the Paleolithic already gave names to familiar territories, mountains, and rivers, and to certain places which from their perspective held a special importance (i.e., were "sacred"), such as the caves of Lascaux and Altamira with their famous wall paintings. However, of such hypothetical Stone Age toponyms no traces exist in the archaeological material that forms the sole source of information for this era. It is said that the culture of the Aboriginal inhabitants of Australia is many thousands of years old, that these Aboriginals never experienced a

Neolithic Revolution, and that in some ways they continue to live in the Stone Age even today. However, this does not mean that their society has not evolved considerably in the course of the centuries, for example on account of technological innovations such as the invention of a most remarkable weapon, the boomerang. The Aboriginals have their own topo- and ethnonyms, but we do not know how old they are; they are possibly the oldest names in the world, but we cannot be certain about this. The term "Aboriginals" itself is obviously a hetero-ethnonym (or exonym), a name given to a people by others; their auto-ethnonym (or endonym), the name they give to themselves, is *Koori,* or sometimes *Murri*, and it means 'humans', 'people'. Their name for Ayer's Rock – the biggest monolith on earth, a gigantic sort of navel of Australia – is *Uluru*, which means 'a place with abundant shadow'. The Pygmies of Africa likewise continue in many ways to live in the style of the Old Stone Age, and it is possible that an auto-ethnonym used by one of their tribes, *Aka*, meaning 'people', originated in that distant era. The name is certainly very old, because an Egyptian fresco of thousands of years BCE shows a Pygmy with the inscription *Aka* (Cavalli-Sforza 1994: 27). Incidentally, *pygmy* is an hetero-ethnonym, coined by the ancient Greeks, first mentioned in Homer, and referring to dwarfs known to be living in distant and exotic lands such as India or Africa: *pygmaios*; its meaning was '[people who are only as tall as] the length of a forearm'.

It was a relatively short step from the Neolithic to the first great civilizations, and those emerged in the so-called "Fertile Crescent", a region stretching from the shores of the Persian Gulf in modern Iraq to Egypt's Nile Valley, and to the Indus Valley. Already in the fourth millennium BCE, cities and city states sprang up in the valleys of the Tigris and the Euphrates, a region the Greeks would much later designate as Mesopotamia, 'land between the rivers'. The first great civilization blossomed in the Mesopotamian land of Sumer, but our history books rarely raise the issue of the identity and origin of the bearers of this civilization. According to the Sahara Hypothesis, however, the Sumerians originated in North Africa, more specifically in the region of the present Sahara Desert. From approximately 8,000 BCE onward, relatively advanced cultures that may be called "Neolithic", if only because they already featured animal husbandry, started to develop there, in what was then still a relatively fertile land. Of this culture, many material remains subsist today, such as rock carvings and paintings that delight travelers who venture deep into the Libyan or Algerian deserts.[18] With the end of the last Ice Age and the accompanying global rise in temperature, however, that region started to desiccate and was gradually transformed into a desert. The desertification process, which would not be completed until approximately 5,000 BCE, triggered a diaspora whereby the "Saharans" emigrated – in numerous waves, and over a long period of time - in all directions (Griffith 2001: 18).[19] Some headed for the Middle East, where they were respon-

---

[18] See e.g. Lhote (1973), *The Search for the Tassili Frescoes*. Some samples of the rupestrian art of the Sahara may be admired in the National Archaeological Museum in Madrid.

[19] Nantet (1998: 173) emphasizes that the desertification process was also interrupted by long pauses. One very long pause was the humid period that lasted from approximately 4,600 to 2,500 BC, and witnessed the emergence in present-day Niger of the so-called Tenerian Culture;

sible, first, for the blossoming of important Neolithic cultures such as that associated with the site of Çatal Hüyük in Anatolia, and second, for the emergence of the first great civilization, the Sumerian one, in Mesopotamia.

Wherever the Saharans settled down, their religious universe revolved around a fertility goddess, the personification of Mother Earth. They believed in an afterlife, and the dead were usually cremated – though sometimes also mummified – since fire was considered to be the "gate" through which the deceased entered the land of darkness and thus returned to the bosom of the Great Mother, who was the Alpha and Omega of all life. These people identified themselves with their religion, and by the term "gate" – *atan* in their Usko-Mediterranean language – they meant not only their religion but also themselves and their land. It could very well be that the Biblical story of Adam and Eve being banished "east of Eden" is an allusion to the migration of Saharans from their original homeland, *Atan* or Eden, to the Middle East. As for the "flaming sword" used by the angel to chase the first humans from Paradise, it may have been a metaphor for the climatic warming that forced the Saharans out of their "paradise-like" *Atan*.[20]

The expulsion of Adam and Eve from the Garden of Eden
(Lucas van Valckenborch, 1594; source: Pauwels [2006: 23])

The age-old "religion of the gate" eventually had to yield to other religions that are more familiar to us: the many varieties of an essentially patriarchal belief in one or more male gods, at home in the heavens rather than on earth, as had been the case of the "chtonic" (earth-based) fertility goddesses. This alternative kind of religion was associated in particular – though not exclusively – with the Indo-European peoples who in the course of the second millennium BCE allegedly also made their

---

see the article by Peter Gwin (2008) as well as *http://en.wikipedia.org/wiki/Kiffian* and *http://en.wikipedia.org/wiki/Tenerians*.
[20] See e.g. the reflections in McKenna (1992: 69-79).

appearance in the Middle East. Into their own traditions, myths, and terminology, these new religions integrated many elements of the archaic Saharan belief system; the fertility goddesses, for example, continued their careers in Greek mythology, albeit as subordinates to Zeus and other male deities, as Hera, Demeter, Artemis, Aphrodite, and indeed also of Athena, whose name may well be a Hellenic variation of the archaic concept of *Atan* (Alonso [*n d*]: 203). The Virgin Mary can similarly be considered a Christian incarnation of the fertility goddess of old, the Great Mother of the Saharans. (The early Christians seem to have concocted the story that Mary died in Ephesus in order to associate her with Artemis/Diana; the temple of that goddess there, known as the Artemision and considered one of the Seven Wonders of the World, had been an immensely popular pagan centre of pilgrimage and had been the sanctuary of an Anatolian fertility goddess before the arrival of the Greeks.) As for the Saharans' "fiery gate" to the underworld, *su-atan* in their language, this became "Satan" in the Hebrew and Christian traditions, a being associated with the underworld and with fire, in other words, with hell.

**The unimpressive ruins of the Temple of Artemis in Ephesus,
one of the Seven Wonders of the Ancient World, with one lonely restored column**
(Photo: J Pauwels, 2008)

If the Sumerians were indeed the descendants of Saharan immigrants in the Middle East, an explanation can be offered for certain Mesopotamian ethno- and toponyms that are familiar to us because of history or the Bible. The name Sumer itself may be interpreted as a combination of two Usko-Mediterranean terms, *su*, 'fire', and *mer,* 'country', meaning 'country of fire' or 'hot land'; a fitting name, because we are dealing with present-day Iraq, a region where it can be extremely hot. The Biblical name of *Samaria* and the Iraqi, Cretan, and Caucasian place names

Samar[i]a have the same origin. Using this methodology, an explanation can also be offered for Ur, the name of the city of origin of the biblical patriarch Abraham. This was one of the very first cities in history, and for this reason the term Ur is even today associated with high antiquity, as exemplified by the German expression *uralt*, 'as old as the city of Ur'. In the Usko-Mediterranean languages of Saharan peoples such as the Sumerians and their Elamite neighbors and relatives – and, incidentally, also in modern Basque – *ur* means 'water'; the toponym referred to a place featuring water, in other words, an oasis.[21]

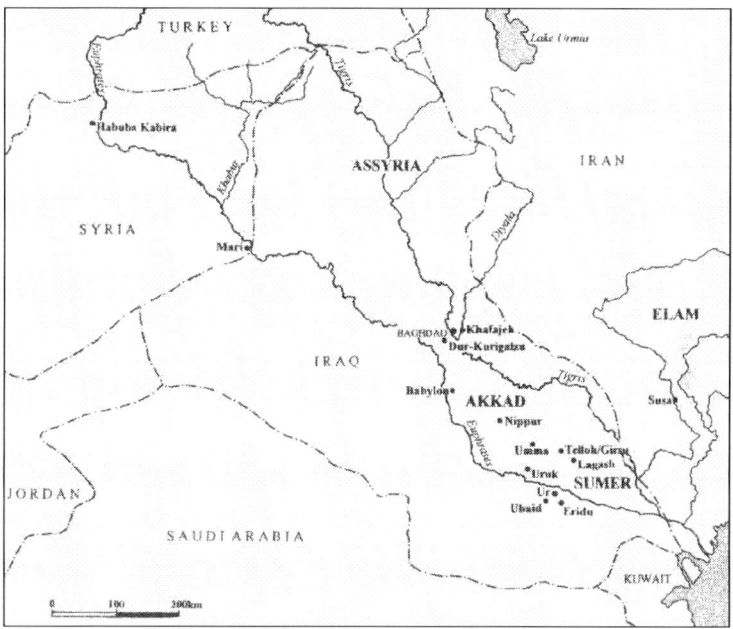

Map of Mesopotamia, with Sumer
(Reproduced with permission from Charles Gates, 2003)

---

[21] According to the linguist John Bengtson, Basque and Sumerian are "relatives" within a subgroup of the Dené-Caucasion family of languages, see S Wells (2002: 171). The connection between Sumerian and Basque was also noted by H G Wells who wrote that "[some] philologists… find Basque… akin to certain similarly stranded vestiges of speech found in the Caucasian, and they are disposed to regard it as a last surviving member… of a very widely extended group of pre-Hamitic languages, otherwise extinct, spoken by peoples of that brunet Mediterranean race [i.e., our "Saharans" -JP] which once occupied most of western and southern Europe and western Asia…" After quoting fellow historian Sir H H Johnston in support of this, and mentioning various other languages which according to Johnston might also have been related to these, he continued: "If this is true, then we have in this 'Basque-Caucasian-Dravidian-Sumerian-proto-Mongolian' group [i.e., our Usko-Mediterranean family of languages -JP] a still more ancient and more ancestral system of speech than the fundamental Hamitic. We have something more like the linguistic 'missing link'". About the Sumerians, H G Wells also wrote that they were probably related to the ancient Iberians, and that their language, related to Basque, "may represent what was once a widespread primitive language group extending from Spain and western Europe to eastern India", see *http://outline-of-history.mindvessel.net/140-the-first-civilizations/1421-early-civilzations-the-sumerians.html* (H G Wells 1919: 131).

The name of the infamous Assyrians may also be of Usko-Mediterranean origin. In that language *Assur* means 'water of darkness', 'dark water'; this was probably a reference to the Tigris, the river that bisected the land of the Assyrians. (We will see later that a number of other rivers have names that mean 'dark water'.) The etymology of Tigris is uncertain,[22] but for the Euphrates – *Purattu* in Akkadian – Semerano suggests that this hydronym is a combination of the Usko-Mediterranean terms *ebu*, 'great' and *buratu*, 'spring'.

The biggest, richest, and most powerful city of Mesopotamia and the entire Middle East was Babylon, a metropolis known far and wide for its monumental buildings, among them *Etemenanki*, the "house of the foundation of heaven and earth", referred to in the Bible as the "Tower of Babel". Even though it is shown to be round on some ancient pictures, this tower was presumably a typical Mesopotamian ziggurat, a step pyramid, with a square base and with garden-like terraces, the so-called "hanging gardens" exalted by the Greeks as one of the Seven Wonders of the World.[23] Babylon's real name was *Bab-Ilani* (or *Babi-Ilu*), 'Gate of the Gods', because its inhabitants believed that it was there that the gods had descended on earth in order to create human beings; the city of Babylon was consequently perceived as the center of the world.

When Egypt was known as Kemit

The first great civilizations originated in the Middle East, in the so-called Fertile Crescent. On one side of this Fertile Crescent lay Mesopotamia, the 'land between the rivers'; on the other side, in the valley of the Nile, there was Egypt, the fabulous empire of the Pharaohs. Like that of the Sumerians, the Egyptian civilization had not appeared out of nowhere: its catalyst had been the arrival of Saharans, driven from their homeland by increasing heat and aridity. It is hardly surprising that these migrants preferred to settle in lands where water was plentiful, and they did indeed find such conditions "east of Eden", i.e., to the east of their *Atan*, namely in river valleys and deltas such as those of Mesopotamia and Egypt, and also in the distant valley of the Indus. Let us cite Arnáiz-Villena and Alonso, the two Spanish proponents of the Sahara Hypothesis, in this context:

> The migration [of the Saharans] to the east produced one of the great achievements of the era of the early civilizations: the colonization of oases and river deltas. It is not a coincidence that the Saharans, chased from their country by increasing desiccation, settled in humid regions, in marshes, and in the deltas of great rivers, i.e. in regions where the combination of nature and human intelligence made it possible for a population to subsist and grow. Consequently, their settlements constituted a string of great oases, not only in the vastness of North Africa but also in the sandy regions of the Middle East and the Arab

---

[22] Semerano claims to recognize in the name Tigris the Akkadian term *egeru* – 'stubborn', 'capricious', 'unpredictable', 'cruel' – so that its meaning would be 'unpredictable, dangerous river'.

[23] For a detailed description of the Tower of Babel, see the excellent essay by Hansjörg Schmid in Kohlmeyer *et al.* (1991: 67-84).

Peninsula. As for the river deltas, it is important to mention not only those of the Nile and of the Tigris and Euphrates, but also of the Indus (Arnáiz-Villena & Alonso, 2001: 179).[24]

A wave of Saharans had migrated from their homeland to the present Sudan, where around 5,000 BCE they were the bearers of the so-called Khartoumian Culture. Khartoum, the capital of Sudan, is situated on a peninsula between the White and the Blue Nile; in the Usko-Mediterranean language of the Saharans, this toponym signified 'city [*kart*] between two waters/rivers [*umm*]'. From Sudan, these Saharans later penetrated into the Nile Valley to the north of the First Cataract, i. e. into present-day Egypt, where the pre-dynastic El-Badari culture of the fifth millennium BCE displayed striking similarities with other cultures that are now deemed to be of Saharan origin. (Prior to 5,000 BCE, during the "early Holocene humid optimum", the Nile valley had been too marshy and hazardous for human occupation.) Thus were created the conditions for the blossoming of the brilliant civilization of Ancient Egypt.[25]

The black alluvial soil of the cultivated land bordering the Nile
(Photo: J Pauwels, 2006)

The language of the Egypt of the Pharaohs was an Usko-Mediterranean idiom, related to Sumerian. In the latter language, the term *nilu* meant 'flood', and it is very likely that this is the key to deciphering the meaning of the name of the Nile, the great river whose annual flood made Egyptian civilization possible. The Nile was indeed 'the flood'; it was 'the [annually] flooding river'. The Ancient Egyptians,

---

[24] On the link between "Saharans" and Ancient Egypt, see also the comments in Guilaine (2000: 257, Nantet (1998: 102-04), and Alonso [*n d*]: 50, note 4). Hagan (2000) similarly postulates North African Berber roots of Egypt's ancient civilization.
[25] See Kuper & Kröpelin (2006: 806), Markey (2006), Arnáiz-Villena & Alonso (2000: 268, 275).

however, often simply referred to the Nile as *iteru*, 'the river', and their Hebrew neighbors seem to have followed their example: in the Bible the Nile is called *Jeor*, meaning essentially 'the [great] river'. For their country, the Egyptians used the term *Kemit*, which meant 'land of the black earth'. It is a name that survives in the terms alchemy, the "Egyptian science", and chemistry.[26] This 'black earth' – *khem*, or *kham*, in Ancient Egyptian – was a reference to the spectacularly fertile alluvial soil of the Nile Valley, whose color contrasted dramatically with that of the sterile sand of the surrounding *desert*, which was itself known as *deshret*, the 'red land'. It was precisely this "gift of the Nile", this combination of water and fertility, which had lured the Saharans – fleeing the "flaming sword" of desiccation – to Egypt, and which made it possible for a brilliant culture to flourish there. According to Semerano, the Semitic root *khem/kham* means 'dark' or 'black', also in the sense of 'burned black'. In the Akkadian language of Mesopotamia, *qamu* signified 'burned', and the Hebrew cognate of this term is *ham*. We recognize this root in the Biblical ethnonym "Hamites", which refers to the descendants of Ham (or Cham), one of the three sons of Noah, namely, the one whose offspring were predestined to populate Africa. In other words, the Hamites were the inhabitants of Africa, the "black" people, the "people with the burned faces".

Ancient Egypt was the land of the "Kemites", and the study of this fascinating culture ought therefore to be known as "Kemitology". Instead, we speak of the land of Egypt and Egyptology. This is Greek terminology, which was later inherited by the Romans and has thus come down to us. The Greeks sometimes did call Egypt *Chemia*, but usually they preferred the term *Higiptos*. This was the Greek version of the Kemitian word *Hetkaptah*, which referred not to the country but to its capital, and more specifically to the most famous temple of this capital. *Het* meant 'abode', and *ka* was the essence, the soul, of a god (or of a human): *het-ka*, 'abode of the soul', was the name of the temple of the god, in this case of *Ptah*, the deity responsible for creation, who was also known as "the sculptor of the earth". The term *Het-ka-ptah* signified 'the abode of the soul of Ptah, god of creation'. To Greek ears this sounded like *Gea-Ptah*, 'land of Ptah'. This term was also used to refer to the city itself, and it is remarkable that its meaning is not very different from that of Babylon, 'gate of the gods', 'gate where the creator gods had descended on earth'. In both cases the name reflected the view of the bearers of the culture that their capital city was the locus of the creation, the centre of the world, or at least of *their* world.

Ptah is believed by some Egyptologists to be identical with the god Nefer, or Neters, a name that inspired the Greek word for 'nature'; according to the Ancient Egyptians, and also according to the Ancient Greeks, nature and divinity were essentially identical. The Egyptian capital, *Hetkaptah,* was also known to the Kemites themselves as *Men-Nefer*, 'city of Nefer'. However, as in the case of the name of the country itself, it was by the Greek version of this term, Memphis, that the capital of Kemit was predestined to become known outside of Egypt (Deroy & Mulon 1992: 153). The metropolis of *Hetkaptah* or Memphis also featured a palace

---

[26] On the Egyptian origins of "chemistry" and "alchemy", see Russo (2003: 197).

for the ruler, a building known as *Per-O*, 'the house [*per*] with the pillars [*o*]'. Gradually, however, this term started to refer to the resident of this palace, and so the ruler of Kemit came to be known far and wide as the "pharaoh". Already at a very early stage, Egypt became famous for its temples, palaces and other monuments, including the spectacular Sphinx of Giza. This sphinx, which is said to be considerably older than the neighboring pyramids, has a human face. Not surprisingly, the meaning of the ancient toponym Giza turns out to be 'the man'. That this is the solution to the riddle of the name of the site of the Sphinx is suggested by the fact that in Basque, a living Usko-Mediterranean language and therefore a kind of "Rosetta Stone" available for deciphering Ancient Egyptian, the word for 'man' is rather similar: *gizon*.

The sphinx at Giza
(Photo: J Pauwels, 2006)

Egypt had another major city, called *Het Amon*, 'residence of the God Amon', by the Egyptians, and *Diospolis*, 'city of Zeus', by the Greeks, who identified Amon with the number one in their Olympian pantheon. However, the Egyptians usually referred to this city as *Waset*, a toponym that combines the terms *was*, 'divine sceptre', and *t[a]*, 'land' as in *Kemit[a]*, 'the black land'; since the divine sceptre was the symbol of power, the name may be interpreted as 'land [or city] of the power', in other words, 'capital'. Waset was also colloquially known as *Niut*, 'the city', in the sense of 'the big city', just as the Romans and Greeks would later respectively refer to Rome and Constantinople as *urbs* and *polis*. Yet another name for Egypt's second metropolis was *ta-ib*, 'land [or city] of the sacred [*ib*]'. The Greeks turned this *ta-ib* into the name that is familiar to us, namely Thebes.[27] When the Romans conquered the country, they installed not one but two army camps within the limits of the city, which thus became known in Latin as *castra*, '[city of] army camps', 'city of castles'. The Arabs turned this into *Al Qusr*, and that gave us Luxor, the modern name of Thebes.

---

[27] Etymologies of Waset and Thebes were provided by the Egyptologist Ihab Shaarawi.

Artist's reconstruction of the western façade of the Ptah temple at Memphis
(Franck Monnier, 2008; source: Wikimedia Commons)

In the fourth century BCE, Egypt was conquered by Alexander the Great and subsequently at least partially Hellenized. After a Roman interlude, featuring performances by historical megastars such as Caesar and Cleopatra, Greeks again ruled the country, but this time the Hellenic masters were the Byzantines, whose state religion was Christianity. Countless Egyptians converted to the new religion, but their liturgy differed from the imperial or "Malikite" (from *malik*, "king") orthodoxy favored by Constantinople. A national Christian church thus emerged in Egypt, and its members proudly called themselves *Aigyptoi*, 'Egyptians'. The Arabs, who conquered the country in the seventh century, turned this term into *Qobt*, and that gave us the familiar term *Coptic*, still used today to refer to Egypt's relatively few remaining Christians. Incidentally, it was while studying the Coptic language, the descendant of Ancient Egyptian, that Gottfried Leibniz, the famous German philosopher and mathematician, who was also an accomplished linguist, was struck by its similarity to Basque (Morvan 1996: 46).

"Egyptians" is the source of the word "Gypsies" – "Gypcians" in 16th-century English - and of that ethnonym's counterparts in some other languages, e.g., *gitanes* in French and *gitanos* in Spanish. This reflects an ancient and widespread, though mistaken, belief that this people originated in Egypt. The generally accepted theory today is that India was their original homeland, whence they started to migrate to Europe and North Africa nearly 2,000 years ago. They may well have reached Europe via the Balkan Peninsula, which could explain why in many European languages they are referred to with a cognate of the Hungarian *Cigány*, such as the German (and Dutch) *Zigeuner* and the Italian *zingari*, though in the latter language *gitani* is also used. According to Semerano, *Cigány* and its variants contain an Usko-Mediterranean root, a variation of the Sumero-Akkadian *ginnu*, 'mountain' but also 'mountain horse' or just 'horse', an animal apparently associated with Gypsies since time immemorial. The term "Gypsies" is a hetero-ethnonym, considered somewhat pejorative by the people to whom it refers. Their auto-ethnonym is "Roma," a plural form of which the singular is "Rom." This term has nothing to do with the city of Rome, the Roman Empire, or the land and people of Romania; "Roma" is said to be derived from the Sanskrit term *dom,* and to have the same meaning, namely, 'men' or 'people'. The Roma family contains many subgroups, one of which is known as the Sinti. The origin of this term remains a mystery, although it is similar to Sindh, the name of a region within the supposed *Urheimat* of the Roma, India-Pakistan.

Gypsy encampment
(Jacques Callot, early 17th century; source: Wikimedia Commons)

Berbers from Libya to Iberia

The Ancient Egyptians were familiar with their neighboring countries and gave them names, some of which survived for centuries, even millennia. The African region to the south of their own empire they called *Kush*, a toponym of unknown etymology. The gold of the famous mask of King Tut Ankh Amun and similar treasures came from there. The Egyptian word for gold was *nub,* or *nebu*, and it is likely on account of this association that Greek and Roman geographers such as Strabo and Pliny named that region Nubia, 'gold country'. However, the Greeks generally preferred the toponym *Aithiopia*, Ethiopia. The Greek word *aithomai* meant 'to burn', and *opsis* was 'face'; Ethiopia consequently means 'land of the people with the burned faces'.[28] This kind of expression was already centuries old when the Greeks adopted

---

[28] For more information on the terms "Ethiopia" and "Ethiopians," see Snowden (1970: 2ff).

a version of their own. We have already seen that the Hebrew ethnonym "Hamites" had the same meaning; the Arabs would later similarly speak of the lands to the south of Egypt as *Bilad As Sudan,* 'country of the blacks'.

The desert to the west of the fertile Nile Valley or, more precisely, "the people whose territories were situated to the west of the Nile", as the historian François Decret (1998: 16) writes, were called *Leba* or *Libu* by the Egyptians. The etymology of this term is uncertain, but what is certain is that the familiar name Libya is derived from it. Perhaps *Leba* was the name of one of the many tribes of Berbers who inhabited that region – and North Africa in its entirety – and continue even today to form the majority of the population between the Atlantic coast of Morocco and the Libyan Desert. Another possibility, to be discussed later, is that the meaning of *Leba/Libu* was 'west', 'land of the setting sun'.

Young Berber woman from the Biskra area of Algeria
(Gustave Le Bon; source: Le Bon 1884)

The present-day Berbers have been thoroughly Arabized and Islamized since the seventh century CE, when the Arabs conquered North Africa. For this reason, the Berbers of Antiquity who were the western neighbors of the Ancient Egyptian Kemites are sometimes referred to as Proto- or Palaeo-Berbers. Ethnically and linguistically, these Berbers of the distant past were closely related to the inhabitants of the Pharaonic Empire. Until fairly recently, the languages of both groups were classified by linguists as "Hamitic", but together with the "Semitic" tongues they are now all said to belong the great Afro-Asiatic group of languages and thus, as seen from our perspective, to the Usko-Mediterranean language family. The Berbers were (and are) also descendants of Saharans, those who had migrated to the north and to the west in order to settle in parts of North Africa, situated along the coasts of the Mediterranean Sea and the Atlantic Ocean, that had escaped the warming that created the Sahara Desert.

The homeland of the Berbers, North Africa, was and is a gigantic land, surrounded by the waters of the Mediterranean and the Atlantic. In their Usko-Mediterranean language, the Palaeo-Berbers had a specific term for 'sea', *ilel*, while 'land' was called *iber*. *Iber* contains the same root as the Sumerian *bireti*, the Akkadian *ep[e]ru*, and the Phoenician *afar*. The meaning of words based on this root is always the same: 'earth', 'land', and more specifically 'land in contrast to water', 'land surrounded by water', therefore occasionally also 'island', though more typically 'mainland' in contrast to the sea and its islands. When using the term *iber,* the Palaeo-Berbers appear to have had in mind their own land, i.e. the homeland of their people, but also 'earth' or 'land' in contrast to water, 'mainland'. Not surprisingly, they also used that word to refer to the great European peninsula that stretched to the north of their own North African homeland, which they named Iberia. In fact, many thousands of years BCE, Iberia was settled by Berbers or other Saharans related to the Berbers; the present-day Spaniards and Portuguese are the descendants of these "Iberians" of Antiquity, as genetic tests demonstrate. (In this sense too, the Iberian Peninsula and North Africa form one single world, a "bicontinent", as Fernand Braudel has emphasized in his masterful study of the Mediterranean.[29]) Like North Africa, Iberia too was a vast land surrounded by the waters of the Mediterranean Sea and the Atlantic Ocean; it therefore amply merited the name Iberia in the sense of 'land in contrast to water', 'mainland'. In addition, Iberia was also a 'mainland' in contrast to the islands scattered in the surrounding seas, for example the Canary Islands and the Balearic Archipelago, which were likewise settled by Palaeo-Berbers. Interestingly, in Antiquity there were other "lands in contrast to water" that were called Iberia, as we shall see later.[30]

It is also noteworthy that the term *iber* may contain the same root as the word *Berber* itself, which meant 'people', more specifically 'independent people' (Arnaiz-Villena & Alonso, 2000: 25). Mircea Eliade, the great expert in ancient religions and myths, has drawn attention to the fact that in many archaic societies, humans were considered as nothing other than the product of "mother" earth, and that a people typically identified with the land it occupied; it would not be a coincidence, then, if Latin words *homo*, 'human' and *humus,* 'earth', are derived from the very same root, as Eliade ([1952] 1980)[31] and others claim. Analogically, in the Usko-Mediterranean

---

[29] Braudel (1990.1: 137). See also Blake & Knapp (2005: 5): "The cultural differences that separate Europe and Africa in the present day are projected back onto the past with little justification".

[30] More will be said about the root *iber* and its significance of 'land in contrast to/near water' in chapter 5, in the section dealing with "primeval hydronyms".

[31] Eliade developed his ideas in numerous books, including, but certainly not limited to, the two

language of the Palaeo-Berbers the term *iber,* 'land', was very closely related to the word for 'people', familiar to us as *Berber*. This ethnonym is not derived from the Greco-Latin word *barbarian,* as is often claimed: it is even possible, though not certain, that the reverse was the case. As we know, to the Greeks (and later the Romans) barbarians were people who spoke an unintelligible language. Such was definitely the case with the inhabitants of North Africa. Their auto-ethnonym made the Greeks think of an unintelligible kind of "babbling"; consequently, its onomatopoeic Greek cognate, *barbaros,* was increasingly used to refer to speakers of foreign tongues in general. The Romans and later the entire "Western" world inherited this Hellenic terminology, including its connotation of inferiority. Another, and ultimately more credible possibility, however, is that the Greeks had learned the word *barbaros* from the Pelasgian indigenous inhabitants of their own country or from their Oriental neighbors; Semerano believes the term to be a Hellenic version of the Sumerian *barbarra,* 'foreigner'. In any event, North Africa, the land of the Berbers, would be known for centuries as *Barbary,* which seemed to mean 'Land of Barbarians'. One can understand why today the proud Berbers prefer to call themselves *Imazighen,* because this ethnonym, meaning 'free' or 'independent' people, is unsullied by pejorative connotations.

The *Imazighen* have never constituted a single, homogeneous people, but rather a veritable mosaic of tribes. These tribes may be said to be the descendants of Saharans who managed to adapt to the desertification of their environment and therefore continue to live in the Sahara and in its periphery instead of migrating to less arid regions. The nomadic inhabitants of the desert, the Tuaregs, are one such branch of the great family of Berbers; their name signifies 'the isolated ones'. Another Berber tribe deserves to be mentioned here, namely the Kabylians of Algeria. However, this ethnonym is not of Usko-Mediterranean origin; its root is the Arabic word for 'tribe', *qabila,* and the name was actually concocted by the French in the colonial era.

Berbers, or at least Saharans related to the Berbers, also migrated to the Canary Islands, an archipelago situated in the Atlantic Ocean on the latitude of southern Morocco. The Romans were familiar with these islands and called them the "Fortunate Islands" (*Insulae Fortunatae*) but also, because of the presence of many dogs there (*canes* in Latin), the Canary Islands or 'Dog Islands'. The Canarian Berbers called themselves *Guancinet* or Guanches, meaning 'people of Tchinet'. Tchinet was the archipelago's biggest island, also known as Tenerife, a name that signified 'white [*ife*] island [*tener*]'. This was an allusion to the perpetual snow on top of Teide, the 3,000-meter-high volcano that dominates the island. This oronym is derived from the Palaeo-Berber term *Eheide,* 'mouth'; the Berbers of Antiquity considered this mountain as a kind of mouth of Mother Earth, a mouth through which smoke and fire rose from the underworld to the heavens. It was probably on account of this that Italian sailors, who in the fourteenth century explored this archipelago on behalf of the Kingdom of Castile, called Tenerife the 'Island of Hell'.

---

listed in the bibliography.

Captured Guanche "kings" presented to Ferdinand and Isabella in 1497
(Photo by GFDL of a painting in Tenerife by an unknown artist; source: Wikimedia Commons)

The Guanches ultimately met a most tragic fate, as their "fortunate" islands became the scene, and they the victims, of one of the more thorough yet ignored genocides of history. In the first half of the fourteenth century, their archipelago was rediscovered by a Genoan explorer, Lancelotto Malocello, after whom one of the Canary Islands was to be named Lanzarote. Malocello's Spanish employers subsequently proceeded to conquer the islands, and in the process the Guanches were expropriated, enslaved, and finally exterminated. Before this "final solution" was a *fait accompli*, the Spaniards were kind enough to try to convert the Guanches to Christianity, and it turned out that for this task Basque priests were eminently suited; indeed, they happened to speak an Usko-Mediterranean language that appeared to be related to the Berber tongue of the Guanches.[32] Incidentally, canary birds did not give their name to the islands, but vice versa. The Spaniards got to know these colorful little songbirds when they conquered the archipelago, and they were to make a lot of money by selling them in Europe.

The Berbers of North Africa, a people to whom our history books hardly ever pay attention, have also bequeathed to us two important toponyms that refer to the part of Africa situated to the south of their own lands, i.e., to West Africa. Because the inhabitants of this region spoke entirely different languages, the Berbers called them *Akal n-Iguinawen,* or *Iguinawen,* 'those who cannot speak', 'dumb people'. This nomenclature gradually spread northward, and so the term *Guinea* was adopted first by the inhabitants of the Iberian Peninsula and later by other Europeans as a synonym for sub-Saharan West Africa. The Berbers were also aware of the existence of the great river that bisects that region, which in Antiquity was known as the 'Nile of the

---

[32] According to Arnaiz-Vilena & Alonso (2002: 195), "Upon their arrival in the [Canary] islands, many [Spaniards] exclaimed: 'these people speak Basque!' It was for this reason that Basques were appointed as bishops for the islands".

Blacks'. They called this river *Ghir-n-igheren,* 'river [*ghir*, also *gher*] of rivers'. When the Romans replaced the Carthaginians as the masters of North Africa and thus became acquainted with this hydronym, they heard the Latin word *niger*, 'black', in it. Consequently, in Europe the 'Nile of the Blacks' became known as the Niger, while it was assumed that the meaning of this hydronym was 'Black River'. In any event, two modern African states owe their name to this river, Niger and Nigeria.

Semites, Hittites, and Aryans

Between Mesopotamia and Egypt lies a vast region that likewise achieved a high degree of development at an early stage in history, even though it did not produce great and mighty empires such as those of the Egyptians and the Babylonians. However, since time immemorial a number of important cities have existed there, cities so old that the etymology of their names – for example, Damascus and Jericho – is mostly shrouded in darkness. For the toponym Damascus, however, Semerano proposes the meaning of 'high fortress', with *tamu* and *saqu* corresponding to the Akkadian terms for 'fortress' and 'high'. (This *saqu* may also hide in the names of the Spanish city, *Sagunto*, located high on a hill, just like Damascus, of the mountainous Greek island of *Zakynthos*, and in *Scotland*, as will be seen later.) Perhaps it was the multiplicity of cities that caused this area to become known as Syria, which is said by some to mean 'land of the walled cities'. On the other hand, the etymology of *Syria* is highly uncertain, and competing toponomastic hypotheses abound. According to one of them, supported also by Semerano, *Syria* is nothing more than an abbreviated version of the aforementioned *Assyria*. According to yet another theory, *Syria* was a cognate of *Tyria*, meaning the hinterland of the great Phoenician seaport, Tyre. This theory appears to receive some support from the fact that Tyre was also known as *Sur*, 'the rock', a toponym that conjures up *Syria*. In any case, in Antiquity the term *Syria* referred to a region that was much more extensive than the eponymous modern state; the territories of present-day countries such as Lebanon, Israel, and Jordan were long considered to belong to the geographical entity known as Syria.

The people who inhabit that part of the world are traditionally said to be Semites, related to, but different from, the so-called Hamitic denizens of Ancient Egypt and the rest of North Africa. Today, however, linguists find the differences between these two groups to be of little or no importance, so they prefer to lump them together into one great "Afro-Asiatic" family of languages. Furthermore, there appears to be a close genetic relatedness between the Hamitic North Africans and the Semitic inhabitants of the Middle East, the Jews and Arabs. According to the Sahara Hypothesis, all these peoples share an *Urverwandschaft*, an ancient and intimate affinity, based on a common Saharan, Usko-Mediterranean origin, and all spoke (and still speak) related Afro-Asiatic languages. It is possible, and even likely, that the Semitic languages emerged as a kind of linguistic synthesis between the Usko-Mediterranean languages of the Saharan immigrants and the tongues of the anonymous people(s) who already inhabited the Middle East before the Saharans' arrival. In this respect it must be kept in mind, first, that from the earliest of times the so-called "Levantine Corridor" figured prominently in the migrations of *homo sapiens* from Africa to the rest of the world, and second, that the existing populations of the Middle East did not virtually disappear during the last Ice Age, as happened in Europe, since that part of the world, in contrast to most of Europe, was not covered by glaciers.[33]

In any case, the language of the Ancient Egyptians did not differ all that much from the Semitic languages of the neighboring Middle East, such as Phoenician, Hebrew, and Aramaic. But within the great Afro-Asiatic ethnic and linguistic family, considerable differences arose in the course of the centuries, for example between nomads and sedentary denizens of cities and oases, between the inhabitants of the coast of the Mediterranean Sea and those of the interior, and also between the devotees of polytheist religions and those who started to believe in one single deity. (Monotheism apparently made its very first appearance with Pharaoh Akhenaton's reforms of the state cult in favor of the god Aton in the middle of the fourteenth century BCE.) The region along the coast, for example, was called Canaan, and was inhabited by the Canaanites, people whom the Greeks would later call "Phoenicians".

The etymology of the term "Canaan" – *kena'an* in Hebrew and represented consonantally as *Kn'n* in Phoenician – is complex. Its original core may well be the Sumerian *kan*, meaning 'west' or 'western lands', which is exactly what Canaan was to the denizens of the Sumerian heartland, Mesopotamia. But the name also resembled the Akkadian *kenu* or *kanu*, which signified 'true' or 'legitimate', and it was in this sense that the inhabitants adopted the name as an auto-ethnym, useful for the purpose of distinguishing between themselves, the civilized rightful inhabitants of the land, and the uncouth nomads who coveted their riches and probably occasionally invaded their homeland. Over time, also, an association arose with palm trees, so that the toponym Canaan acquired the connotation of 'land of palm trees' and the palm tree became the symbol *par excellence* of the land.

The inhabitants of Canaan were predominantly craftsmen, merchants, and sailors who were at home in seaports such as Byblos and Sidon, strung out along the coast of the modern state of Lebanon. The Canaanites were polytheists, but ethnically and linguistically they were closely related to the tribes of their own hinterland, known as "Hebrews". The latter, however, would long maintain a very different, predominantly nomadic lifestyle. In any event, there was preciously little difference between the Semitic languages of the Canaanites/Phoenicians and the Hebrews. "The early Israelites," write Israel Finkelstein and Neil Asher Silberman (2005: 135) "were – irony of ironies – themselves originally Canaanites!" The name of the Hebrews is almost certainly a cognate of the Canaanite ethnonym *Ibrim*, which means 'people on the other side', i.e., on the other side of the Lebanon Mountains and/or the Jordan River. The Hebrews appear to have been the original nomadic inhabitants of the

---

[33] S Wells (2002: 98-99, opines that "modern humans" may have permanently settled in the Middle East "around 45,000 years ago". See also *http://dienekes.blogspot.com/2007/04/mtdna-dispersal-via-horn-of-africa-vs.html*.

interior of that part of the Middle East, a vast region stretching from the Jordan to the Euphrates and the Tigris; according to the Bible, they were the descendants of the Patriarch Abraham, a man from the Mesopotamian city of Ur, and of his son, Isaac. (Abraham's name contains the Usko-Mediterranean root *aba*, 'father', and the meaning of the name Abraham is 'high father', 'tribal ancestor', in other words: 'patriarch'.) In any event, in the course of the centuries the Hebrews became known by that name even in Egypt, if indeed a reference to the *Apiru* or *Habiru* in sources from the time of Pharaoh Akhenaton refers to them, as is commonly accepted.

The call of Abraham
(Julius Schnoor [or Schnorr] von Carolsfeld, ca. 1855; source: Pauwels [2006: 41])

The Hebrews, too, were originally polytheists, just like all other inhabitants of the Middle East of yore. (And they also appear to have engaged in human sacrifices, as is suggested by the Biblical story of Abraham preparing to sacrifice Isaac.) But already in the time of the legendary patriarch from Ur, his son Isaac, and his grandson Jacob, they developed a predilection for one single god in their pantheon, namely Yahweh. According to the Bible, Israel – 'he who has seen God [*El*]'[34] – was the name Jacob had received from Yahweh himself. Thus the Hebrews also became known as the Israelites or "children of Israel," at least those who chose to follow Israel's example in worshipping only Yahweh, because polytheism long retained the loyalty of quite a few Hebrews, as the episode of the Golden Calf illustrates. In fact, the cult of Yahweh initially did not amount to a genuine mono-theism; it can be more accurately described as a monolatry (or henotheism), that is, a predilection for, and the exclusive cult of, one single deity, something that did not preclude the belief in other gods and goddesses.[35] It was only after a sojourn in Egypt, where they may

---

[34] The etymology of *Israel* is a matter of controversy. Semerano claims to recognize the Akkadian root *isarum* in this name, meaning 'divine justice', so that *Israel* would mean 'God is just'. He also claims that *Isaac* derives from Akkadian *issakkum*, 'territorial ruler', while *Jacob*, descended from Akkadian *aqabb*, 'to order', would mean 'I, Yahweh, have ordered this'.

[35] See e.g. Leeming (2004: 91), Kirsch (2004: 28-30).

have become acquainted with the ideas of Akhenaton, that the Hebrews, under the charismatic leadership of Moses, embraced a strict monotheism, predicated not only on the exclusive worship of one deity but also on the belief in the existence of only one God.

Moses in front of the Pharaoh
(Persian painting of unknown date by Hayder Haterni; source: Wikimedia Commons)

According to the Bible, the Hebrews subsequently left the Pharaonic Empire in order to settle permanently in the land of Canaan, or at least in a part of that land, there to create a state of their own.[36] A special identity was thus developed by the descendants of Isaac and followers of Moses, an identity that henceforth differed dramatically from that of their close relatives along the coast, the Canaanites.

Moses[37] is supposed to have brought the Israelites from Egypt to the Canaanite "land of milk and honey" during the reign of Pharaoh Ramses II, i.e., in the thirteenth century BCE. This coincided with the invasions of the so-called "Sea Peoples", some of whom settled permanently along the coasts of the eastern Mediterranean. The Israelites, then, were certainly not the only migrants in the troubled times that the end of the Bronze Age happened to be. At approximately the same time, the southern part of the land of Canaan was invaded or infiltrated by the Philistines. Between the two groups of newcomers a conflict soon arose, of which the Biblical story of Goliath

---

[36] Some archaeologists and Bible experts now cast serious doubt on the Biblical story of the Exodus from Egypt and the conquest of Canaan, see Finkelstein & Silberman (2005).

[37] According to Semerano, the name "Moses" is related to the Babylonian *massu*, 'guide' or 'leader', a word whose Egyptian cognate may also be recognized in the names of Pharaohs such as Tutmosis and Ramses.

and David provides an echo. The Hebrews called the Philistines *Pelishtim*, which, according to Semerano, signified the 'lords' (*pelu*, or *belu*, as in the name of the god Baal, 'god, the lord') of the 'city or cities' (*isitu* or *asitu*). This Biblical episode reflected a rather typical conflict for the ancient Middle East, one between nomads, in this case the Israelites, and sedentary "city folks".

Egyptians battling Philistines and other "Sea Peoples"
(Source: Arthus Evans, 1921, via Wikimedia Commons)

If the Philistines were indeed newcomers, they appear to have been firmly established in the southern Canaanite cities by the time they got into trouble with the Israelites. After all, that area became known as Palestine, 'land of the Philistines'. The Greeks were familiar with this term in the time of Herodotus, in the fifth century BCE. The modern Palestinians seem to be descendants not only of the Philistines mentioned in the Bible, but also of the original Canaanites and of Hebrews – Canaanites from the other side of the Jordan – who did not follow Isaac and Moses on the path to monotheism. It is a major irony of history that the Palestinians are closely related to the Israeli Jews, as is suggested in the Bible and as genetic tests appear to demonstrate.[38]

According to the Bible, the Israelites founded a mighty kingdom in Canaan, associated with the names of David and Solomon. The Egyptians would undoubtedly have noticed the existence of such a state right on their doorstep, but their sources fail to make any reference to it, which casts considerable doubt on the Biblical story.[39] It is certain, however, that in Canaan/Palestine a number of Hebrew states or statelets

---

[38] The Biblical reference to this relatedness is to be found in Griffith (2001: 85). For the genetic tests, see the study by Arnáiz-Villena, Gomez-Casado, & Martinez-Laso (2002).

[39] According to Finkelstein & Silberman (2005: 159), "There is hardly any reason to doubt the historicity of David and Solomon. Yet there are plenty of reasons to question the extent and splendor of their realm".

did temporarily exist. One of them covered the area around Jerusalem and was called Juda. In the Aramaic *lingua franca* of the Middle East, it was known as *Jehud*, which, according to Semerano, meant 'Yahweh is my joy'. Its inhabitants were known as *Jehudim*, and thus appeared the term "Jew". This ethnonym, a powerful statement of monotheistic faith, was to eclipse "Israelite" and "Hebrew" after the traumatic experience of the Babylonian Captivity. The term "Jew" thus began to refer to all those who worshiped no God but Yahweh. In any event, Canaan/Palestine remained a region with a heterogeneous population: with polytheists and monotheists; with Canaanites, Philistines, and Israelites; with city folks, merchants, and nomads; with languages such as Canaanite and its Semitic relatives, Hebrew and Aramaic. The waters were muddied even more by the fact that the region of Canaan/Palestine had no clear borders with the rest of what was called Syria, nor with Egypt, Mesopotamia, or Arabia.

In Canaan/Palestine too, there existed a number of cities and sites that were considered by at least some part of the population to be "the center of the world", or for some reason or another enjoyed the reputation of being sacred, as was the case with Babylon and Memphis. Mount Tabor, for example, was generally considered to be the 'navel' (*tabbur*) of the 'world' (*haaretz*); its full name happens to be *tabbur haaretz*. Since the earliest times, Canaan not only featured a sacred mountain, but also a sacred city. This city, presumably founded by the Canaanite clan of the Jebusites, was originally known as *Urusalim*, an Akkadian construction meaning 'roof' (*uru*), in other words 'temple', of 'friendship' (*salimu*). This term developed into *Awsham* and eventually – after the Hebrews conquered the city, possibly around 1,000 BCE – was displaced by its Hebrew cognate, *Jerushalim*. Jerusalem was constructed on two hills and was therefore also known as *Zion*, a toponym in which – as in *Sinai*, the name of a mountain with two peaks – the Akkadian *sina* and/or the Hebrew *snaim*, 'two', can be recognized, at least according to Semerano.[40]

The Bible also mentions the Anatolian empire of the *Chittim*. When Luther produced his German version of the Bible, he rather inaccurately translated this ethnonym as *Hethiter*, and thus we have come to speak of the "Hittites". These were a people whom conventional historiography and linguistics claim to have been Indo-European, albeit on the basis of extremely dubious evidence. It is now argued rather convincingly that, like all or most of their Middle-Eastern neighbors, the Hittites were of Saharan origin and therefore spoke an essentially Usko-Mediterranean language, albeit one that – for reasons to be discussed later - reflected a measure of Indo-European influence.[41]

---

[40] The Phoenician settlement of Tharros in Sardinia is located on a peninsula that prominently features two hills and is called Sinis. Switzerland has an old town called Sion built on two peaks. These both appear to provide support for Semerano's interpretation of Zion and Sinai.

[41] See Arnáiz-Villena & Alonso (2001: 47ff). Also Semerano (1984: 87-99, and 2005: 18-20). Kazanas (2005: 1) writes of the Hittite language that "it has some I[ndo-]E[uropean] relics but is otherwise flooded with Mesopotamian, Hurrian and Assyrian elements".

Bas relief with gods of the underworld near the former city of Hattusas
(Photo: J Pauwels, 2008)

The Hittites called themselves *Hatti*, which – according to Semerano – meant 'mighty people' or, to use a notorious German term, *Herrenvolk*. Their capital, situated in the vicinity of the modern city of Ankara and known in Turkish as Bogazkale (or Bogazköy), was *Hattusas*, 'city [*essu, isu*] of the Hatti'. The Hittites were the ancestors of the modern-day Turks and Kurds, peoples who today – 3,000 years later – differ from each other in many ways and do not get along very well, but who appear to display a remarkable genetic proximity. In the second millennium BCE the Hittite Empire revealed itself to be a powerful rival of Pharaonic Egypt, and it often came to war between the two, as it did over the control of strategically important Palestine. The invasions of the Sea Peoples during the early twelfth century BCE allegedly brought about the collapse of the state of the *Chittim*.

Ruins of the city wallss and so-called Royal Gate of Hattusas
(Photo: J Pauwels, 2008)

Eastern Anatolia, a region encompassing the upper reaches of the Tigris and Euphrates rivers as well as the Caucasus mountains, was temporarily the cradle of the Urartu Empire. Its inhabitants were the ancestors of the modern Armenians, a people of Usko-Mediterranean origin just like the Turks, Kurds, and other neighbors such as the Georgians and Chechens. As we have already seen, the root *ur* signifies water, and the toponym Urartu had the meaning of 'land between the waters'. This was an appropriate name, since we are dealing with a territory situated between the Mediterranean, Black, and Caspian Seas. The name of Mount Ararat is virtually synonymous with Urartu and is based on the same roots, so that this oronym may be interpreted as 'great mountain of the land between the waters'. The inhabitants of Urartu called themselves *Hay*, 'the people', 'our [own] people', and *Hayastan* is the name by which the Armenians continue to refer to their homeland today. In Mesopotamia, however, the inhabitants of Urartu were informally known as *A(he)rimanin,* which meant 'foreigners'. Later, in the time of the great Persian empire of the Achaemenids, the land of these *Arimanin* became known far and wide as *Armina* or *Arminya* The Greeks co-opted this Persian name in the form of *Armenioi*, and this is why, eventually, the entire world came to call the land of the Hay 'Armenia'.

Georgian militiamen
(Artist: unknown, 1887; source: Project Gutenberg via Wikimedia Commons)

Like Spain, Armenia's neighboring state of Georgia was also known in Antiquity as *Iberia*. The Greeks were familiar with two Iberias, Spain in the west, and Georgia in the east. We already know that the toponym *Iberia* was of Usko-Mediterranean origin and meant 'land', 'mainland', or 'land surrounded by water'. This term was appropriate in the case of Spain, and it was equally appropriate in the case of Georgia, a piece of real estate tucked between the waters of the Black Sea and the

Caspian Sea. The Georgians have always called themselves *Kartmanybi*, 'Kartvelians', and their country *Sakartvelo,* which means 'valley between the mountain peaks'. However, for some unfathomable reason the Persians and Arabs called the Georgians *Gurj,* and their country *Gurji*, and it was this nomenclature that gained international acceptance. The Russians inherited it when they conquered this Caucasian region, using their own version of the Persian-Arab name, *Grusija.* In "Western" countries this became *Georgia*, but the name of the land has nothing to do with some mythological George nor Saint George, even though the latter was inevitably adopted as the country's patron saint; there is also no connection whatsoever with the British King George, after whom a former British colony in North America, now a Southern US state, was named.

It is generally known that the inhabitants of Iran, a country formerly called Persia, are Muslims but not Arabs, and that their language is not Semitic but belongs to the Indo-European family. An Indo-European people allegedly settled in this country in the middle of the second millennium BCE. They called themselves *Arya* or *Airiya*, which in Persia's ancient language, Avestan, meant 'noble people'; later, in Middle Persian, this became *Eran*, and thus the terms *Aryan* and *Iran* are said to have originated. While in the European context one no longer speaks of "Aryan" or "Indo-German[ic]", the term "Indo-Aryan" remains in use in the context of Iran and India.

The Persian Aryans consisted of a number of tribes that were related yet differed in some ways from each other, for example the Medes and the Parthians, who lived in the north of modern-day Iran, and also the Persians themselves, the inhabitants of an area in the southwest of present Iran. This was a "highland", contrasting sharply with the "lowland" of Mesopotamia. Down there, among the highly civilized Babylonians, the eastern highlands were referred to in Akkadian as *parsu*, the 'separate' or 'different' land. And so the inhabitants of that Pars (or Fars) became known as Farsi or Parsi, in other words, as *Persians*. Their foremost urban centre was also known as Pars, but the Greeks called it Persepolis, 'city of the Persians'.

Ruins of Persepolis, with the so-called Apadana Staircase
(Photographer and date unknown; source: www.visipix.com)

Among the Aryans, the Medes – from the Akkadian *madu*, 'mass of people', or *hoi polloi* to use a Greek expression – were originally the leading tribe, but then the Persians took over, and the city of Pars became the capital of the huge empire of the Achaemenids, soon known abroad as *Persia*. At home, on the other hand, one preferred the term *Eranshar,* 'land of the Aryans', or *Eran* (Iran) for short. The rest of the Middle East, inhabited by Semites, was known as *An-Eran,* literally 'non-Iran', 'land of the non-Aryans'. In 1934 the country officially changed its name from Persia to Iran. This was done by order of Reza Shah, who had founded the Pahlevi Dynasty about a decade earlier and was the father of the last Shah. Reza Shah was a fan of Hitler, who happened to idolize all things "Aryan".[42] Incidentally, the Persian *Arya* not only inspired the term "Aryan", but is also etymologically related to the German word *Herr*, 'lord', or 'master'. Hitler considered the Germans to be an "Aryan" *Herrenvolk*, that is, a 'master race'.

Persia, then, was (and is) the 'land of Aryans' in a region predominantly inhabited by Semites. At least, this has been the conventional wisdom ever since the triumph of the Indo-Europeanists and their "Aryan Model" of history and linguistics in the nineteenth century. Our Spanish and Italian guides, however, beg to differ, and to differ radically. According to Arnáiz-Villena & Alonso, Persia had already been settled thousands of years BCE, just like the rest of the Middle East, by people of Saharan origin. Furthermore, the arrival in Persia of the Indo-Europeans did not amount to a massive migration but rather to an "elite invasion", resulting in "language replacement" but not in significant "gene replacement". Thus, while the Persians did eventually adopt a new, Indo-European language, ethnically they were and remained an Usko-Mediterranean, more specifically Semitic people, closely related to the unquestionably Semitic inhabitants of neighboring Mesopotamia.

Semerano goes even further: he insists that the so-called "Aryan" migrations of the middle of the second millennium BCE – not only in Iran but also in Europe! – are merely a figment of the Indo-Europeanists' imagination. Consequently, he too considers the Persians to be Semites, and in addition he claims to recognize clear traces of a Semitic origin in their supposedly Indo-European language. With respect to the ethnonym *Aryans*, he rejects the theory that it means 'noble people' and interprets it, like *Persians*, as a Mesopotamian term signifying 'inhabitants of the "highland"' – *al(i)u* or *ar(i)u* in Akkadian. In addition, this name also suggested a link with Akkadian *aru* as well as its Aramaic (and also Hebrew) cognate *aher*, 'foreigner', already identified in "Armenians". With this nomenclature, the highly civilized denizens of the Middle East used to refer to their aggressive – and supposedly nomadic, but not necessarily ethnically and linguistically different – neighbors living in the high country, who regularly raided the Mesopotamian lowlands. Semerano (1984: 655) concludes mercilessly that "wanting to identify the word Aryan as the name of the Indo-Europeans is a pure illusion". So by what name

---

[42] It was actually Hjalmar Schacht, "Hitler's banker", who, convinced of the Aryan origin of the Persians, encouraged the Shah to rename his country Iran, see *http://en.wikipedia.org/wiki/Hjalmar_Schacht#cite_note-14*.

did the Persian "Aryans" refer to themselves? Semerano claims that they did not use an Indo-European but a Semitic, Usko-Mediterraneam term, namely, *belu*, 'lords'. So they were a *Herrenvolk* after all!

The name *Iran* itself, *dixit* Semerano, has nothing to do with "Aryans". He claims it is an ancient Mesopotamian (more specifically, Akkadian) term, *harranu* or *hiranu,* meaning 'high (caravan) road', yet another reference to the highlands to the east of the Mesopotamian valley, inhabited by pesky "Aryans". Those highlands included a plateau but also a mountain range, the Zagros. According to Semerano, that oronym is simply a variant of the Akkadian term *zaqru*, 'height' or 'mountain' which, incidentally, happens to be related to the *acro* in *acropolis*, Greek for 'upper city'.

The Zagros mountains border the Iranian plateau to the west. Even more impressive mountains stretched from the eastern frontiers of Iran to the dizzying heights of the Pamirs and Himalayas. The original settlers of that land were also of Saharan origin and spoke an Usko-Mediterranean language, but they were joined in the course of many millennia by all sorts of newcomers, presumably including Indo-Europeans, resulting in a mosaic of ethnic groups and a multiplicity of languages. However, if we can believe Semerano, even today the ancient Usko-Mediterranean toponomastic legacy lives on in names such as Afghanistan, 'settlement [*appu*] in the mountains [*ganinu*]'or 'settled/inhabited mountains', and Kabul, 'mountain [*kapum*] city [*alum*]'.

Into, and out of, India

Many thousands of years BCE, people of Saharan origin also settled in India. There they did not invade virtually empty spaces, as was the case in post-Ice Age Europe, but a land that was already inhabited, and inhabited even much more densely than the Middle East. Humans had arrived in the subcontinent during earlier exoduses of *homo sapiens* from Africa, including the primeval one, probably approximately 60,000 years ago (S Wells 2002: 72-73). They must have found India a true "Garden of Eden" on account of its tropical climate, fertile soil, lush vegetation, etc. Consequently, thousands of years BCE, India was already the huge human reservoir it has remained ever since, a mosaic of multiple ethnicities, skin colours, languages, and – last, but not least – religions.[43]

Purely demographically, the Saharans were a mouse jumping onto the back of the Indian elephant. However, their arrival appears to have functioned as a catalyst for the emergence of the first great Bronze Age civilization on the subcontinent. This civilization – whose paramount archaeological sites are those of Mohenjo-Daro and Harappa, revealing great, complex, and prosperous cities – was based in the vast valley of the Indus River and its tributaries,[44] a region in the Indian northwest; it is

---

[43] This treatment of India is based primarily on the recent study of Michel Danino (2006) and on the series of essays edited by D N Tripathi (2005).
[44] And of the great Vedic river, the Saraswati which, on account of tectonic activity, disappeared in

therefore referred to as the Indus Civilization, though the term Harappa Civilization is also used. The script used by the "Harappans" has not yet been deciphered, and about their language nothing can therefore be stated with certainty. However, there are reasons for believing that they were either Saharans or, more likely, as in the case of the Semites of the Middle East, a people that had originated as a fusion of Saharan newcomers and an anonymous "indigenous" population. First, it is logical that migrants coming from Africa would have entered India via the Indus Valley. Furthermore, while much of India - and particularly the lush tropical south - was already inhabited, the vast spaces of the Indus Valley may not have been densely populated because, while crisscrossed by rivers descending from the Himalayas, they were extremely arid. So there was still room there for Saharans who, while in Mesopotamia, had become acquainted with sophisticated irrigation technologies. And indeed, the Indus Civilization, which flourished in the third millennium BCE, follows chronologically on the heels of the Sumerian Civilization of Mesopotamia, and reveals many similarities with it, especially with respect to hydraulics. We also know that the Harappans maintained lively trade relations with the land of Sumer, via the Persian Gulf as well as by land.

According to the conventional, but now increasingly abandoned "Aryan Invasion Theory" (AIT), developed in the 19th century by German, French, and Victorian British scholars with an undeniably Eurocentrist and even racist point of view, the Harappans were a dark-skinned indigenous, so-called "Dravidian" people. Their Indus Civilization ceased to exist in the course of the second millennium BCE, when a wave of presumably light-skinned (and preferably tall and blond) Indo-European or "Aryan" warriors burst in from an "original homeland" somewhere to the north or west of India, destroying the Harappan cities and forcing the surviving Dravidians to migrate to the south of the subcontinent. This is supposed to explain why languages classified as Dravidian, such as Tamil, continue to be spoken today by the predominantly dark-skinned denizens of the Indian south, while the languages of northern India, such as Hindi, are predominantly Indo-European. The main problem with this "invasionist" theory is that there is not a shred of archaeological, genetic, or any other type of evidence for such an Indo-European invasion of India. And the disappearance of the Indus Civilization is now known to have been caused by environmental problems determined by human as well as natural factors, including shifts in the course of rivers (Danino 2006: *passim*).

Sanskrit (or "Old Indic"), India's ancient language, is classified as Indo-European and is supposed to have been brought to the subcontinent by the Aryan invaders. And the famous wisdom literature written in that language, the books known as the Vedas, are said to have been written around the middle of the second millennium BCE, at the earliest. However, now that it is as good as certain that an Aryan invasion never occurred, it is very likely that languages later to be classified as Indo-European, such as Sanskrit, were already spoken in large tracts of northern India, before the arrival in the Indus River Valley of our Saharan migrants. And these migrants –

---

the early second millenium BCE.

relatively small in number – appear to have adopted Sanskrit, much as Frankish invaders would adopt Latin when they conquered Gaul at the time of the collapse of the Roman Empire. Some Indologists are indeed convinced that Sanskrit was the language of the Indus Civilization, and that the Vedas originated in the context of that civilization, i. e., in the course of the third millennium BCE. However, since the Saharan invaders came from Mesopotamia, elements of Semitic - and therefore, from our perspective, Usko-Mediterranean - Mesopotamian languages such as Sumerian and particularly Akkadian presumably also slipped into Sanskrit. This is what is believed by Sanskritologists such as Malati J Shendge, and also by Semerano.

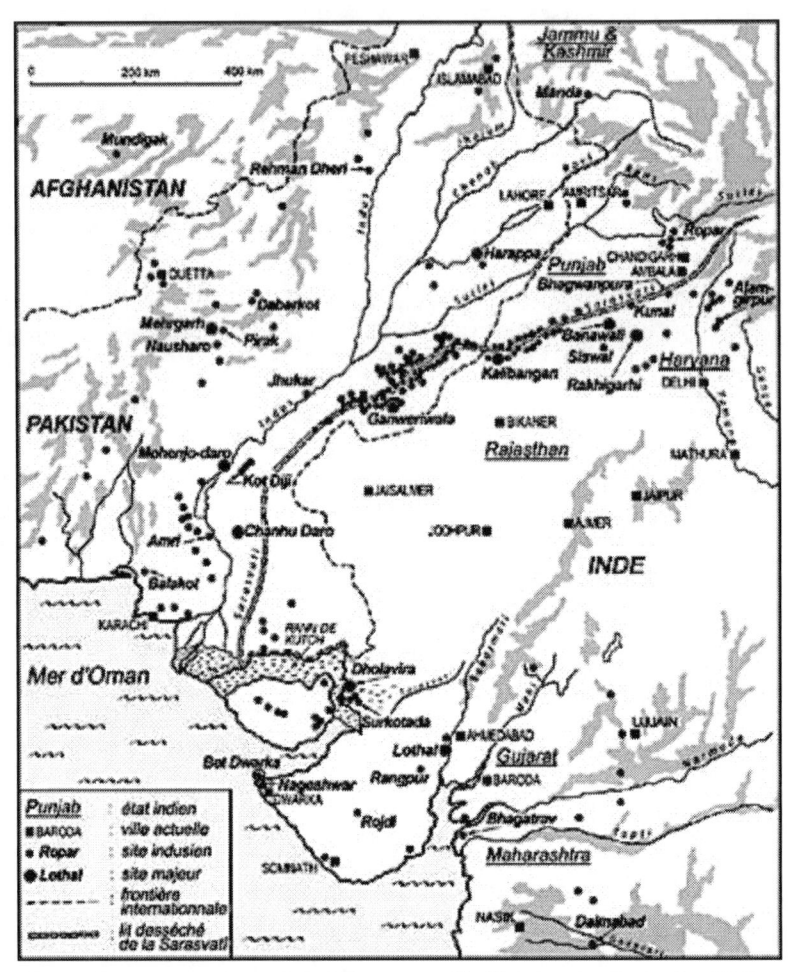

Map of important sites of the Harrapan Civilization in the Indus Valley
(Michel Danino, 2006; source: Wikimedia Commons)

The name Sanskrit itself, writes Semerano (2005: 27-28), may be understood with the help of Akkadian as meaning "writing of the community". As for the Vedas, Semerano claims that this term is a cognate of Akkadian *wadum*, 'to know'; the Vedas, in other words, are the 'words of wisdom', the 'books of knowledge'. Such an interpretation is necessarily speculative, but it is certainly plausible. Ultimately more important for our purposes, however, is the fact that the supposedly Sanskrit name of the Indus contains the Usko-Mediterranean root meaning 'water', related to the Semitic *ayn*, 'water' or 'spring', which will be discussed later. To the denizens of the Harappan Civilization, the Indus was as important as the Nile was to their Kemitic cousins: it was the water in the sense of 'the great water', 'the water of waters', so it makes sense that this is what they called it. The river, then, gave its name to the country as a whole because the valley of the Indus and its tributaries constituted the historical – as opposed to prehistorical, demographic - heartland of India. (Incidentally, it was only after the demise of the Indus Civilization that the Ganges Valley would also start to play an important role in the history of that country.)

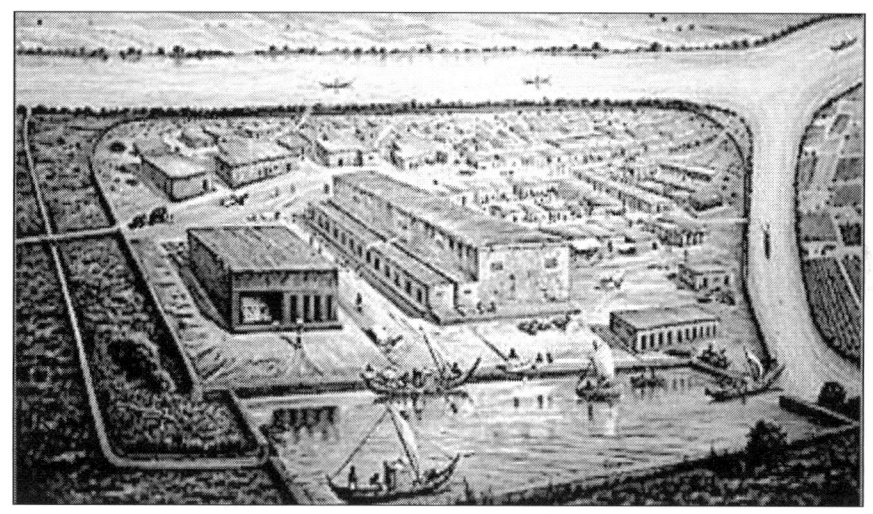

Artistic conception of Lothal, a Harrapan city
(Archaelogical Survey of India)

The Indus Valley happened to be the part of the subcontinent that bordered on the great civilizations of the Middle East, starting with Sumer. To India's neighbors of the Fertile Crescent, the name of this river would for many centuries conjure up the civilization located in its valley and the country in its entirety. In Babylon, Niniveh, Persepolis, and the like, one spoke of *Hindush*, that is, the land of *Hind*, the land of the Indus. (This was also the meaning of the later, Middle Persian toponym *Hindustan*.) The Greeks inherited this Persian terminology, but because the Greek alphabet did not have the "h", they spoke of *India*, and it is this Greek version that has come to us via Latin. The name India, then, is not an auto-ethnonym, but a hetero-ethnonym. The Indians themselves used – and continue to use – other terms, especially *Bharat*. This Sanskrit term is found in one of the Vedas, and means something like 'sages', 'wise people'. *Bharat* thus means 'land of the sages' (Deroy & Mulon 1992: 227). In Persian, the Indus Valley would eventually also become known as *Panch Ab*, 'land of the five [*panch*] waters [*ab*]', a reference to the five major tributaries of the Indus, the Jhelum, Chenab, Ravi, Sutlej, and Beas; the British were to take over this nomenclature in the form of *Punjab*.

With the demise of the AIT, we have also come to view the Dravidian languages in a new light. The theory that some type of proto-Dravidian was the language of the Indus Civilization, and that Dravidian languages are spoken in southern India today because the arrival of the Aryans drove the "Dravidians" away from their homeland to areas further south, is no longer credible. It now seems likely that Dravidian languages such as Tamil had been at home in India's south since time immemorial, just as Indo-European languages had been part of the linguistic landscape of the northern part of the subcontinent for a very, very long time. However, the Dravidian languages are not as drastically different from India's Indo-European languages as the AIT would have us believe, and reflect a measure of Sanskrit influence. Conversely, Sanskrit appears to have been influenced by Dravidian languages, with Dravidian loan words allegedly slipping into Sanskrit "from the beginning" (Mallory 1991: 44). In addition, numerous linguists have drawn attention to the affinities between India's Dravidian languages and Sumerian, Elamite, and even ancient Egyptian.[45] This suggests that Saharans may also have settled in areas south (and east) of the Indus Valley and/or that the advanced civilizations of the Middle East may have exerted a measure of linguistic – as well as cultural and also religious – influence on the southern half of the subcontinent. In any event, Semerano, citing Mesopotamian cognates, interprets Tamil, the name of India's leading Dravidian language, to mean 'brotherhood' or 'community'. As for the term "Dravidian", he proclaims it to be a combination of two cognates of the Akkadian terms *dor*, 'generation' or 'people', and the aforementioned *wadum*, 'to know', so that its meaning would be identical to that of "Bharat", namely 'wise people'. However, according to an alternative etymology, the meaning of dravida was never ethnic or racial but always purely geographical, referring to the southern part of India, and attested ancient versions of it - *dramira, dramila* and *dramida* – appear to suggest that this term was synonymous with the word *tamil*, from which many scholars derive *dravida*)Nagaswamy 1993: 84-85).

The people of the south may have been considered "wise" by the Harappans because the southern "aboriginals" had developed village cultures that were sufficiently ancient and interesting to command the respect even of the admittedly more advanced denizens of the cities of the Indus Valley. Keeping in mind that the terms Tamil and Dravidian did not originally denote languages, let alone ethnicities, as they do today, we should also allow for the possibility that the Harappans referred to their neighbors to the south as a "community" (Tamil) led by "wise men" (Dravidian), presumably some kind of shamans or gurus. Looking at things that way, one cannot help thinking of the similarity of the term *Dravidian* with the (presumably Usko-Mediterranean) name given to the "wise men" or shamans of ancient Gaul, the *Druids*.

The AIT is being abandoned because there is no archaeological or other evidence that supports it, while there is much genetic evidence that contradicts it. However, while an Aryan invasion of the subcontinent never happened, there is a very real

---

[45] See *http://fr.wikipedia.org/wiki/Dravidiens#Th.C3.A9orie_africaine*.

likelihood of historical migrations from the huge human reservoir that India has been since time immemorial, to regions not only further east, but also further west, including Europe. Such a scenario is postulated by the so-called "Out of India Theory" (OIT). The Indo-European family of languages, then, may well have originated in India – as the term in fact seems to suggest! - and spread from there to Europe.[46] Instead of some hypothetical "proto-Indo-European" language, allegedly spoken in the equally hypothetical Indo-European "original homeland", one of India's ancient languages, Sanskrit, adopted by the Saharan migrants who established the subcontinent's first great civilization, may well be the "grandmother" of all Indo-European languages, the Indo-European *Ursprache*, as "Indophile" European scholars like Friedrich Schlegel suspected before the emergence and triumph of the "Indophobe" AIT in the middle of the 19th century. In this case, it would be an irony of history that the adoption of an indigenous Indian language by Saharan migrants who originally spoke an Usko-Mediterranean tongue, functioned as catalyst of the emergence of an entirely new family of languages, one that would sweep westward out of India, to Iran and ultimately Europe, there to become the Indo-European "superstrate" languages that would submerge the Usko-Mediterranean linguistic "substrate". (Indo-European languages also swept northeastward into the Asian interior, as attested by the existence - from the sixth to ninth centuries - of the Tocharian people and language in the Tarim Basin of western China; perhaps it was these migrants who left behind the mysterious Tarim or Xinjiang mummies.)

Although recent research suggests that families of languages may also originate and/or spread through slow, long-term linguistic "convergence" and other similar "complex cultural processes",[47] one would normally associate the spread of the Indo-European languages from India to Europe (and elsewhere) with migrations. One such historical migration from India to Europe is well known, namely that of the Roma or "Gypsies". They presumably left their homeland "in the early centuries CE", writes a Greek Indologist, Nicholas Kazanas, and he adds that "groups of [Indians] could have left at earlier periods also" (Kazanas 2005: 6). As for the migrations that presumably brought Sanskrit-based Indo-European languages to Europe, they are most likely to have occurred well before the Gypsies first left their homeland, but soon after environmental degradation forced the denizens of the Indus Civilization to abandon their cities, in other words, in the first half of the second millennium BCE. Groups of Harappans are known to have migrated east, namely, to the Ganges Valley, at that time; there is no reason why other Harappans could not have headed west, towards Iran, Mesopotamia, Anatolia, and beyond. The hypothesis of a Harappan migration via Iran and other parts of the Middle East to Europe between 2,000 and 1,500 BCE also accords with the fact that Indo-European languages - for example Mycenaean Greek - appeared in Iran as well as in Europe in that millennium. This timing may also account for the Indo-European influence on the Usko-Mediterranean language of the Hittites, whose civilization blossomed in

---

[46] See e.g. the essay by D N Tripathi (2005).
[47] Danino (2006: 282-84), referring to studies by Nikolai S Trubetzkoy, Andrew Garrett, Hans H Hock, Kenneth Kennedy, and others.

Anatolia, half way between India and Europe, in the same second millennium BCE. According to experts such as B B Lal, "Indo-European" Hittite was a "minority language". introduced by an invading elite coming from India, whereas the "basal [i.e. indigenous] language was non-Indo-European" (Lal 2005: 56). The hypothesis of one or more Indian migrations, possibly in the form of "elite invasions", into the Middle East in the second millennium BCE, receives additional support from the fact that Hittite documents of about 1,400 BCE invoke Vedic deities and cite countless names of Indian origin (Shastri 2005: 101-03).

In Europe, then, the Sanskrit-based Indo-European languages appeared on the scene on account of impulses originating in distant India, either in the form of "linguistic diffusion" or similar "complex cultural processes" or, more likely, in the form of migrations. And so, wrote H G Wells in 1919, referring to what we call the Usko-Mediterranean tongues, "language groups that, eight or ten thousand years ago, had extended over western and southern Europe, completely vanished before Aryan tongues" (1971: 131). In reality, however, the Indo-European languages did not triumph quickly and easily, and they did not do equally well everywhere in Europe. In Italy, the Etruscan substrate resisted the onslaught of the Indo-European Latin language of the Romans until the time of Augustus (63 BCE – 14 CE). And the Usko-Mediterranean Basque tongue has managed to subsist until the present. Furthermore, languages originating in tropical India never seem to have had much interest in Europe's northern reaches, thus allowing the survival there of Finnish, Estonian, and other so-called Finno-Ugric languages. Finally, some parts of Europe seem to have witnessed the emergence of "fusions" between the new, Sanskrit-based "superstrate" languages and the existing Usko-Mediterranean "substrate" languages; it has earlier been suggested that the Celtic languages may well constitute such a linguistic "fusion" or "synthesis". However, even where Indo-European tongues triumphed, they never triumphed completely. Their vocabularies adopted many words from the Usko-Mediterranean substrate, as has been demonstrated in the case of Dutch. But most important, from our perspective, is the fact that virtually everywhere Usko-Mediterranean names of peoples, lands, cities, mountains, lakes, and rivers have survived until the present time.

Admittedly, the hypothesis of the adoption of Sanskrit by the Saharan founders of the Indus Civilization, of Sanskrit as the grandmother of all Indo-European languages, and of a westward proliferation of the Indo-European languages from India through demic migrations or cultural diffusion, is only that: a hypothesis. But can we do much better at this point, given the near-collapse of the AIT with respect to India, the lack of unanimity among the experts with respect to an Indo-European *Urheimat*, and the purely hypothetical nature of so-called "proto-Indo-European"? The hypothesis presented here will hopefully have at least some heuristic value, in other words, it may provide inspiration to linguists, geneticists, archaeologists, etc., who are trying to resolve the mysteries of the origin - and original homeland, if any - of the Indo-European languages as well as their historical "triumph" over the Usko-Mediterranean linguistic substrate in parts of the Middle East, particularly Iran, and in most of Europe.

2

Phoenicians in the land of rabbits

Between Mesopotamia and Egypt

The Greeks, pretty competent sailors and merchants themselves, revealed a bit of jealousy by calling their keenest competitors *Phoinikès,* 'Phoenicians', which allegedly meant 'people of the purple [*phoinos*]'. They supposedly did this because the Phoenicians, whose auto-ethnonym was Canaanites, long enjoyed a monopoly over the production of the dye for this beautiful and noble color, and made a fortune from its sale. (The secret of the purple color was locked away in the murex, a shellfish that abounded in the coastal waters of Phoenicia.) But there exists another, more credible explanation, namely that *Phoinikès* was the Greek version of the name by which Phoenician people were known in the Middle East. Of the true meaning of this Usko-Mediterranean hetero-ethnonym, the Greeks may well have had no idea, but it gradually acquired the connotation of 'purple' on account of the Greeks' association of their Phoenician competitors with the production and sale of this dye. The Phoenicians, then, were not named after the Greek word for purple, as conventional wisdom has it. Instead, it was the other way around: *phoinikos*, the Greek word for purple, meant 'the Phoenician color'. (In analogous fashion, the Greeks, who had learned the art of navigating by night from the Phoenicians, called the North Star *Phoinikè*, that is, 'the Phoenician star', and the palm tree, the great symbol of the Phoenicians, *phoinix*, 'Phoenician tree'.) Semerano claims to recognize in the term *Phoinikè* the Akkadian word *panu*, which meant 'front' or 'face', also in the sense of the 'face' of a country, in other words, its coast. As a translation of the ethnonym that was adopted by the Greeks in the form of *Phoinikès*, the Italian linguist suggests 'people of the coast'. As far as the Babylonians and other Mesopotamians were concerned, the people who called themselves Canaanites were indeed inhabitants of the coast. It should come as no surprise that the Greeks adopted Mesopotamian terminology because, like the Phoenicians, they too engaged in intensive trade relations with Mesopotamia and were quite familiar with its metropolis, Babylon, whose Hanging Gardens were cited by Herodotus as one of the Seven Wonders of the World.

The Semitic people known as the Phoenicians were at home in an area of the Middle East that was long known in Europe as 'the Levant', that is, the land where the sun rises. We are dealing with the east coast of the Mediterranean, more specifically the coast of Lebanon, a country bearing the name of the mountain range that screened the relatively small world of the Phoenicians from areas further east. Some etymologists believe they recognize in the name Lebanon the ancient Semitic root *leb*, which signifies 'white' (or 'silver') and supposedly alludes to the snow that covers the highest peaks of these mountains throughout the year. As for the Phoenician coast, it was dotted by a string of seaports that would each in turn play the leading commercial and political role in the Phoenician universe: Byblos, Sidon, and Tyre. And also modern-day Beirut, whose original name, *Beryta,* may have had the meaning of 'well' – *beroth* in Phoenician – on account of the abundance there of freshwater springs. Semerano, however, considers this toponym to be a variant of the term *iber*, already familiar to us and meaning 'land surrounded by water' or 'peninsula'. The historical core of the Lebanese capital is indeed located on a small promontory jutting out into the Mediterranean.

For hundreds of years, the Phoenicians performed the profitable role of middlemen between the two great cultural centers of early Antiquity, Mesopotamia to the east and the Nile Valley to the southwest. They controlled the traditional trade route, which stretched overland from the upper reaches of the Euphrates to Canaan itself, and hence by sea to the Nile delta. Only much later, after the camel had been domesticated in the middle of the second millennium BCE, was it possible to establish a direct overland route between Mesopotamia and Egypt via the Syrian and/or Arab deserts and the Sinai Peninsula; this turned out to be the precondition for the emergence of Arab peoples that will be discussed later. Already at a very early stage, the Phoenicians were accomplished sailors, and in this capacity they made an extraordinary contribution to what has been called the "domestication" of the Mediterranean Sea, the vast "interior sea" that separated the three continents known to the Ancients: Europe, Asia, and Africa. At the dawn of the third millennium BCE, Byblos sent ships loaded with cedar wood from the mountains of Lebanon to the land of the Pharaohs. That empire happened to suffer from a chronic shortage of quality lumber for the construction of palaces and temples, whose pillars originally consisted of tree trunks. Sailing along the coast, the Phoenicians gradually developed the navigational techniques that would eventually permit them to tackle the open sea, to navigate by night with the help of the North Star, and thus to become totally familiar with the eastern Mediterranean, stretching between Egypt and Greece. The clever Canaanites did not just develop sophisticated navigational technology; they also constructed excellent ships, whose hulls were caulked with tar. They had become acquainted with that product – oxidized petroleum, also known as bitumen or naphtha – in neighboring Mesopotamia, modern-day Iraq, where it bubbles out of the ground in many places. Bitumen could also be found in Phoenicia's immediate hinterland, namely in the Dead Sea, known in Antiquity not only as the 'salt sea' but also as the 'tar sea'. The Phoenicians probably also sold tar to the Egyptians, who used it to mummify their dead; the word 'mummy' is actually derived from the Semitic term *mum*, a synonym for tar or naphtha.

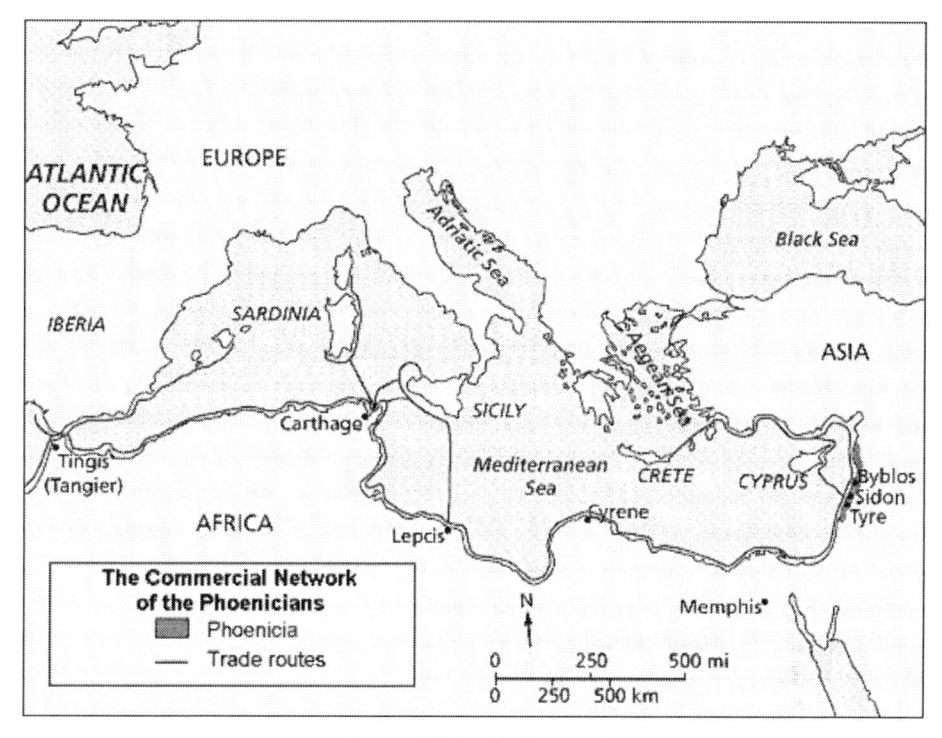

(Source: Wikimedia Commons)

By trading with the empire of the Pharaohs, the inhabitants of the city of Byblos got to know the hieroglyphic script as well as papyrus. Thus they developed the first books, and this major technological innovation became internationally known by the name of its birthplace. *Byblos* would in due course be adopted by the Greeks as the word for 'book'. Furthermore, an epic story that originated among the Jews in neighboring Palestine and that – in contrast to the usually orally transmitted stories – was in fact written down, became known as the 'Bible', that is, 'the book'. The businesslike Phoenicians did not find the Egyptians' hieroglyphic system of writing to be practical, however, so by the end of the second millennium BCE they invented the alphabet, a revolutionary system of writing that the Greeks would take over from them a few hundred years later. The term "alphabet" stems from the first two Phoenician letters, *aleph* ('ox') and *beth* ('house'). In their adoption of the alphabet the Greeks, whose typically Indo-European language featured fewer consonants and more vowels than the Semitic languages, simply took a number of letters that had symbolized consonants to the Phoenicians and used them for vowels.

The Minerals of Hispania

In Egypt and Mesopotamia there was not only a great demand for lumber, but also for gold and silver – picture the treasure of King Tut! – as well as other minerals such as copper and tin, which were the basic ingredients of bronze, an alloy used to produce weapons, statues of deities, and all sorts of other objects. It is no coincidence that the term 'Bronze Age' is a synonym for Early Antiquity, but even after the end of the Bronze Age, that is, during the Iron Age, bronze remained in great demand; the strong, shiny and beautiful material would long continue to be used for the manufacture of statues and ceremonial objects.

Phoenician merchants could be counted on to supply the minerals necessary to make bronze. Initially they were able to find them in their own part of the world, for example in neighboring Anatolia, and copper was plentiful on an island that appears to be anchored like a ship off the Phoenician coast, Cyprus. This toponym is descended from the Greek name *Kypros*, meaning 'copper island'. (However, in this case too the reverse is possible, namely that the Greek word for copper comes from the name of the island where that mineral could be found.) When the Anatolian and Cypriot mines were exhausted, the Phoenicians were forced to look elsewhere for gold, silver, copper, and tin. The search for these minerals would cause them to explore and get to know the entire Mediterranean Sea and even the waters beyond the strait where the very salty Mediterranean waters mix with those, less saline, of the Atlantic Ocean. (The higher salinity level of the Mediterranean, incidentally, is due to that sea's high evaporation rate combined with a relatively low inflow of fresh water from rivers.) The Canaanites, then, may be said to have "domesticated" the Mediterranean Sea. Just as the Spaniards would later discover in the Eldorado of the New World the gold and silver they craved, about one thousand years BCE the Phoenicians discovered in the Mediterranean "Far West" a "land of unlimited possibilities," that is, a land with a virtually endless supply of sought-after minerals: gold, silver, tin, and copper. This "Eldorado" of the Phoenicians was the afore-mentioned Iberia, inhabited by a people closely related to the North African Berbers and therefore speakers — like the Semitic Phoenicians themselves — of an Usko-Mediterranean language. The Phoenicians did not call this land Iberia, however, but gave it a name of which Spain is the modern English cognate. In order to explain this, however, a few things must be said about rabbits and hares.

During the last Ice Age, glaciers covered Europe down to the Pyrenees. When the ice cap slowly withdrew to the north, approximately ten thousand years ago, many people and animals followed it and migrated to the northern regions of Europe. Not the rabbits, however, who stayed to the south of the Pyrenees, on the Iberian Peninsula, because these little animals were unable to cross either the waters of the Bay of Biscay or the Pyrenees Mountains. The bunnies continued to hop around in Spain, where on account of their well-known fecundity they multiplied spectacularly. In the eyes of the Spaniards, the rabbit has always been a truly indigenous animal, and *conejo* has been a culinary specialty there since time immemorial. In northern Europe, on the other hand, rabbits were introduced only during the Middle Ages.

Hares have been found inside and outside Iberia for ages, and were already known to the Ancient Egyptians. This other bunny differs from rabbits in some crucial ways. For example, the hare does not live in burrows, but in nests above ground. Unlike contemporary North Americans, who tend to believe that hares and rabbits are essentially the same animal, the Romans were keenly aware of the difference; the fast hare was known in Latin as *leper* (which produced the French *lièvre*), while the sexually hyperactive rabbit had a totally different name, *cuniculus,* a term that referred not only to the hairy beastie in its little underground tunnel, but also to that little tunnel itself. (*Cuniculus* was derived from an Usko-Mediterranean word – *kunin* in Sumerian, *kuninu* in Akkadian – for 'waterpipe', 'tube'.[48]) From the Latin *cuniculus* are derived the Italian *coniglio*, the Spanish *conejo*, the Old French *conyn*, the German *Kaninchen*, the Dutch *konijn,* and finally the Old English *coney*, as in Coney Island, 'rabbit island'. In puritanical times, this nomenclature would be phased out in favor of terminology of a lower erotic voltage, such as 'rabbit' and the French *lapin*, but that is a different story.

The creature that gave Spain its name[49]
(Albrecht Dürer, 1502; Source: Wikimedia Commons)

When the Phoenicians arrived in Spain three thousand years ago, they were struck by the omnipresence of rabbits. These furry little animals reminded them of hyraxes, a kind of groundhog that was a familiar sight in their own country; in the Semitic language of Phoenicia, these were called *shaphan,* which meant 'the hidden ones'. The Canaanite explorers used this same term to refer to the rabbits of the Iberian Peninsula, and that land soon became known as *Ishaphanim* or *Ishaphania*, 'land of rabbits'. From the Carthaginians the Romans would inherit this nomenclature,

---

[48] Many Etruscan towns featured underground systems of waterpipes, known as *cuniculi*, and the Romans took over the terminology together with the technology, see Lombard (1991: 150, footnote 1), and *http://fr.wikipedia.org/wiki/R%C3%A9publique_romaine*: "les zones cultivées du Latium s'étendent grâce à l'assainissement des marais par le creusement des *cuniculi* dont on trouve encore les vestiges."

[49] Although this picture is generally known as 'the rabbit', Dürer in fact entitled it 'a young hare'.

Latinizing it as *Hispania*.⁵⁰ To the Romans as well, the Iberian Peninsula was 'rabbit land'; the poet Catullus, for example, described Iberia as *cuniculosa*, 'abounding with rabbits'. The Latin term *Hispania* eventually produced the Spanish *España*. In Hebrew, a Semitic language very closely related to Phoenician, the original Phoenician name for Spain led to *Sepharad*, and Jews who settled in Spain (until they were expelled in 1492 by the "Catholic Kings", Ferdinand and Isabella) thus became known as "Sephardic" Jews. According to the Sephardic tradition, Jews first arrived in Spain with the Phoenicians. This happened either in the time when King Solomon is supposed to have lived, approximately 1000 BCE, or about four hundred years later, in 587 BCE, when Nebuchadnezzar destroyed Jerusalem and emigration to the "Eldorado" of the Canaanite neighbors constituted an interesting alternative for Jews to that nasty Biblical exile in Babylon.

There are admittedly other theories about the origin of the name 'Spain'. It is also possible, for example, that the term *Hispania* is derived from the Phoenician *sphan*, 'north', and would therefore have the meaning of 'northern region' (or 'northern coast'), that is, the region to the north of the Strait of Gibraltar. (The Phoenicians were also interested in Morocco's Atlantic coast, an area they presumably referred to as 'the south'.) Yet another theory suggests that the Phoenician root *sapan* signified 'border' or 'extremity', and also 'treasure'. This term was used to refer to the distant land on the far side of the Mediterranean Sea where the Canaanites found "treasures", that is, the minerals that were the object of their desires. And Semerano believes that 'Spain' is a cognate of the Akkadian *sapannu*, 'sunset', 'west', 'land of the setting sun'. However, it is obvious that such down-to-earth hypotheses can hardly compete with the picturesque rabbit conjecture.⁵¹

Allegorical representation of Hispania with a rabbit at her feet.
Roman coin from the time of Emperor Hadrian.
(Source: www.museumoflondon.org.uk)

The Phoenicians were interested mainly, if not exclusively, in the many important minerals hidden in Spanish soil. They were experts in the matter, and the brown waters of a river that flows into the Atlantic Ocean near the seaport of Huelva undoubtedly revealed to them the presence of copper and iron ore further upstream.

---

[50] MacDonald (2001: 448); for more on the hyrax, see Slifkin (2004: 99ff), and *http://en.wikipedia.org/wiki/ Hyrax*.
[51] For a concise but excellent treatment of this theme, see Bendala (2000: 145-48).

We have no idea what the local Iberians or the Phoenicians themselves called that river, but eventually it received the revealing name by which it is still known today: Rio Tinto, 'Red River'. Copper was indeed to be found on the upper reaches of the Rio Tinto, namely in the mountains that bear the evocative name Sierra Morena, 'brown mountains'. From the coast it was also possible to penetrate the interior via the wide and fertile valley of another river, known in the language of the indigenous Iberians as *Tertis*; it is now called the Guadalquivir, and this is the Spanish version of the name given to the river by the Arabs when they conquered Spain in the eighth century, *Wed-al-Kebir*, the 'great river'. The *Tertis* was also known as the 'silver river', and Strabo and Pliny reported that its sources were located in the *mons argentarius*, the 'silver mountains'. They had in mind the aforementioned Sierra Morena, which abounded not only in copper but also in *argant*, as silver was called in the language of the Iberians, a term that survives in the French word *argent*.

Hercules visits Tartessos

When the Phoenicians arrived in the country we now call Spain, it had already been inhabited for centuries by a people of Saharan origin, closely related to the Palaeo-Berbers of North Africa. These people called their homeland Iberia, as we saw earlier, and present-day archaeologists and historians speak in this context of the Iberian people, the Iberian culture, and the Iberian language. Like Ancient Egyptian, that language belonged to the Hamitic group within the Afro-Asiatic family of languages and therefore differed relatively little from the Semitic Canaanite tongue of the Phoenicians. It may be said, then, that the Iberians and Phoenicians were distant relatives of a sort, who came together after having been out of touch for a long time.

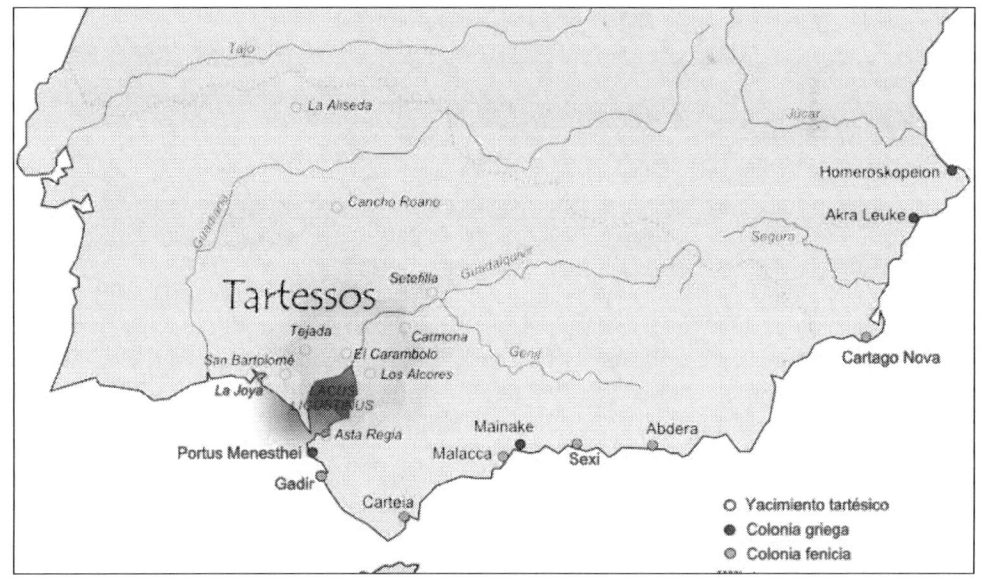

Phoenician settlements in the land of Tartessos
(Source: Wikimedia Commons)

The Phoenician merchants were interested primarily in the Atlantic coastal regions of modern Andalusia, where copper and silver and other minerals abounded. They – and later also the Greeks – referred to that particular part of Iberia as Tartessos, and archaeologists assume that an eponymous city must have existed in the vicinity of the city now known as Huelva, situated near the mouth of the aforementioned Rio Tinto. The Tartessians were excellent sailors and merchants themselves, having been at home for a very long time on the coastal waters of the Atlantic Ocean and even the dangerous Bay of Biscay. Thus they were able to supply the Phoenicians also with tin, a mineral they themselves fetched in Portugal, Galicia, the Morbihan region of Brittany, and above all in the distant British Isles, known to the Greeks – in whose language tin is called *kassiteros* – as the *Kassiterides* or 'tin islands', more specifically on the Isles of Scilly and in Cornwall. Furthermore, using an overland route known today as the *Via de la Plata*, the 'silver road', silver and gold were brought to Tartessos from parts of northern Spain, such as the gold mines of Las Medulas near the city of Léon, predestined to be mined by the Romans to the very last ounce of *oro*.[52] (Incidentally, the root of the name Scilly appears to be of Usko-Mediterranean origin, a cognate of the Akkadian *sikli.* 'sunset' or 'west', so that the Isles of Scilly are 'the western islands'; the origin of the name Cornwall will be discussed later.)

The Lady of Elche
(Photo: Luis García, 2006; source: Wikimedia Commons)

The Phoenicians never "colonized" Tartessos in the same way that European powers would later colonize distant lands full of mineral wealth. However, they engaged in intensive trade relations with that Iberian region, and exerted considerable cultural influence on it. This is reflected in the so-called "orientalizing" style of many Tartessian *objets d'art* that may be admired in the superb archaeological museums of Seville and Madrid, for example the magnificent golden 'Treasure of El Carambolo' in the museum of the Andalusian metropolis on the banks of the Guadalquivir and the famous bust of the Lady of Elche in the National Archaeological Museum in Madrid. As they often did elsewhere, the Canaanites

---
[52] On Tartessos, see the study by Jorge Alonso (n.d.).

settled in ports of trade – or *emporia*, to use the Greek terminology – situated on strategically and commercially favorable sites, preferably on small offshore islands. Around the year 1000 BCE, they founded their most important emporium in Tartessos. They called it *Gadir* – 'wall' and therefore also 'walled town', 'fortress', or 'citadel' – and we now know this seaport by its Spanish name, Cadiz. In the course of Antiquity *Gadir* was to be Hellenized as *Gadeira* and Latinized as *Gades*. It is no coincidence that the Latin term is plural, because the city comprised a number of little islands; the city proper was located on one of them, and on another was the temple of the Phoenician deity, Melkart. However, on account of thousands of years of silting up, the former Phoenician fortress town is now situated at the tip of a peninsula. With its Phoenician antecedents, incidentally, Cadiz can and does claim to be the oldest city in Europe.

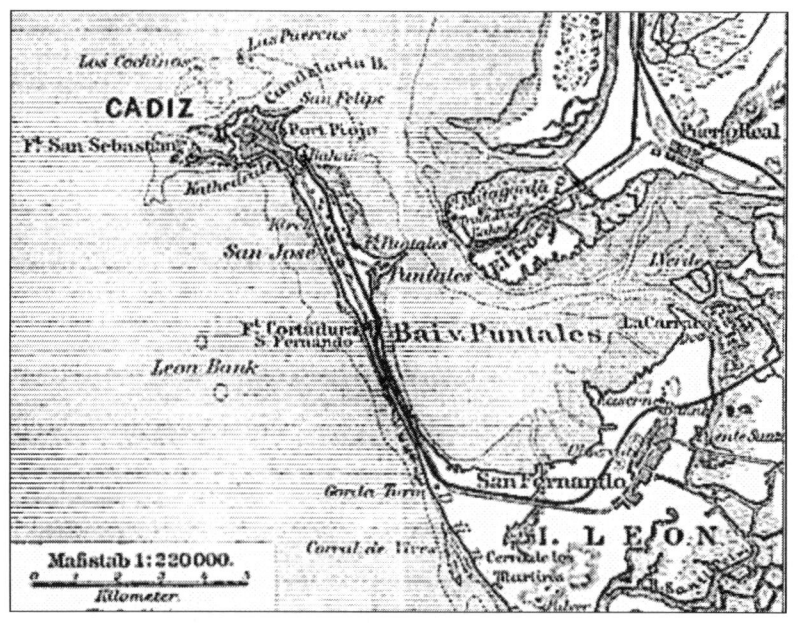

Plan of Cadiz in 1888
(Meyers Konversations-Lexicon; source: Wikimedia Commons)

Gadir enjoyed a wonderful location, on the coast and in the immediate vicinity of the mouths of the Guadalquivir and the Rio Tinto, respectively the silver and copper rivers, and very likely also close to the most important trade center of the Tartessians. The emporium was situated on the Atlantic coast, but not far at all from the familiar Mediterranean Sea, and also not far from the Moroccan coast, where the Phoenicians likewise engaged in trade — for example in gold, ivory, and ostrich feathers and eggs — and founded emporia. In the interior, and above all in the fertile valley of the Guadalquivir, the Phoenicians also founded a number of trading posts. One was given the name *Sepil(ia)*, or *Sfela*, which meant 'low-lying place', 'city in the lower plain'; the Arabs would later transform that term into *Ishbilia*, and thus originated the name of Seville. Further upstream, still on the banks of the Guadalquivir but close to the copper-rich mountains of the Sierra Morena, the Phoenicians founded *Kart Tuba*, the 'great [*tuba*] city [*kart*]'. This *Kartuba* would later be called *Corduba* by the Romans and *Kurtuba* by the Arabs; we now know it as Cordoba. *Nomen est omen*, goes the Latin proverb, and *Kart Tuba* would indeed become a great city; in 1000 CE – when the Phoenicians had admittedly long ago departed from the Iberian scene – Cordoba was one of the three biggest cities in Europe, with Constantinople and Palermo completing the trio.

King Solomon
(The Bible of Charles the Bald, 880 CE; source: Wikimedia Commons)

When the Phoenicians began to trade in Spain around the year 1,000 BCE, Byblos had long since ceased to be the leading seaport in their own homeland. For a while Byblos had been succeeded in this role by Sidon, but by the end of the second millennium BCE the city of Tyre had become the great metropolis of Canaan. Its name signified 'rock', reflecting the fact that Tyre was situated on a rocky little offshore island; the town's present Arab name is *Sur*, which has the same meaning. *Sur* is in fact a very ancient Semitic, i.e. Usko-Mediterranean term, *surum* in Akkadian and *sur* in Hebrew. Tyre was cited by the authors of the Bible as the hub of a great (though mostly commercial) empire and as a fine and powerful city; its lord, Hiram, was allegedly a contemporary of King Solomon. This Phoenician New York featured a great temple that was dedicated to the local version of the god Baal, known in Tyre as 'Baal Melkart' or 'Melkart' for short. The name Melkart signified 'king [*malik*] of the city [*kart*]'. Inside the "holy of holies" of this temple there was no statue of this deity, but instead an abstract symbol representing him. Semitic people tended to be "aniconistic", that is, they typically rejected "craven images" in favor of abstract representations of deities, known as *bethels*. (The term *bethel* stems from *beth-el*, 'house of the god'.) According to an ancient tradition, King Hiram made architects available to his royal colleague, Solomon, in order to build a similar looking temple in the latter's capital, Jerusalem; it was in the *sanctum sanctorum* of this temple that the Ark of the Covenant found a home.

Tyre
(Photo: French Air Force, pre-1934; Source: Wikimedia Common)

Remarkable in the case of the façade of the temple of Tyre – and, according to ancient traditions, likewise in that of the temple of Solomon – was a great entrance flanked dramatically by two bronze pillars, an arrangement that differs greatly from that of the later, more familiar Greek and Roman temples with their multiplicity of pillars, their colonnade or "peristyle". According to Bernal, those two pillars functioned as "spiritual lightning rods" that were supposed to ward off the evil deity, Booz or Boaz (Bernal 1996: II.168). An alternative theory holds that they symbolized the equilibrium between the powers of good and evil – the "yin" and "yang," in Chinese terms – in the dualistic cosmos of the Canaanite people. The twin pillars were twisted and decorated with vines, and therefore resembled what are called "Solomonic columns". As in the case of the Temple of Melkart in Gadir and Solomon's Temple in Jerusalem, these columns were crowned with "Proto-Aeolic" capitals featuring an anthemion ('flower'), also known as a palmette, that is, a radiating, fan-shaped ornament suggestive of the leaf of a palm tree, the symbol of Canaan. Today nothing is left of the once famous Temple of Melkart, but three thousand years ago that building was known throughout the civilized world, and to the inhabitants of Tyre and the Phoenicians in general it served as a source of pride and a symbol of their city, much as the Twin Towers once did for New York. Like the Manhattan Twin Towers, the Temple of Melkart with its twin pillars fell victim to the wrath of the enemies of those who took pride in it; in 332 BCE the Greeks, led by Alexander the Great, destroyed the symbol of Tyre together with the rest of the city after a long siege.

Proto-Aeolic capitals, rescued from the ruins of Carthage and elsewhere, put to new use in the famous Kairwan Mosque colonnade
(Photo: J Pauwels, 2009)

On the other side of the Mediterranean Sea, approximately 4000 kilometers away from their home port, a distance that under optimal circumstances could be covered in three months – a gigantic kind of mirror image of their familiar temple of Melkart revealed itself to Phoenician sailors on their way to Tartessos, namely, two oversized "pillars" that flanked the watery "gate" that led from the Mediterranean *mare nostrum* to the mysterious Atlantic Ocean. This "gate" was the narrows known today as the Strait of Gibraltar; on the European side loomed the steep rock of Gibraltar, while on the African side the admittedly less spectacular and lesser known but nonetheless impressive peak of Jabal Musa may be admired. In the Palaeo-Berber, Usko-Mediterranean language of the Tartessians, these twin mountains were called Calpe and Abila. According to Semerano, the former toponym probably combined the Usko-Mediterranean terms *kallu,* 'top' or 'crown', and *appu,* 'peninsula', giving us a meaning akin to 'steep rock jutting out into the sea'; and Abila was supposedly a cognate of the Akkadian *abullu* and the Hebrew *abul*, 'gate', an allusion to the geographical fact that this site marked the gateway from the Mediterranean to the Atlantic and vice versa. In any event, the Phoenicians baptized those twin mountains the Pillars of Melkart in honor of the "patron saint" of Tyre, who also happened to be the protector of the city's diligent merchants. Because the Greeks identified Melkart with their demigod Hercules (or Heracles), the Greeks as well as the Romans later referred to the twin peaks as the Pillars of Hercules.

In order to perfect the symmetry on both sides of their familiar Mediterranean world, the Phoenicians constructed an enormous temple of Melkart just beyond the "gateway" to the Atlantic Ocean, that is, in their Tartessian emporium, Gadir. Within this temple they installed the *bethel* of the deity – in the Hellenistic era it would be replaced by an anthropomorphous statue of the *Hercules Gaditanus* – and the entrance was of course adorned by a pair of pillars, just as in the case of the sanctuary in Tyre. The idea behind all this, according to the historian Denis van Berchem, was that "the presence of their god would turn this faraway corner of the world which they claimed for themselves into [...] an extension of their own fatherland". However, with this remarkable edifice the Phoenicians simultaneously erected an appropriate monument commemorating the truly "Herculean" task they themselves had accomplished, namely, the "domestication" of the entire Mediterranean Sea from the Levant to the confines of the great ocean in the west. This temple, which was to become famous in the Greek world as the *Herakleion* of Gadir, would exist for approximately one thousand years. During the final years of the Roman Empire, however, Christianity became the state religion, and that opportunity was used by fanatical and intolerant zealots to raze the temple to the ground. The site of the *Herakleion* was given the name of St. Peter, the Christian incarnation of Melkart/Hercules. As in Tyre, so in Cadiz: not a trace remains of the great temple of Melkart.

A Phoenician base in the dusty land

Gadir was the New York of the New World of the Phoenicians, but in the distant Land of Rabbits the Canaanites also founded other emporia, for example *Malaka*, the modern-day city of Malaga. Perhaps this name is descended from the same *malik*, 'king', that hides in Melkart, which would make the meaning 'queen', that is, 'queen of seaports'. However, it is more likely that its root is a homonym of *malik*, namely *malaka*, meaning 'haven', 'refuge'. (The Arabic cognate is *malga*, and Arab sailors would later give that name to a seaport in the Far East, Malacca.) Another seaport where Phoenician ships en route to or from Tartessos could find protection against the waves and winds of the often dangerous Mediterranean had a name with an almost identical significance, 'haven' or 'well protected harbor': Malta. But to the Greeks this Phoenician toponym conjured up their word for honey, *melita,* so they concluded that its meaning was 'Honey Island'. That this Greek etymology is the conventional wisdom in Malta today is perhaps due to the fact that the island produces much honey of excellent quality.

The Phoenicians normally called on Malta and on the western part of the neighboring island of Sicily on their way from their homeland to distant Tartessos. This voyage usually took them from their home port via Cyprus to the south coast of Turkey and the Greek islands, and hence to Malta and Sicily; from Sicily they continued to the south of Sardinia, the Balearics, the east coast of Spain, Malaga, and Gibraltar. This route was taken because within the Mediterranean Sea the currents run counter-clockwise. For the return journey, preference was consequently given to a southern route along the coast of North Africa. What was to develop into the paramount port of call along this route was founded in 814 BCE in the vicinity of present-day Tunis, more or less halfway between Tartessos and the Levant. The name given to this emporium was Carthage, in Phoenician *Kart Hadasht,* meaning 'new city', more particularly, 'new Tyre'. When between 700 and 600 BCE Tyre and the other cities in the Canaanite homeland were overwhelmed by neighboring powers, first the Assyrians and then the Babylonians under Nebuchadnezzar, the Phoenician possessions on the other side of the Mediterranean Sea found themselves to be independent, whether they liked it or not. And so the seaport of Carthage, favorably situated in the heart of the Mediterranean world rather than the Atlantic outpost of Gadir, developed into the great metropolis of the "West Phoenicians". The vast region that would come under the domination of Carthage is called the "Carthaginian" Empire in our history books, but their Roman neighbors and rivals spoke of the *Puni* (or *Poeni*; the adjective being *punicus/a, poenicus/a*) and the "Punic" Empire. The long and bloody wars (264-241, 218-202, and 149-146 BCE) in which Rome and Carthage fought over supremacy in the western Mediterranean were described by the Latin author, Livy, as the three "Punic" Wars. *Puni* and *Punici* were simply Latin cognates of the Greek word *Phoinikè*. As far as the Romans were concerned, the Carthaginians obviously were and remained Phoenicians.

Delenda est Carthago — 'Carthage must be destroyed' — was the slogan of the hawks on the banks of the Tiber, and in due course Carthage was indeed wiped off the face of the earth by Rome. For many hundreds of years, however, this proud West Phoenician city dominated a gigantic region stretching from the Atlantic coast of Spain via Sardinia and Sicily to the Libyan Desert. Just like their East Phoenician predecessors, the Carthaginians founded emporia on strategic sites, and quite a few of these developed into important cities. Spain was again the stage of much activity of this nature. The most renowned family of Carthage, the Barcids, of which Hamilcar Barcas as well as the famous Hannibal were members, thus founded in the northeast of the Iberian Peninsula a seaport that still bears its name, Barcelona. (Incidentally,

Hamilcar signified 'Son of Melkart', and Hannibal was 'Honor to our god', or Gottlob, as one would say in German.)

View of the ruins of Carthage
(Photo: Patrick Verdier, 2004; Source: Wikipedia Commons)

Along the same eastern Mediterranean coast of Rabbit Land, the name of the city of Carthagena, 'Little Carthage', reflects yet another Punic colonial initiative. After the Second Punic War, most Spanish possessions of Carthage were taken over by Rome, but in North Africa itself the ancient Phoenician culture and language – the *lingua punica* – would continue to exist long after the city's destruction. At the time of the church father Augustine (354-430 CE), the Carthaginian version of the Phoenician language was still spoken there. The Punic tongue of North Africa only died out in the course of the seventh century, when the Arabs conquered that part of the world and introduced not only a new religion, Islam, but also a different Semitic language, Arabic, admittedly a close relative of Phoenician.

According to some, the toponym "Africa" is of Arab origin and is a derivation of the Arabic word *afar,* 'dust'; Africa is therefore the 'dusty' or 'sandy' land. However, the Romans already used the term *Africa* in order to refer to the hinterland of Carthage, that is, more or less the territory of modern-day Tunisia, long before the Arabs started to exert a measure of influence in that part of the Mediterranean world. Like Ancient Greek, Latin was hardly influenced by the Arabic language. In Antiquity, Arabic did not play a role of importance even in the Middle East; the regional *lingua franca* there was another Semitic language, namely Aramaic, said to have been the tongue spoken by Christ. It was only with the emergence of Islam in the seventh century CE that Aramaic was displaced by Arabic as the leading language of the region. Furthermore, the Romans must have become familiar at an early stage with the northern part of the "black continent"; it is therefore highly improbable that they would have had to borrow a name for that familiar land from the inhabitants of the distant Arab Peninsula. In Antiquity, the latter were still a relatively parochial people, whose knowledge of Africa was restricted to Egypt – a special case – and of course to the part that happens to lie close to them, on the other side of the Red Sea, a region for which they had a name that lives on today: *Bilad As Sudan*, the 'land of the black people', or "Sudan" for short. Finally, why would the Arabs have given to a far away and foreign land a name that applied equally well to their own desert-like, dry, and "dusty" homeland? When in the seventh century CE the Arabs did get to know (and conquer) areas now called Tunisia, Algeria, and Morocco, they were struck not by the dryness but by the relative fertility of that region, which is after all blessed with a Mediterranean climate. This was reflected onomastically in the name they gave to that area, *Al-Jazair,* the fertile and therefore eminently habitable "island" between three seas: the Mediterranean Sea, the Atlantic Ocean, and the great sand-sea, the truly "dusty" Sahara, which did in fact remind them very much of their own homeland. That Arab nomenclature for North Africa, the "island," lives on today in the name of Tunisia's neighbor, Algeria, known in Arabic as *Al-Jazair*.

It is very likely that the name "Africa" was given to the hinterland of Carthage by the Phoenicians who founded that colony. *Afar* – "dust," "sand," "earth" – is indeed not exclusively Arab, but is a term that already existed in the Phoenician language and in its close relative, Hebrew, as well as other languages of the Semitic branch of the Afro-Asiatic family. Like the aforementioned Palaeo-Berber word *iber*, *afar* was a cognate of the Akkadian *eperu*, and the significance in all cases was "land [in contrast to water]". In a recent book, Semerano pays a lot of attention to this term, and identifies it as the word for the "earth," "clay," or "dust," from which God created man according to the Bible, the "dust" of which man is made and to which he or she must inevitably return after death (Semerano 2001).

The hypothesis that the Phoenicians were the originators of the term "Africa" is quite plausible. Their own homeland, Canaan, enjoyed a Mediterranean climate, and so did virtually all emporia founded by the Phoenicians in their "new world" in the west. The dryness and "dustiness" of great parts of North Africa must have made an impression on them, particularly wherever the desert reached the immediate vicinity of their colonies. This happened to be the case in Carthage. A dramatic contrast existed there between the fertile surroundings of the city itself, known for its lush gardens and orchards, and the steppes and desert in the interior. This dichotomy may well have inspired the truly rational Phoenician-Carthaginian nomenclature – "Africa," "dusty land" – for the hinterland of Carthage. The term "Africa" was taken over by the Romans, and thus originated the Latin version, *Africa,* which for a long time used to refer exclusively to the region around Carthage, modern-day Tunisia. The Roman commander Scipio was honored with the title *Africanus* for having defeated the Carthaginian enemies in their own "African" neighborhood in Zama, in 202 BCE; this victory, "away from home," so to speak, was all the more remarkable since in the earlier "home game" the Romans had almost been crushed by Hannibal. For other regions of Africa, including parts of North Africa, the Romans used other names; the neighbors of Carthage in present-day Algeria and Morocco, for example, were said to inhabit *Numidia* and *Mauritania,* and the regions thus named were considered not as parts of *Africa*, but as separate and equivalent geographical areas. Like the Ancient Greeks, the Romans used to refer to the African continent in its entirety as *Libya* or *Ethiopia.*

It is most likely, then, that the credit for having coined the term "Africa" should go to those great, albeit frequently underestimated explorers of Antiquity, the Phoenicians. If the "dark continent" does indeed bear a Phoenician name, it would only be appropriate, even though when using this nomenclature the Canaanites had in mind not the continent in its entirety, but only the arid hinterland of their Carthaginian colony. The Phoenicians have indeed made a considerable contribution to the Ancients' geographical knowledge of Africa. At an early stage already, they became familiar with the north coast of the "black continent" from the Nile delta to the Pillars of Hercules, and it did not take long before the Atlantic coast of Morocco was a *mare cognitum* to Phoenician sailors. *Dor,* or *dir,* as in *Gadir,* the Phoenician word for fort, can be identified even today in toponyms along the Atlantic coast of Morocco, such as Mogador (now known as Essaouira) and Agadir; Agadir is actually a Berber version of the Phoenician *Gadir,* 'walled town'. The Carthaginians later took over the role of the Phoenicians in the region known as Guinea, and in the fifth century BCE a Carthaginian admiral, Hanno, undertook a spectacular journey along the West African coast, apparently all the way to Cameroon. (The gorilla skins he brought home to Carthage and donated as a kind of *ex voto* to a local temple were still there when, hundreds of years later, the Romans conquered the city.) According to an ancient tradition, around the same time another Carthaginian, Himilco, led a similar seaborne expedition in a northern direction, presumably in an attempt to reach the fabulous "tin islands," and it is said that he went as far as Brittany. The Phoenicians are also believed to have been familiar with the Red Sea, where they allegedly carried out expeditions on behalf of King Solomon, for example to mysterious lands such as Ophir and Tarshish. However, by far the greatest African achievement of the Phoenicians was unquestionably their famous circumnavigation of the entire African continent around 600 BCE. This undertaking amounted to yet another truly Herculean feat. It was a three-year odyssey, which the majority of historians today believe did indeed take place, and it was carried out on behalf of an Egyptian Pharaoh, Nacho (610-595 BCE).

Something must also be said about the term "Sahara". This word is ssometimes claimed to derive from the Arab *sahr,* '[the color of a] fawn', and this is not a bad way to describe the color of the sands of the great North African desert. Over time, the term "Sahara" supposedly took on the meaning of sand sea'. This too is a conventional explanation, against which one can cite the historical fact that the Berbers of North Africa, who had been familiar with this desert for centuries, did not need the Arabs – who only showed up in North Africa in the seventh century CE – to provide them with a name for such a prominent feature of their environment. It is far more likely, then, that the name "Sahara" would be of Berber or possibly Phoenician origin, but its etymology is buried below the dust left behind by thousands of years of history.

A "sand sea" of dunes in the Western Sahara
(Source: not traced)

A great expert in the history and cultures of the Mediterranean Sea, the Croat Predrag Matvejević (2000: 108), tips his hat to the Phoenicians: "The glory they earned on account of their distant voyages", he writes, "has proved to be more durable than bronze". Today the Phoenician, or rather Canaanite, people no longer exist, but their descendants are still at home in many places along the coast of the Mediterranean Sea they "domesticated" and were entitled to call *Mare Nostrum* long before the Romans would make that boast: in the south and east of Spain, in Morocco and Tunisia, on islands such as Mallorca, Sardinia, Sicily, Cyprus, and Malta (where a modern version of their language continues to be spoken), and naturally also along the eastern seaboard of the Mediterranean, in the land known as Canaan in the Bible. This Canaan has also ceased to exist, or rather, it still exists but no longer bears the name of the people who called themselves Canaanites. In the course of the centuries their homeland was conquered, occupied, and colonized time and again by foreigners. The first foreign invaders were the cruel Assyrians, who were followed by Nebuchadnezzar and his Babylonians, the Achaemenid Persians under Cyrus, Alexander the Great's Greeks and Macedonians, the Romans and Byzantines, Arabs, Seljuk Turks, "Frankish" crusaders and Kurdish fighters for Allah, Ottoman Pashas, and finally, in the twentieth century, French colonial masters. Virtually without exception, these outsiders spared no effort to recast the inhabitants of the Levant in their own image, succeeding to a greater or lesser degree. The result of this convoluted historical development is a small country with a dynamic and cosmopolitan population. Since the departure of the French at the end of the Second World War this country bears the name of the Lebanon Mountains, formerly crowned with a legendary cedar forest, that used to constitute the eastern border of the Phoenician world.

3

Between Ashiwa and Atlas: The *Oikoumene* of the Greeks

Land of the Rising Sun, Land of the Setting Sun

Like their Phoenician competitors, the Greeks also revealed themselves to be great international travelers and merchants, discoverers and colonizers. They too discovered new lands and settled in a "new world" in the west, and had to devise all sorts of new names for peoples, regions, cities, and rivers; in this process, however, existing indigenous ethno- and toponyms were frequently Hellenized. Ancient Greece also produced philosophers, scientists, geographers and historians, such as Plato, Aristotle, Herodotus, Eratosthenes, and Ptolemy. These intellectuals developed certain theories with respect to the earth in general and the continents and seas in particular, and they came up with concepts and names that are still familiar to us.

The Mediterranean as the centre of the world, linking Asia, Europe, and Africa
(Drawing in Isidorus' *Etymologiae*, 623CE, first printed in 1472; source: Wikimedia Commons)

The Greek word for the earth, for example, was *gaia,* or *gè,* and this is the root of terms such as *geography* and *geology*. The earth features water as well as land, and the part of the earth inhabited by humans was known to the Greeks as *Oikoumene*. This term – in which the Greek word for house, *oikos,* can be recognized – was probably first used by the philosopher Democritus around 400 BCE. The *Oikoumene* was perceived as being round, and a gigantic "river", the *Okeanos,* encircled it like a snake wrapped around a tree; this "ocean" also separated the land from the air, the earth from the heavens. Furthermore, a sea divided the inhabitable part of the earth into three continents: Europe, Asia, and Africa. This sea, which not only separated but also connected the three continents, was of course the Mediterranean. The term "Mediterranean Sea", however, would only be introduced by the Romans, and is in fact a sort of misnomer, as has been explained by an expert in the field, Predrag Matvejević. The Latin term *mediterraneus* – like its synonym, *meditullius* – was the opposite of *maritimus* and signified 'in the middle of the land'; in principle, therefore, the term referred to a place *on* land, not to something *between* lands.[53] It is widely known that the Romans liked to refer to the Mediterranean Sea as *mare nostrum*, 'our sea', but that was something the Greeks had already done before them. However, the Greeks usually called the Mediterranean the 'inner sea' (*entos thalassa*), while the Ocean was known as the 'outer sea' (*éiso thalassa*). The Mediterranean 'inner sea' was perceived to belong to the familiar world of humans, the *Oikoumene*, but not so the Oceanic 'outer sea'. Of the great ocean sea, one had empirical knowledge only in the west, where each and every evening its turbulent waters could be seen to swallow the sun, symbol of life *par excellence* among archaic peoples. On account of this, the ocean was associated with darkness, the underworld, and death; it hence functioned as a symbol of death.

Diving from the Pillars of Hercules into the western "sea of death"
(Greek fresco of ca. 470 BCE on a tomb at Paestum; source: Wikimedia Commons)

The Romans would inherit this vision, even though they would become quite familiar with the Atlantic's coastal waters; for them the Mediterranean Sea was the familiar *Mare Nostrum*, but the ocean was the *Mare Tenebrum*, the terrifying 'sea of darkness'. (The Arabs too would later call the Atlantic Ocean 'sea of darkness', *al bahr al zulumat*.) The Pillars of Hercules symbolized not only the geographic end of the familiar world of the Romans and Greeks, but also the frontier between life and death. These pillars were associated with the saying *nec plus ultra,* '[there is] nothing beyond'; nothing, that is, that was familiar to them in terms of both space and

---

[53] Matvejević (1998: 14; 2000: 206). According to Deroy & Mulon (1992: 309), the term *Mare Mediterraneum* was first used "as a true toponym" by Isidorus of Seville in the 7th century AD.

time. Paestum is famous for its Greek temples, but the local museum features an equally wonderful Greek fresco that used to decorate a tomb; it shows the deceased diving from the Pillars of Hercules, the physical end of the world and thus simultaneously the symbolic end of life, into the waters of the ocean, the sea of death.

As Martin Bernal has demonstrated so impressively in *Black Athena*, the wisdom of the Greeks was nurtured primarily by knowledge, myths, and traditions originating in the southern and eastern lands where the very first civilizations had originated thousands of years before Plato attended kindergarten, namely Egypt and Mesopotamia. It was long believed that philosophy constituted an original contribution by the Greeks, amounting to a *rational* – and presumably typically "Western" – way of thinking, one that owed nothing to the traditional, supposedly purely *mythical* thought of the easterners. We now know better: in intellectual matters too, the Greeks once sat at the feet of their wise Asian and African neighbors, and consequently it does not make sense to proclaim philosophy a "Western" invention.

It is no coincidence that Greek philosophy first made its appearance in Ionian Greece, in cities such as Miletus, with thinkers like Thales, Anaximandros, Anaximenes, and Heraclites. Indeed, Ionia functioned as the Greek window on the world of the Babylonians, Assyrians, Persians, and other Orientals. The fact that the Greeks learned a great deal from the easterners and Egyptians is also reflected in the terminology used by the Ionian "natural philosophers". The word "nature" itself is of Egyptian origin, as we saw earlier. Also of particular interest, as seen from our perspective, is the fact that a key term of Greek "materialist" philosophy – and therefore of embryonic scientific thinking – is related to a Semitic word encountered frequently in the eastern wisdom literature – including the Bible, as our Italian linguistic guide, Semerano, has demonstrated in a recent and fascinating book, *L'infinito: un equivoco millenario*. That term is *afar* (or *apar*), the 'earth', 'clay', 'dust', or 'matter' that makes up not only humans themselves but the entire cosmos of which they are an infinitely small part. Of this *afar/apar*, which happens to be the core of the toponym *Africa*, is derived the Greek word *apeiron*, used by the Ionian philosopher Anaximandros to refer to the earth or dust – in other words, the *matter* – "of which everything is made and which everything must become again", both the infinitely big (the stars in the heavens) and the infinitely small (the billions of grains of sand). (On account of this, *apeiron* has sometimes been translated inaccurately as 'infinity'.[54]) Ionian natural philosophy, the basic principles of Greek "materialist" philosophy, and therefore the "rudimentary principles" and the "secularization" (that is, the de-mythologization) of science, as Semerano puts it, had been directly inspired by Mesopotamian and other eastern antecedents.

Mesopotamian and Egyptian ideas also inspired Greek cosmology and eventually Greek geography. Not so long ago Babylonian world maps were unearthed, and these reveal a remarkable similarity with much younger Hellenic cosmographies. The concept of the ocean as a kind of snake, wrapped around the land and separating it from the sky, already familiar to the Babylonians, was in fact of even more ancient,

---

[54] Semerano (2001: 32, 43ff). See also the remarks in Bottéro (1998: 175-85, 201, 214).

Sumerian origin, at least according to Martin Bernal. He believes, furthermore, that the word *Okeanos* itself echoes the Sumerian combination *a-ki-an*, the 'water [*a*] between the land [*ki*] and the heaven [*an*]', and that it is from the Sumerian *ki* (or sometimes *gu*) that the Greek word for 'earth', *gè* or *gaia*, was derived (Bernal 1996.2: 301). As mentioned earlier, the Greeks also learned a few things from the Egyptians, for example a word with the meaning of 'great water': *Atlas*. According to Bernal, in the land of the Pharaohs this term was originally used to refer to great rivers such as the Nile or the Euphrates. Eventually, however, *Atlas* conjured up the Mediterranean, or at least the eastern basin of that sea, which was familiar to the Egyptians. The seafaring Greeks borrowed this Egyptian term; to them too it probably originally signified the eastern Mediterranean, then the Mediterranean Sea in its entirety, and ultimately the seemingly endless mass of water that could be glimpsed beyond the Pillars of Hercules. To the Greeks, the *Okeanos* was the 'great water', the "Atlas", *par excellence*, and thus these two terms became synonymous.

On the shores of the huge mass of oceanic water, at the very end of the world, somewhere in North Africa to the south of the Pillars of Hercules, there was a mountain range that would eventually also acquire the name Atlas. The reason was that, in the mind of the Greeks, its high peaks shared the neighboring ocean's primordial function, namely, separating the earth from – or linking it to? – the heavens. The Atlas Mountains were said to touch the sky, to rise like "pillars that support the heavens". (Here too there is a remarkable similarity with the Babylonian world view, which postulated high mountains in the extreme west, on the edge of the Ocean, there "to support the heavens" [Bottéro 1999: 163].) When used to refer to the mountains, the name *Atlas* eventually acquired the significance of 'mountains at the end of the world', 'mountains on the edge of the ocean'. The Atlantic Ocean does not owe its name to these mountains, as we are often told; on the contrary, they received the name Atlas because they were situated near the Ocean and, like the *Okeanos*, conjured up the end of the (inhabited) world, the *Oikoumene*, and separated the earth from the heavens.

The term "Atlantic Ocean" is intrinsically tautological, because *Atlas* was, originally at least, simply a synonym for *Okeanos*. However, the name *Atlas* would be used increasingly to refer to the Moroccan mountain range alone, perhaps because the great mass of water at its feet already had the unambiguous nomenclature *Okeanos* available to it. At the dawn of the era of the Great Discoveries, Columbus and company still spoke of the "great ocean sea" when they had in mind the Atlantic Ocean. But as new oceans were discovered, it became necessary to differentiate the world sea of Antiquity from the new upstarts. Thus originated the appellation "Atlantic Ocean", and thus originated the belief that the name of this particular ocean is due to the mountains on its shores, instead of vice versa.

A vast and distant land, a great water, the setting sun, snow-covered mountain peaks, *Atlas, Okeanos*: these were vital elements in the cosmology of the Ancient Greeks. Moreover, as seen from the Hellenic perspective, all of these things were to be found in the west, in the "far west" of their world, beyond the Pillars of Hercules. The Greeks had preciously little empirical knowledge about that region, if only because the Phoenicians – and later the Carthaginians – did not normally tolerate competitors over there. (Only on very rare occasions was it possible for Hellenic sailors to slip through the Punic blockade of the Strait of Gibraltar; those who did, like Pytheas of Marseilles, returned home with fabulous tales.) The Greeks' far west was therefore a mysterious world, reputed to be the habitat of gods, heroes, and monsters, the antechamber of the underworld, and the theatre of all sorts of myths whose main ingredients happened to be the aforementioned cosmological elements. In those myths we meet the giant Atlas, for example, a Schwarzenegger working out by hoisting a massive globe on his shoulders. This theme was already centuries old during Plato's lifetime: the ocean, named Atlas, supported the heavens, and a mountain personified by a giant named Atlas supported the earth.

Atlas supporting the Earth
(Artist: Rubens, 1613; source: Wikipedia)

To the Greeks, the mythological Pillars of Hercules simultaneously conjured up the ocean and the mountains that were to be found in their immediate vicinity; according to Mircea Eliade, pillars were archetypical symbols of a connection between heaven and earth. And in these ancient myths we of course also meet Heracles (Hercules), the Greek Melkart, who travels west to perform his great labors. It is in the west that Hercules seeks the Apples of the Hesperides, symbols of the minerals of Tartessos and of the unreachable Kassiterides, the tin islands. Of Hercules it was also said that he had used his enormous club to split the mountain that had blocked the way from the Mediterranean Sea to the Atlantic Ocean in two, thus opening up a strait flanked by two half-mountains, the Pillars of Hercules. This myth amounted to a veiled compliment to the Canaanite competitors of the Greeks, who had succeeded in a truly heroic fashion in finding a way from the familiar "inner sea" to the mysterious "outer sea". Indeed, because of the strong east-flowing current in the Strait of Gibraltar, an enormous physical effort is required to row into the Atlantic waters. Even when occasional easterly, so-called "Levanter" winds make it possible to hoist a sail, this passage amounted to a truly Herculean labor.

We should not forget the age-old legend of Atlantis, the utopian kingdom that was swallowed by the oceanic waves. This was supposedly an "Atlantic" island, but it is far from certain that we should imagine a location somewhere in the Atlantic Ocean. The reason for this is that for many centuries the term Atlas simply conjured up some "great water", that is, an impressive river or sea. It is most likely that the toponym "Atlantis" referred to an Aegean island called Thera. Thera almost certainly owed its name to the Phoenicians; in their Semitic language *tira* meant 'settlement', 'village', or 'town', so the name signified something like 'the island with the city'. During the Middle Ages, the presence of a chapel dedicated to a martyr, Irene, popular in Italy, caused Thera to become known among Venetians and Genoans as *Santa Irena* or *Sant Erini*, and thus originated Thera's modern name, Santorini. During the first half of the second millennium BCE, this island was a possession of the fabulous Minoan Empire, based on the island of Crete. At that time, neither the Egyptians nor the Greeks – who had not even arrived yet in the land named after them – were familiar with the distant *Okeanos* that would later be called "Atlantic". The term Atlas then still signified simply the sea, the Mediterranean Sea, and probably only the eastern part of that sea, that is, the waters between Egypt, Greece, and Asia Minor; indeed, the western basin of the Mediterranean would long remain a *mare incognitum*. Thera is situated in the middle of the "great [Mediterranean] water" familiar to the Greeks of the archaic era. This corresponds perfectly with the supposed location of Atlantis, at least if we accept the modern translation – or interpretation – of Plato's famous remarks in this respect. The traditional interpretation of the philosopher's text described Atlantis as being "greater than Asia and Africa combined". This implied that the island could not possibly have been located in the Mediterranean Sea and ought therefore to have been situated in the biggest of all bodies of water, the *Okeanos*. Moreover, in Plato's time, the term "Atlas" was no longer associated by the Greeks with the eastern basin of the Mediterranean, but with the distant western ocean. Consequently, it is very likely that Plato's contemporaries assumed that an island named Atlantis had to be located somewhere in the endless waters beyond the Pillars of Hercules. However, it is now rather convincingly argued that Plato used ambiguous key words whose correct interpretation is that Atlantis was not "*greater than* Asia and Africa combined" but situated *halfway between* Asia (Minor) and Libya (meaning North Africa to the west of Egypt), which is exactly where Thera is to be found. Thera, then, was Plato's Atlantis. And indeed, just like the legendary Atlantis, Thera was swallowed by the sea, at least partially, on account of a spectacular volcanic eruption that took place at the earliest in 1628 BCE and at the latest in 1450 BCE.

In the middle of the second millennium BCE, the so-called Mycenaean Civilization flourished on the Greek mainland. Its name refers to one of the great centers of the Late Bronze Age in Greece, Mycenae, whose impressive ruins attract numerous tourists to this site in the region of Argolis. According to Semerano, "Mycenae" means nothing other than 'dwelling place', 'foundation' – *makanu* in

Akkadian, *makon* in Hebrew. The toponym is of Usko-Mediterranean origin, but the Mycenaean Greeks were an Indo-European people. They are considered to be the direct ancestors of the present-day Hellenes and, like the latter, they revealed themselves as extremely capable sailors. Before them, at the time of the Usko-Mediterranean Minoan civilization on the islands of Crete and Thera, the eastern Mediterranean Sea had already been thoroughly explored, and the Minoans had probably already ventured as far as Italy.

Mycenean woman accepting necklace, fresco, Mycenae, ca. 1500 BCE
(Photo: Marsyas, 2005; source: Wikimedia Commons)

Of the Mycenaean Greeks we know with certainty that they undertook regular voyages to the western basin of the "inner sea". They traded in Sicily and Sardinia, and also on the Italian mainland. However, the progress that was made at that time was lost during the twelfth century BCE as a result, perhaps, of invasions by Dorian Greeks and by the so-called "sea peoples". These events were accompanied by wars and the destruction of cities, not only in Mycenaean Greece but also in Egypt and throughout the Middle East, where the Hittite Empire collapsed. Then a "dark age" descended on Greece, which was to last nearly half a millennium. Nevertheless, a vague memory of the great Mycenaean voyages to the west lived on in Greece in heroic legends that would crystallize in the eighth century in the form of a great epic poem, the *Odyssey*. This opus was the creation of a literary genius, Homer, or, as Mark Twain remarked sarcastically, "someone else with the same name". Incidentally, in the name "Homer" Semerano claims to recognize a Babylonian word, namely *zammeru*, 'singer' or 'bard'.

In a very similar fashion, Homer's *Iliad* echoed memories of a Mycenaean expansion from the Greek mainland towards the east, namely, to the far side of the Aegean Sea. This region had been known to the Greeks since time immemorial as Anatolia (*Anatolè*), which means 'land of the rising sun'. (An alternative version of that name was *Natalia,* 'land where the sun is born'.) This Greek nomenclature has probably inspired a term with the same meaning, "Levant[e]", used by Europeans in general, and Italians in particular, to refer to the 'land where the sun rises', that is, the

Middle East, and more specifically the coast of Lebanon. Among archaic peoples the east was closely associated with the sunrise, with dawn, and the west was intimately connected with the sunset, with the evening. The Ancient Greeks were by no means the only archaic people who considered time and space as two dimensions of the same reality, like Einstein. A specific moment of time was associated with a specific geographic space, and vice versa. Since the sun rises in the east, the east was the 'land of the morning'. The south is where the sun may be seen at noon, so the south was often called 'mid-day'; this is still the case in France and Italy, for example, where the south is known respectively as *le midi* and *il mezzogiorno*.

Anatolia had been inhabited for ages by Usko-Mediterranean peoples, such as the Hittites. Against some of them, ensconced in city-states far less powerful than the Hittite Empire, the Mycenaean Greeks waged war, whereby the aim was to secure control over the Dardanelles and access to the Black Sea; another issue may have been control over overland trade routes from the Aegean to Mesopotamia. In the thirteenth century BCE, the Greeks fought a particularly nasty conflict with Troy, and ended up destroying that city. This war was the subject of the *Iliad*, an epic so named because Troy was also known to the Greeks as Ilion. According to Semerano, the latter toponym hides an Usko-Mediterranean word – *ilum* in Akkadian, *elum* in Assyrian – meaning 'upper part of a city', 'citadel'; and the name Troy itself reflects the Akkadian *tarum*, 'to circle [with a wall]', and therefore means 'walled city'.

According to some specialists in ancient history, however, there existed another urban center in western Anatolia; like Troy, this city formed a kind of buffer state between the world of the Greeks on the one side and that of the Hittites and other easterners on the other, but presumably it was even more wealthy and powerful than Troy, until it was destroyed by the Hittites around 1,500 BCE. No one knows exactly where it was situated, but it may have been the site that would later be known to the Greeks as Assos, whose impressive ruins may still be admired near the Aegean coast to the south of Troy. While the name Assos conjures up the Mesopotamian term *essu* or *isu*, 'city', the city-state in question was supposedly called *Ashiwa* or *Assuwa* in the language of the Hittites, and the Greeks used this name to refer to Anatolia and eventually to the entire land mass to the east of the Aegean and Black Seas. Anatolia, then, was the original "Asia", but when the entire continent received that name, the Anatolian peninsula became increasingly referred to as Asia Minor, 'little Asia'.[55]

This hypothesis is interesting and not at all incredible. However, an alternative theory, proposed by Semerano, enjoys a competitive advantage, namely, that of being less complicated.[56] The toponym Asia, *dixit* Semerano, was simply the Greek version of the Semitic – i.e., Usko-Mediterranean – word *asu* (or *wasu*), meaning "sunrise", the same *asu* that the English term *east* has been derived, the French *est*, the German *Osten*, etc. In the Akkadian language, the opposite of *asu* was *wasitu*, 'sunset', and

---

[55] According to Schwertheim (2005: 9), the term Asia Minor first appeared in ancient literature in the early 5th century AD.
[56] According to the great historian of science, Thomas Kuhn, simplicity and "elegance" enhance the persuasive power of a scientific theory or "paradigm".

this *wasitu* lives on in the term for the direction where the sun goes down in countless languages, including the English *west* and the French *ouest*. The ancient Greeks, then, developed two equivalent terms to refer to the land of the rising sun: on the one hand, the Usko-Mediterranean nomenclature "Asia"; and on the other hand, their own translation of this name, "Anatolia". (Incidentally, the term *[w]asu* signified 'rising' in a very general sense, not only the 'rising' of the sun but also the 'rising' of rivers, in other words, it could also mean 'spring' or 'river', as we will see later, when hydronyms such as *Thames* and oronyms such as *Vesuvius* will be dealt with.)

The ruins of Assos
(Photo: Gregorof, 2006; source: Wikimedia Commons)

It is obvious that those who used nomenclature such as 'land of the sunrise' or 'land of the sunset' had in mind distant regions, lands inhabited not by themselves but by other peoples. As Mircea Eliade has emphasized so frequently in his brilliant essays about ancient myths and religions, archaic peoples believed virtually without exception that they themselves inhabited *the center of the world*. Alternative names for the rather trite 'center of the world' were 'navel of the earth' and 'place where the gods descended on earth'.[57] Mesopotamia, and the Middle East in general, was the cradle of the very first great civilizations. That region was referred to by the Greek outsiders as the 'land of sunrise', and very probably they had inherited this terminology from the indigenous inhabitants of their own land, the Usko-Mediterranean "Pelasgians", whose language was related to the Semitic languages of the Middle East, as we will soon see. However, it is extremely unlikely that the inhabitants of the Middle East would have called their own land the "land of sunrise". Did they not inhabit the center of the world, or at least of the civilized world of that time? Was Babylon not "the place where the gods had descended on earth"? The

---

[57] Japan, "the land of the rising sun", is no exception to this rule. The Japanese considered China as the cradle of all culture and wisdom; consequently, they did not hesitate to borrow this nomenclature from their Chinese neighbors, to whom Japan was indeed "the land of the rising sun".

easterners had no reason whatsoever to call their own land "land of the sunrise" but, conversely, they had very good reasons for calling western lands such as that of the Greeks the "land of the sunset", or "land of the evening". The proud Babylonians, Phoenicians, and other Semitic inhabitants of that region appear to have called themselves *qad'm,* which – just like the term "Dravidian" – meant something akin to 'wise people', 'elders', or 'leaders'. To the Greeks and other less-civilized people of the western periphery of the civilized world, however, that term gradually took on the meaning of 'easterners'. The easterners were the wise men, the wise men came from the east. We are dealing here with the end of the second millennium BCE, but it may be said that at that time the "light of wisdom" had been "dawning" in the east for many thousands of years! *Ex oriente lux,* indeed.

The Phoenicians played an extremely important role in the task of carrying the brightly shining torch of civilization to western lands. Already in the first half of the second millennium BCE, according to Bernal (1996), they performed a kind of *mission civilisatrice* in certain regions of Greece, for example in Thebes, where vague memories of "wise people from the east" would long live on in the legend of the founder of the city, Cadmos, a name in which the aforementioned root *qad'm* can be identified. From these Phoenician visitors the Greeks borrowed eastern nomenclature, also with respect to themselves and their country. The easterners called the west the "land of the setting sun", and their Semitic word *ereb(u),* meaning 'sunset', 'darkness', 'west', or 'evening', was turned into *Europe* by the Greeks. The Greek myths confirm in their own peculiar way that the term *Europe* originated in the east, namely from – or at least via – Phoenicia. Indeed, in Greek mythology Europa was a princess from the Phoenician seaport of Tyre, kidnapped by Zeus – himself disguised for the occasion as a handsome bull – and brought to Greece, that is, to the west. Cadmos was Europa's brother, and he traveled to Greece to seek his sister, to no avail as it turned out. Despite this, he took advantage of the opportunity to found Thebes. The Greeks – and westerners in general – inherited a great deal from their Semitic neighbors in the east, starting with the name of their own so-called continent. Incidentally, the root *ereb,* meaning 'sunset' or 'darkness', is also hidden in the name of Erebos, the ferryman who in Greek mythology ferried the deceased to the underworld and even personified Hades, the land of death and darkness.

It is possible that the root *ereb,* signifying '[land of the] setting sun' or 'west', is also concealed in the toponym used by the Ancient Egyptians to refer to the people and the region to the west of their own Kemit, *Leba* or *Libu.* As in all other Afro-Asiatic languages, the vowels are not important here; in addition, one has to keep in mind that in the Egyptian hieroglyphs the *l* and the *r* were interchangeable.[58] *Leba* or *Libu* can therefore also be pronounced "rebu" or "ribu". A remarkable similarity is thus revealed with the familiar term *ereb.* Obviously, nothing is hereby "proven", but this conjecture is undoubtedly rather plausible. Was Libya not the "west," the "land of the setting sun," to the Ancient Egyptians, just as Greece and the rest of Europe were to the Phoenicians, Babylonians, Assyrians, and others?

---

[58] I thank the Italian Egyptologist Federico Poole for an extremely useful tip in this respect.

The Golden Fleece and the Apples of the Hesperides

When sometime around 800 BCE Homer put to papyrus his epic poems, the Greeks had already emerged from the long night of the "Dark Age" that separated their own time from the Mycenaean era. From their home ports on the Greek mainland, the Greek islands, and along the Hellenized Ionian west coast of Anatolia, voyages were again undertaken to faraway lands. Trade was a major objective, but so was emigration, since chronic overpopulation bedeviled the Greek homeland. Consequently, Hellenic colonies soon mushroomed along the shores of distant lands, but not where the Phoenicians had already settled; Greek newcomers were emphatically not welcome in places where the Phoenicians had gained a toehold.

To the north of the Hellenic world, however, there lay a region in which the Canaanites never displayed much interest. It was therefore a "land of unlimited possibilities" for the Greeks, even though to reach it one had to sail through two dangerous straits somewhat reminiscent of the "Pillars of Hercules" on the other side of the Mediterranean Sea. The first strait was the Hellespont, the 'Sea of Helle'. Helle was a mythological personality who had drowned in these waters. "As was so often the case, the legend was produced by the desire to explain an unusual name", write the French onomasticians Deroy & Mulon (1992), and they propose an alternative etymology:

> Probably, Hella was a prehellenic term referring to the mainland part of the Greek Peninsula, that is, the area to the north of the Peloponnesus and the islands [...] Homer, in the Iliad, conjures up the memory of an era when the names Hellas and Hellenes designated this northern region. It is only much later that these names began being used for the Greek islands and the Greek Peninsula. Consequently, to the Greeks the Hellespont was originally the 'northern sea,' and the term in all likelihood referred also to the Sea of Marmara and even the Black Sea, then still barely known (Deroy & Mulon 1992: 218).

The Sea of Marmara and the Black Sea are discussed below. Meanwhile, it should be noted that in all probability we are also dealing here with pre-Hellenic toponyms.

The Hellespont was also known as the Dardanelles. The reason for this is that according to a Greek myth Dardanos, son of Zeus and founder of the Trojan royal dynasty, started his career on the shores of this strait as lord of the region around the city of Troy, situated on the Asian side of the Hellespont and known as the Troad. However, very likely the term "Dardanelles" emerged only in the Middle Ages. At the narrowest point of the Hellespont, there lay a fortress called *Dardanello,* after Dardanos, by Venetians and other Italian sailors; the site developed into the town now called Çanakkale. Since there happened to be a very similar-looking fort on the other side, it became customary to use the plural and speak of the *Dardanelli,* the Dardanelles. On the European side of the Dardanelles there is a peninsula that was called Chersonesos by the Greeks; this happened to be a rather banal name, meaning nothing other than 'peninsula'. (*Chersos* meant 'earth' or 'dry land' and *nesos,* 'island'; therefore Chersonesos signifies 'land-island', that is, 'peninsula'.) The Chersonesos is known today as the Gallipoli peninsula. This name, which is well known for the unsuccessful Allied troop landings there of the spring of 1915, is derived from the Greek *kalè polis*, 'the beautiful city'. Gallipoli is the Italian version of the name, presumably likewise popularized by Venetian and/or Genoan sailors. The area is now in Turkey, and is called Gelibolu in Turkish. The Chersonesos was only a small part of a vast region known to the Greeks as *Thrakè*, Thrace. According to Semerano, this toponym reflected the Akkadian combination *dor-iku*, - *dor* or *dur*, 'fortresses', and *iku*, 'land' (Latin *vicus*), i.e. 'land of the fortresses'. This was supposedly a reference to the fortresses that already dotted the shoreline of the strategically important Dardanelles in a very distant past. Such military installations must have had a commander, *tartanu* or *tardennu* in Akkadian, and this is almost certainly the key to the etymology of the term Dardanelles.

The Dardanelles
(Engraving of 1705 by an unidentified artist; source: Pauwels 2006)

Sailing through the Dardanelles, one reached a sea known to the Greeks as *Propontis*, the 'anterior sea', because it provided a foretaste of a much greater sea even further, the Black Sea. This 'anterior sea' of the Hellenes featured Marmara (or Marmora), the 'marble island', where much of the marble used for the construction of temples was quarried; this sea therefore also became known as the Sea of Marmara. A second strait connected the Sea of Marmara with the Black Sea, namely, the Bosporus. This Greek term supposedly had the meaning 'ford of the cow'.

According to a Greek mythological explanation reminiscent of the story of Europa, it was there that Zeus, in the guise of a white cow, brought yet another love interest, Io, from Asia to Europe. More realistic is the theory that we are dealing with some variation of the Greek verb *buzo*, meaning 'to squeeze', so that the meaning of Bosporus is basically 'place where the land squeezes the water'; in other words, a strait. However, it is very likely that the *Bosporos,* to use the Greek term, already had a name long before the Hellenes appeared on its shores, and in this case the toponym was almost certainly Pelasgian, in other words, Usko-Mediterranean. According to Semerano, *poros* corresponds to the Akkadian *buru*, meaning "spring," 'pond', or 'water' in general; this term could easily be confused with a near homonym, *bur*, meaning 'calf', hence the story of the cow. As for the first part of *Bosporus*, Semerano views it as a cognate of the Akkadian *ba'u*, 'to cross'. The Bosporus, then, would be 'the crossing of the water', 'the crossable water'.

Here is another sample of mythological etymology: on a little peninsula between the Sea of Marmara and an inlet of the Bosporus, the so-called Golden Horn, an adventurer from Megara named Byzas founded a city; as "Byzantium", it would bear his name for many centuries and then, renamed Constantinople in honor of the Roman Emperor Constantine, it would serve for one thousand years as the capital of the Eastern Roman or "Byzantine" Empire. The Oracle of Delphi had ordered Byzas rather cryptically to found a colony "across from the blind". Poor Byzas had no idea what this was supposed to mean until his travels took him to the Greek colony Chalkedon (now Kadiköy), situated on the Asian shore of the Bosporus. Facing this settlement on the European side was an inlet that formed a perfect natural harbor, and its waters teemed with fish. Obviously, Chalkedon's founders had been *blind* to the wonderful opportunity on the other side of the water, so that is where Byzas founded Byzantium, presumably somewhere in the middle of the seventh century BCE.

In this case too, a less quaint but more convincing etymology is available. *Byzant,* or *Wissant*, was the name given to this site by its pre-Hellenic, Pelasgian and therefore Usko-Mediterranean inhabitants. Its meaning was 'horn', and this name was clearly inspired by the form of both the peninsula on which the city was founded and the inlet of the Bosporus that is still known today as the Golden Horn. The Greek colonists had no idea what this toponym signified, so they concocted the story of the adventure of Byzas. They also adopted a "secret" name or nickname for the city – *Anthusa,* the Greek word for 'blossom'. Knobloch (1995) suggests that the choice of this name may have been influenced by the fact that its first three letters "lie at the heart of Byz*anth*ium". (He also points out that, at the time of Julius Caesar, the high society of the Roman capital adopted a Latin version of this nickname, as a result of which *Flora* became a code word for Rome in Patrician circles. Long before Byzantium became a "second Rome" under the name Constantinople, Rome, in the guise of *Flora,* had become a "second Anthusa" and thus a "second Byzantium".) Semerano offers yet another etymology for Byzantium. He regards this toponym as a variant of Akkadian *abusatu*, 'warehouse' or 'port of trade', 'emporium'.

After a difficult passage through the crooked, turbulent, and windy Bosporus, the Greeks emerged into the Black Sea, which they knew as the *Pontus Euxeinos*, the 'hospitable sea'. This was possibly a hopeful euphemism, a semantic attempt to exorcize the dangers of a sea that – in contrast to the familiar Aegean Sea, perhaps? – was actually a very dangerous one and ought therefore to have been known as the *Pontos Axeinos* or 'inhospitable sea'. However, it is suspected that the original Greek name for that sea was not *axeinos* but *axeanos*, 'black' or 'dark'. In doing so they followed the example of the Semites and Persians of the Middle East, who associated this color with the north, while white was associated with the south. In Turkish and Arabic, the Mediterranean Sea is still called the 'white sea': *Ak Deniz* and *Bahr al Abyad*, respectively (Matvejević 2000: 211). In the Black Sea too, Mycenaean sailors had probably carried out voyages of exploration half a millennium or more before Byzas. The legend of Jason and the Argonauts kept alive the (vague) memory of these undertakings; however, very likely it also reflected the interests of the Greeks who sailed into that sea in the seventh century BCE in order to explore, to trade, and to colonize its shores. As in the case of the Phoenicians in Hispania, minerals such as gold served as the magnet that attracted the explorers. Were Jason and his comrades not looking for the "golden" fleece, a sheepskin made of gold? Gold was indeed to be found on the northern shores of the *Pontus Euxeinos*, and the Scythians who lived there were excellent goldsmiths. With the aid of stones, the Scythians fastened sheepskins to the bottom of fast flowing streams in order to collect minuscule particles of gold; hence the legend of the golden fleece. The Black Sea shores also witnessed a lively trade in amber, honey, wax, furs, and slaves, products that were transported via great rivers such as the Danube and the Dnieper. The Greek traders obtained this merchandise primarily in exchange for olive oil and wine. Amber was known as the "gold of the north"; rubbing it over wool generated static electricity, so the Greek name for amber, *elektron*, has given us the term for the particle behind "electricity".

As for the etymology of "Scythians," this was an Usko-Mediterranean term related, according to Semerano, to the Akkadian term *saquti,* plural of *saqu* and meaning 'lords' or 'rulers' or something similar. The Scythians also liked to refer to themselves as the 'people [*umma*] of lords [*hazanu*]', but to the Greeks this quixotic *umma-hazanu* conjured up a more familiar Semitic term, namely, *ama*, 'girl'. Thus originated the legend of the female warriors, the Amazons. Scythian young women did in fact participate eagerly in warlike activities and, according to Herodotus, could only marry after they had killed an enemy in battle.[59] Such facts were undoubtedly known to the Greeks and must have reinforced their interpretation of the term "Amazon". The vast expanses of far eastern Europe and the Pontic steppes were not only inhabited by the Scythians by also by a people the Greeks called the Sarmatians. This was yet another Hellenic version of an Usko-Mediterranean ethnonym, meaning 'kings [*sarru*] of the land [*matu*]'.

The Greeks also sought opportunity in the western basin of the Mediterranean Sea. There they arrived in a region where their Mycenaean predecessors had already come to do business, and where all kinds of tantalizing opportunities continued to

---

[59] On the Scythian women warriors, see Christian (1998: 143-44).

beckon the eager traders they happened to be. However, the Phoenicians had turned up in the western Mediterranean before the Greeks, not only as merchants but also as colonists, so Hellenic enterprise in the west faced a serious obstacle, namely the presence of capable and sometimes dangerous competitors.

The Greek word for 'evening', and also for 'west', was *hesperos*, a term whose Latin cognate was *vespera,* the root of the term vespers, 'evening prayers'. The Greeks used to refer to the west in general as *Hesperia*, 'land of the evening'; conversely, as we have already seen, the east was known to them as *Anatolè*, 'land of the morning' or 'land of the rising sun'. The Greeks had become familiar with the Asian 'land of the morning' at an early stage, but the distant 'evening land' remained *terra incognita* for a long time. *Hesperia* was actually a very general label, used primarily in literature and also in mythology, which featured, for example, the aforementioned Hesperides or 'ladies of the west'. The term *Hesperia* indicated the lands on the other side of the Mediterranean Sea in general, but the western land *par excellence* was Spain. However, on account of the preponderance of the Phoenicians in the "land of rabbits", and particularly in the Tartessian south, the Greeks never managed to establish a major presence in Spain. In particular, the regions beyond the Pillars of Melkart/Hercules – Tartessos with its desirable minerals – remained to them a mysterious region on the shores of the immense "outer sea". As far as the Greeks were concerned, the Rock of Gibraltar might as well have displayed a sign proclaiming "no admittance", and *Nec plus Ultra* was indeed the motto conjured up in Hellenic minds by the Pillars of Hercules. The Romans would later also associate these Pillars with the expression *Nec plus Ultra*, but interpreted it in the sense of 'there is nothing beyond'; indeed, the beginning of the Atlantic Ocean heralded the end of the Romans' very own sea, their *Mare Nostrum*, and therefore in some sense also the end of the Roman world.

In spite of all this, in the sixth century BCE the Greeks did succeed in acquiring a toehold in Spain, namely, on the rugged Catalan coastline known today as the Costa Brava, the 'wild coast'. There, far away from the Canaanites in Gadir, they founded a colony called *Emporion*; the banality of that name, 'trading post', matched that of the *Kart Hadasht* of the Phoenicians and the Greeks' own *Neapolis*. The site, now called *Ampurias* in Spanish and *Empuriès* in Catalan, was well chosen, because it enabled the Greeks to trade with the Iberian inhabitants of the interior of northern Spain; thus they were able to acquire minerals such as tin from Galicia and gold from León. The Greeks did not come up with a new name for Spain, as the Phoenicians did when they coined the expression "land of rabbits", but simply adopted the nomenclature of the indigenous population: "Iberia". They also followed the example of the locals when they referred to the great river of northern Spain, along which the precious minerals reached the Mediterranean coast, as *Iberos*, Ebro. The Usko-Mediterranean root of this hydronym was very likely an Iberian cognate of the same Akkadian word *buru* (or also *beru*) that hides in *Bosporus*, meaning 'well', 'pool', 'pond', or any 'body of water'. In spite of the similarity of Ebro and Iberia, it is unlikely that the *iber* of Iberia hides in Ebro, since *iber* always refers to land near, or in contrast to, water, and never to water itself.

Unfortunately for them, the Greeks' Iberian adventure was to be short-lived. With the emergence of the Carthaginian Empire and the establishment of Punic bases such as Barcelona in the same part of the peninsula, they were eventually forced to vacate their Spanish *Hesperia*. Fortunately, in the western basin of the Mediterranean Sea the Greeks possessed a base of much greater interest than Ampurias, namely, Marseilles. *Massalia* was founded around 600 BCE by pioneers from the Ionian city of Phocaea, and this provides the basis for the claim that Marseilles is the oldest city in France. The name of the settlement reflected an indigenous Ligurian toponym, a cognate of the Akkadian *maslu*, meaning 'half', 'half-circle', or 'half moon', *mezza luna* in Italian, a reference to the shape of the harbor. From this port, the Greeks were able to trade with the inhabitants of southern Gaul, particularly with the denizens of the region now known as Provence. The possession of :Marseilles also permitted the Greeks to compete with the Phoenicians and (later) the Carthaginians in the long-distance trade with the faraway British "tin islands". Indeed, as Fernand Braudel has noted, France is an isthmus between the Mediterranean and the Atlantic, an isthmus that was already crossed by two major trade routes when the Greeks appeared on the scene (Braudel 1990.1: 261-69). The most important of these was the one that started at the mouth of the Rhône, followed the Rhône and the Saône rivers upstream into Burgundy, and descended the Seine all the way to the English Channel, thus eventually reaching the tin mines of Cornwall. A second route took the Greeks from the Mediterranean in the vicinity of Narbonne via a relatively hospitable highland known as the Seuil the Naurouze to the valley of the Garonne River, the estuary of the Gironde, and on to the Bay of Biscay, Brittany, and finally, Britain.

Their city's privileged location at a stone's throw from the mouth of the Rhône permitted the Massillians to take full advantage of the trade opportunities available via the Rhône Valley. Incidentally, the Gallic suppliers of tin were compensated primarily with wine. Amphoras were used to transport wine via the aforementioned waterways, and amphoras of Hellenic origin have been discovered just about everywhere in the Seine-Rhône corridor. The most spectacular specimen is the so-called "Vase of Vix", which makes it worthwhile to go off the beaten path and visit the historical museum in the Burgundian town of Chatillon-sur-Seine. Viticulture would only be introduced in Gaul much later, during the Roman era, so it can be said that the Greeks taught the French to drink wine.

Not only Marseilles – the Greek *Gadir* – but many other Hellenic colonies emerged on France's Mediterranean coast, as a considerable number of toponyms reveal. One of these settlements was dedicated to the goddess of victory, Nike, and this *Nikaia* is known today as Nice. The name of the nearby town of La Napoule shares the same etymology as Naples: it also originated as a Greek *Neapolis*, a 'new city'. Yet another Hellenic foundation along the *Côte d'Azur* was *Antipolis*, today known as Antibes. This meant 'the city on the other side', that is, the port situated across from Corsica. Ships heading for Corsica from Marseilles used to follow the coast to the cape just outside of Antibes, Cap d'Antibes, then sail directly to their destination; the same route was taken on the home journey.

As for the toponym Corsica, its etymology is far from certain, but there is no shortage of hypotheses. According to some, its meaning is 'mountain[s] or rock[s] rising from the sea'; others prefer the equally romantic 'island covered by forests'. Corsica's grandiose landscape is characterized by both mountains and forests, but the former of these two hypotheses appears the most convincing. The reason for this is that *ker* was an Usko-Mediterranean root signifying 'rock' or 'mountain', as we shall see later. Its Sumerian variant was *kur*, which happened to be conjured up very clearly in the first part of the name the Greeks sometimes used to refer to the island, *Kurnos*. (The second part of this toponym seems to be a form of the Greek word for island, *nesos*.) Normally, however, the Hellenes flattered the island that would some day witness the birth of Napoleon with a name of their own, *Kallistè,* 'the most beautiful island'. This attribute is echoed today by the local tourist board, which proudly promotes Corsica as *l'ile de beauté.*

During the sixth century BCE, the Greeks temporarily maintained a toehold on Corsica in the form of a colony named Alalia, situated on the eastern coast just south of the modern city of Bastia. Bastia itself originated only during the Middle Ages as a fort, a "bastion", constructed by the Genoans, who were then the masters of the island. However, in 535 BCE the Greeks abandoned their base on Corsica after a war against the Carthaginians and the Etruscans. As for the region around Marseilles on the French mainland, the permanent conflict against the Carthaginians would later drive this isolated Greek colony into the arms of the archenemy of the *Puni*, the Romans. With the ultimate triumph of the latter, Marseilles and surroundings were incorporated into the Roman Empire.

Etruscans and other Pelasgians

The Greeks, just like their Phoenician competitors, ventured to the western basin of the Mediterranean Sea in search of minerals. Copper, lead, iron ore and such also happened to be found in Italy, more in particular, in the central part of that country as well as on islands such as Elba. This mineral wealth is reflected onomastically even today in toponyms such as Portoferraio ('harbor of iron'), the capital of Elba, and Piombino ('lead city'), a port in the vicinity of Livorno. A stone's throw from Portoferraio, one can visit the ruins of the Etruscan settlement of *Populonia*, whose name is derived from the Usko-Mediterranean *bullulum,* 'to melt', 'to alloy'; *Populonia* was the 'crucible'. (A metallurgical center in France has a name with exactly the same meaning, *Le Creusot*.) To the south of Volterra lie the Monti Metalliferi or 'metal mountains', a hilly region where already in Antiquity copper as well as iron were mined; its name conjures up similar mineral-rich mountains, for example Spain's Sierra Morena and Germany's *Erzgebirge* or 'iron-ore mountains'.

Italy had great mineral wealth, but the Greeks faced a problem: the country's mineral deposits were concentrated in the homeland of the Etruscans. This highly civilized people knew how to use these minerals and was keenly aware of their value, so it was not prepared to make them available to the Hellenic merchants in return for trinkets. (An impressive example of the Etruscans' skill in bronze casting is the so-called "Chimera of Arezzo" in the National Archaeological Museum of Florence; another splendid Etruscan bronze sculpture was the famous Roman she-wolf suckling Romulus and Remus.) With the Etruscans, then, the Greeks were not able to develop the highly profitable kind of trade relations the Phoenicians enjoyed with the Tartessians;[60] in addition, the Etruscans' fertile, densely populated, and relatively urbanized country hardly offered any opportunities for Greek colonization. Furthermore, the Etruscans maintained close cultural and commercial relations with the Phoenicians and later the Carthaginians, so in principle they did not look favorably upon the Greek competitors of their Punic partners.

The Hellenes called the Etruscans the *Tyrrhenoi* or the *Tyrsenoi*, supposedly because they had been the companions of Tyrsos, the son of a king of Lydia in Anatolia; according to the legend, Tyrsos had founded a colony in distant Italy at the time of the Trojan War. The coast of the land of the Etruscans, known today as Tuscany, overlooks a stretch of the Mediterranean Sea the Greeks referred to as the "Tyrrhenian Sea", that is, the 'Sea of the Etruscans'. It was a most sensible nomenclature, because the Etruscans did in fact consider that part of the Mediterranean Sea as their very own *Mare Nostrum*, and they were determined to keep these waters to themselves, as they demonstrated only too clearly when, with the help of their Carthaginian allies, they expelled the Greeks from Alalia, an emporium the Hellenic interlopers had founded on the eastern, Tyrrhenian coast of the island of Corsica, virtually within sight of the coast of Etruria/Tuscany itself.

The Chimera of Arezzo, in the National Archaeological Museum of Florence
(Photo: Lucarelli; source: Wikimedia Commons)

---

[60] In exchange for valuable painted Attican vases and other ceramics, however, the Etruscans proved in fact quite willing to provide the Greeks with minerals and other goods.

The Etruscans had been at home in central Italy for hundreds of years when the Greeks first made their acquaintance.[61] Already thousands of years BCE, Saharan emigrants had settled not only on the Iberian and Italian Peninsulas, but on virtually all the islands of the Mediterranean Sea and on its northern shores. These settlers are now credited with the emergence of important civilizations such as that of "Minoan" Crete in the second millennium BCE,[62] and indeed also that of the Etruscans. These migrants spoke Usko-Mediterranean tongues related to Hamitic and Semitic languages such as Ancient Egyptian, Sumerian, and Phoenician. In the course of the second millennium BCE, then, the so-called Indo-Europeans are supposed to have appeared on the scene from their *Urheimat* in some northern or northeastern *terra incognita*, as we have already seen. They settled just about everywhere in Europe and penetrated deep into the Mediterranean basin. In doing so, they expelled the Saharans from their habitats, or else assimilated them, or else again were assimilated by them; in any event, virtually without exception they imposed their Indo-European languages on the indigenous population. (The Basques, who continue to speak an Usko-Mediterranean language, constitute the great exception that confirms this rule; it is in this sense that Friedrich Engels called the Basques "the last representatives of the ancient Iberian race" [Morvan 1996: 75].) In their myths, legends, literature, and religion, however, the newcomers – or the hybrid peoples that originated as a kind of ethnic fusion of the newcomers with the Usko-Mediterranean substrate – kept alive the memory of the sometimes highly civilized yet strange people – the *Urvolk* – who had been the original inhabitants of their lands, and who were called *pelasgoi*, 'Pelasgians' by the Indo-European Greeks. This term appears to have originated as the auto-ethnonym of a people who had migrated from the Sahara to settle in, and claim ownership of, the Greek – and not only the Greek – islands and mainland. It was a combination of the Usko-Mediterranean terms for 'lord' (*bel*, *pelas*) and 'people' (*ga'u* in Akkadian, *goy* in Hebrew), meaning something akin to 'lordly people', or *Herrenvolk*, to use an all too familiar German expression. Coincidentally, *pelasgos* strongly resembled *pelargos*, 'stork', a Greek composition of Usko-Mediterranean origin that contained the same initial element plus *arhu*, 'journey' or 'road', giving us the meaning 'lords of the journey'. The latter epithet was not only appropriate in the case of the great migratory birds but also in that of the Saharan people who in a distant past had crossed over from Africa to Europe, an event of some historical magnitude, whose memory was perhaps kept alive by the conspicuous arrival each spring of storks from Africa.

---

[61] It is not known precisely when the ancestors of the Etruscans arrived in Italy. However, it is generally accepted that they developed the so-called Proto-Villanova- and Villanova-cultures of the late Bronze Age and the early Iron Age in Italy, i. e., shortly before and after 1000 BCE.

[62] In *An Outline of History*, H G Wells referred to "the early Cretans" as "a race akin to the Iberians of Spain and Western Europe and the dark whites of Asia Minor and North Africa" and, citing H H (Harry) Johnston, he also mentioned the possibility that "ancient Cretan" was related to Basque as well as Caucasian languages, see *http://outline-of-history.mindvessel.net/150-sea-peoples-and-trading-peoples/152-the-aegean-cities-before-history.html*.

The Saharans did not always and everywhere allow themselves to be pushed aside by the Indo-European newcomers. The Phoenicians and the majority of the other highly civilized peoples of the Middle East were "Pelasgian" and remained so, even though Indo-European tribes allegedly invaded the part of their world that would later be known as Iran, a name supposedly meaning 'land of the Aryans'. In the western basin of the Mediterranean too, considerable Pelasgian pockets survived for a long time despite the coming of the Indo-Europeans, for example in Italy, where the famous Etruscans were definitely a non-Indo-European nation. When the Greeks arrived on the Italian shores, they immediately identified the Etruscans as Pelasgians.

The Greeks called the Etruscans *Tyrrhenoi* or *Tyrsenoi*, allegedly because the latter were descendants of a Lydian prince named Tyrsos. According to Semerano, however, the Hellenes used this term to refer not only to the Etruscans, but to the Pelasgians in general; he interprets the term as a combination of two Usko-Mediterranean words: *tur*, 'to roam', 'to travel', 'to do business' and *ursani*, 'warriors'. The Greeks, so Semerano argues, considered the Pelasgian peoples in general, the Pelasgian Phoenicians in particular, and undoubtedly also the Pelasgian Etruscans, as aggressive and dangerous competitors. The reverse also applied, as we will see when we will deal with the meaning of the Pelasgian term for the Hellenes, namely, "Greeks".

Fresco of a banquet from the "Tomb of the Lions" in the Etruscan necropolis of Tarquinia
(Unknown artist, 5th century BCE; photo: J Pauwels, 2009)

Tyrsenoi and the cognate *Tyrrhenoi* were exonyms. The Pelasgian inhabitants of Central Italy obviously did not use this nomenclature; they called themselves *Rasenna*. According to Semerano, this auto-ethnonym contains the Usko-Mediterranean root *ras,* meaning 'head', also in the figurative sense of 'lord' or 'leader'. And *enna* appears to have been a variant of *inu,* or *enu,* 'human beings'. The Etruscans viewed themselves as "lords," that is, 'lords of the land'. Their Roman neighbors, on whom they would long exert a considerable influence, called the Etruscans *Etrusci.* In this ethnonym, Seremano claims to identify two Usko-Mediterranean roots: first, *etr* (*atr* in Ugaritic, *atra* in Aramaic), as in the Latin *terra* or the English *earth*, meaning 'land'; second, *isqu* or *esqu*, 'property'. The meaning of "Etruscans" is 'owners of the land'. The indigenous inhabitants of the land, then, were the 'lords' or 'owners' of the land. Conversely, the lords or owners of the land were its "inhabitants"; indeed, the Usko-Mediterranean root for 'inhabitants' was *tus* – as in the Sumerian *tus*, 'to inhabit' – a term we encounter in yet another Greek name for the Etruscans, *Tuskoi*, of which the Latin *Tusci* was derived. Thus the Romans used not only *Etrusci* but also *Tusci* for the people; and for the land of that people they also used *Tuscania*, the Latin ancestor of the present Italian toponym *Toscana* and its international cognates. A synonym for *Tuscania* was *Etruria*, yet again an Usko-Mediterranean name in which *etr*, 'land', is married to *re*, 'community; *Etruria* thus means 'the community of the [people of the] land'.

Terracotta Etruscan figures in the Museum of Volterra
(Photo: J Pauwels, 2009)

The Usko-Mediterranean language of the indigenous Etruscan people differed radically from the languages of the Indo-Europeans who descended on Italy in the course of the second millennium BCE, the so-called "Italic" peoples, such as the Romans, Umbrians, Samnites, Sabines, etc. In light of this, we can understand a little better why the Etruscans got along just fine with the Phoenicians and Carthaginians, who belonged to the same Usko-Mediterranean ethnic and linguistic family. The aforementioned anti-Greek alliance of the Etruscans and the Phoenicians / Carthaginians thus happened to be based on a deeply rooted ethnic-linguistic affinity.

In Italy there were other peoples who spoke Usko-Mediterranean languages, who were related to the Etruscans, and whose territories belonged to the sphere of influence of this politically, economically, and culturally sophisticated people. As an example we can cite the Sards, a mysterious people that was mentioned in Egyptian sources as one of the infamous "Sea Peoples", as were the Etruscans themselves. Today the memory of the ancient Sards lives on in the name of the island of Sardinia. According to Pausanias (1971), this island was called *Ichnoussa,* 'stepping stone', by the Greeks, because its shape conjured up a human footprint. More important for our purposes is the fact that this second-century CE author also cites ancient traditions according to which the island had originally been settled by migrants from Libya, Iberia, and even Minoan Crete, thus implying that its inhabitants were "Pelasgian", i.e., Saharan migrants; one Greek author thus referred to the Sards as *Sardolubues*, 'Sardo-Libyans' (Pausanias 1971.1: 448). As for the etymology of "Sards" (and "Sardinia"), this name derives from *sarru*, 'lords', and either *danu*, 'powerful', or dunum, 'towns', and therefore means 'lords of the towns (or fortresses)'.

The Sardic family included sub-groups such as the *Baleri*, who lived on an archipelago that received their name: the Balearic Islands. Their name meant "lords [*bel*] of the land [*ara*] or of the mountains [*harru*]'. The name of one of those islands was represented by the consonants *Ybsm* by the Phoenicians and Carthaginians, which meant the 'arid island' according to some, and 'island of pines' according to others. However, Semerano claims that the toponym is derived from (*a*)*busu*, meaning 'warehouse' or 'emporium', a reference to the commercial activities of the Phoenicians. Via its Greek cognate, *Ebyssos*, this term ultimately gave us the island's present name, Ibiza. The Romans knew the two biggest Balearic Islands as *Balearis Major* and *Balearis Minor*: Mallorca and Minorca. To return for a moment to the word *Sards*, we can recognize that term in the name of the region Cerdagne (Spanish: Cerdaña), situated in the Pyrenees on both sides of the French-Spanish border, and in the name of the national dance of Catalonia, the *sardana*.

On the Italian mainland, along the coast of the province of Liguria, and also along the French *Côte d'Azur* all the way to the outskirts of Marseilles and even on the island of Elba, there lived yet another Usko-Mediterranean people, the Ligurians. The Greek version of their name was *Ligues*, in which one can recognize a cognate of the Akkadian *lihmu*, 'still water', 'marsh', 'area with much water or near the water'; in other words, the Ligurians were the 'people of the coast', or something similar. We know that the Romans also called this people the *Ilvates*. In this word the root *ilva* can be identified, an equivalent of *erva*, *erba*, or *ereb*, which we already met when the meaning of "Europe" was discussed; its meaning was "[land of the] sunset." ("Elba", the name of an island that was once inhabited by Ligurians, is allegedly a mere cognate of this *ilva*.) The Ligurians or *Ilvates*, then, were the inhabitants of the land of the setting sun, the land of the evening, the west – at least from the perspective of the Etruscans and, later, the Romans. Incidentally, even today the western part of the great arch formed by the Ligurian coast is known in Italy as the *Riviera del Ponente*, the 'coast of the setting sun'; facing it on the eastern side is the *Riviera del Levante*. The Riviera is a rocky coast that abruptly separates the blue waters of the Mediterranean from towering mountains. The name of the Ligurian capital, Genoa, onomastically reflects this reality, because it contains an Usko-Mediterranean root for 'mountain', *gin(nu)* or *gen(nu)*. The same root also hides in the name of the Swiss city of Geneva.

The Pelasgian ethnic mosaic in Italy also included the Raetians, sometimes referred to as North Etruscans or "Etruscoids". Already in the nineteenth century a

British etymologist, Isaac Taylor (1893: 35), wrote that "there are reasons to believe that they belong to the ancient race of Etruscans".[63] This people originally inhabited the area north of Etruria, that is, the Po Valley. Their name – and that of their territory, Raetia – contains an Usko-Mediterranean root meaning running water or river, *ratu[m]* in Akkadian and *rahat* in Hebrew. The name Raetia signified 'land of the river(s)' and this was a reference to the mighty Po and its tributaries. The Raetians migrated to the "Raetian" Alps when Celtic tribes coming from Gaul invaded Northern Italy in the fifth century BCE. Like the Sards and the Etruscans themselves, the *Raeti* were eventually assimilated by the Romans, and under the influence of Latin their language slowly evolved into the present-day Raeto-Romansh, one of the official languages of Switzerland together with German, French, and Italian.

Speaking of the Alps, the Etruscans, Ligurians and Raetians must have been familiar with those mountains long before the Romans appeared on the scene. It is therefore extremely improbable that this oronym originated as a Roman word meaning 'white mountains', just because it resembles the Latin word for 'white', *albus*. Can there be any doubt that the Etruscans and Etruscoids already had a name for the mountain range that bordered their lands so dramatically to the north? Very likely, this name was some form or other of *alb*, an Usko-Mediterranean root which – in its Sumerian version, *halp(u)*, for example – referred to water, rivers, snow and ice, and above all to the combination of mountains and water, in other words, to the mountains or hills where rivers rise and whence they flow towards the valleys and the sea. Many great rivers of the land of the Etruscans, Raetians, and other Pelasgians did indeed rise in the Alps, and of course also in the Apennines, for example the Po. As for the etymology of "Apennines," the core of this oronym is likely another Usko-Mediterranean root, namely, a cognate of the Akkadian *appu* and the Celtic *penno*, meaning 'tip', '[mountain] peak'.[64] The name of the mountain range that forms the backbone of England, the "Pennines," may be supposed to have precisely the same origin and significance. And might this not be the reason why in Scotland the names of so many mountain peaks are prefixed with "Ben"? Finally, it is worth noting that the Romans baptized that area of the Alps where the highest mountain peaks were to be found, such as the very "peaked" Matterhorn, the *Alpes Penninae,* a name that survives as "Pennine Alps".

Descending the Po, one eventually reaches the Adriatic Sea in an area where its shores were once inhabited by the mysterious *Veneti*. According to some authors, the "Venetic" people belonged to the ethnic family of the Illyrians, whose homeland consisted of the entire coastal region to the north and east of the Adriatic Sea, from the Po delta to the modern states of Albania and the confines of Macedonia. The Illyrian family included many other tribes, for example the *Pannones*, after whom a large area corresponding more or less to the combined territory of present-day

---

[63] The origin and language of the Raetians is discussed in Pajarola (1997), especially in Chapter V.
[64] *Apu* could also mean 'point', 'tip', 'prickle', and 'spine', and we find the same root in the Latin *apis* and French *abeille*, 'bee', and the English *bee* and *apiculture*.

Austria and Hungary was called *Pannonia* by the Romans, and the Dalmatians. According to Semerano, the root at the core of the toponym Pannonia was *panu*, '[water's] edge', and the toponym presumably referred to the lands bordering on the Danube. The Dalmatians were another Illyrian group. The name of their land means 'irrigated' or 'watery [*dilum*] land [*matu*]', a reference to the Adriatic coastline of modern Croatia with its countless inlets, peninsulas and islands.

Like the Etruscans, the Illyrians were a Pelasgian people, that is, a nation of Saharan origin speaking an Usko-Mediterranean language. Evidence of this survives in onomastic fossils such as *Zagora Dalmata*, the 'Dalmatian Mountains', a name in which one can recognize the Usko-Mediterranean root *zaqru*, 'mountain', already mentioned when the Iranian Zagros chain was cited. (Incidentally, the same ancient root *zaqru* obviously also hides in the names "Zagoria", high hills in northern Greece, "Zakros", a rugged and mountainous landscape in eastern Crete, and "Zagora", a town in Morocco with a mountain – the *Jabal Zagora* – rising up dramatically on its outskirts.) Like the Etruscans, Sards, and Raetians, the majority of the Illyrians were gradually Romanized and thus started to speak their own version of Latin, the so-called "Balkan Latin". Later still, the Illyrians were marginalized and/or assimilated by the Slavs who invaded their lands in the sixth and seventh centuries CE and who are considered to be the ancestors of the Serbs and Croats.

As Predrag Matvejević has observed, the wave of Slav immigration covered the indigenous Illyrian substrate with a demographic layer "which sometimes happens to be relatively thick, but sometimes also extremely superficial" (Matvejević 2000: 283). Indeed, here and there along the eastern shores of the Adriatic Sea – *l'altra sponda,* 'the other shore', they say in Venice – as well as deep in the interior of the Balkan Peninsula, pockets of people survive who may be considered descendants of the Illyrians of Antiquity. The Macedonians are sometimes cited in this context, and even more so the Albanians. Macedonia's original Pelasgian name was *Emathia* (*E Madhja* in Albanian), meaning the 'high', 'great', or 'mighty land'. According to Semerano, this toponym incorporates the root *dan(n)u*, 'mighty', which we will meet again when dealing with hydronyms such as Danube; this is more obvious in the case of the Greek and Latin cognates, *Makedon* and *Macedonia.* In all likelihood, Macedonia was called the 'great country' because it was a vast region in comparison to the Greek heartland, which happens to be a relatively small peninsula.

As for Albania, in this toponym we encounter once again the ancient root *alb*. This is hardly surprising, because here too we are dealing with a country dominated by mountains from which countless streams and rivers flow to the Adriatic. The term "Albania" first surfaced in chronicles of the eleventh century; it referred to the region around Durrës (Durazzo in Italian), in other words, not to the entire modern state of Albania, but only to its historical heartland. The Albanians themselves also use the toponym *Arbenia* to refer to that specific part of their country, and the ethnonym *Arber* to refer to its inhabitants; to them too, *Arbenia* (or *Arberia*) is virtually a synonym for 'mountain'.

The Albanians call themselves *Shkupetar*, and their country *Shkupenia* or *Shkuperia* . It is generally believed that *Shkupetar* means 'eagles', but that is a typical example of folk etymology. More credible is the hypothesis that *Shkupetar* is a form of *shkyipoij*, 'to understand', and means 'people who understand [our language]', 'people who speak our language'. This kind of nomenclature was rather typical in the case of archaic peoples, and we will see later that the term "Slavs" – the ethnic "family name" of the Albanians' neighbors – means something analogous: 'people who can speak'. According to Semerano, however, *Shkuperia* is an ancient Usko-Mediterranean term, to be interpreted as 'high [*saqu* in Akkadian] land [*eperu*]', which happens to be the same meaning as the term Albania.

"Albania" and its cognates in other languages, toponyms referring to a land of mountains and rivers, happened to be common onomastic currency in Antiquity. Greek geographers such as Strabo also cited an "Albania" in the Caucasus, inhabited by a people known as the *Albanoi*. And already thousands of years ago, the Scottish highlands were known as *Alba(n)*. This term, which remains the Gaelic name for Scotland, was rendered in Latin as *Albania*. During the Middle Ages, *Rex Alban* was a title used by the Scottish kings, considered synonymous with *Rex Scotiae*. This ancient term would survive in English as "Albany", the title of a dynasty of British lords; it was after a scion of this family that a town in New York State's Hudson Valley was named.

Between the Black Sea and the Caspian Sea; another Iberia and another Albania
(Unknown cartographer, 1522; source Wikimendia Commons)

One has to keep in mind that in the course of time the ancient root *alb* sometimes mutated into *arb*, and that the *n* of *Albania* could on occasion turn into an *r*. Have we not just seen that the Albanians themselves call Albania *Arbenia* and not *Albenia*, and that they also use the toponym *Arberia*? Thus we can understand that the Latin name of the French province of Auvergne, *Arvenia*, was an equivalent of *Albania,* in other words, a toponym in which the Usko-Mediterranean root *alb* is tucked away and which refers to a combination of mountains and water; we do indeed encounter this combination in that part of France, since Auvergne is situated in the middle of the mountain range known as the Massif Central, blessed with abundant springs whose waters end up in bottles bearing labels such as Perrier and Vichy. According to some, "Armenia" is also a cognate of *Albania,* and it is possible that the Ancient Greeks had this mountainous land in mind when they talked about an *Albania* in the distant Caucasus. Finally, it is possible that the root *alb* is also hidden in Lebanon, then name of a country, to be sure, but a name that was originally used to denote a range of snow-covered mountains.

With the Illyrians in general and the *Veneti* in particular, the Greeks maintained lively trade relations and their ultimate object of desire in this trade revealed itself to be amber. This product from the coastal regions of the Baltic Sea was transported along ancient trade routes through Eastern and Central Europe to the harbors of the Black Sea, as we have already seen, and also to those of the Adriatic Sea. In this respect the northern coast of the Adriatic – 'the head of the Adriatic' (*caput Adriae*), as the Romans put it – was obviously privileged. There, in the region inhabited by the *Veneti*, was where the Greeks found the harbors where they could fetch the cherished *elektron*. The city of Venice, however, later to be celebrated as the "bride of the Adriatic Sea", did not yet exist. The hub of the amber trade was the town of Adria, enjoying a privileged location close to the mouths of the Po and Adige rivers, and located right on the Adriatic coast, from which today it is separated by about twenty kilometers; according to the Italian historian Lorenzo Braccesi, Adria was at one point a genuine "thalassocracy", a 'queen of the sea'. As far as the Greeks and other foreign merchants were concerned, then, the sea they had to cross to reach this important destination was the "Sea of Adria," in other words, the Adriatic Sea. Braccesi elaborates as follows:

> Adria had a double commercial role. The city attracted the goods that were transported there via the Po and the [Venetian] lagoon from the other side of the Alps, and sent them in turn via the Greek trade routes towards the Aegean Sea. It is on account of this unique function that Adria gave its name to the Adriatic Sea. And so it was inevitably this sea that became the route along which the cultural influence of Greece spread to the Po Valley and even to the north of the Alps (Braccesi 2003: 74).

The inhabitants of Adria belonged to the nation of the "Estruscoid" *Veneti* and spoke an Usko-Mediterranean language, related to Sumerian and Akkadian. There is nothing mysterious about the toponym Adria if one knows that in the Mesopotamian idiom of the Sumerians *aduru* – a word incorporating the aforementioned root *ur*, 'water' – signifies an 'elevated site in the middle of a marsh or an irrigated region'; the site of Adria fits this description to a T. Incidentally, the name of the nearby town of Padua (*Padova* in Italian, *Patavium* in Latin), contains a root related to the Akkadian *pattum*, 'canal', and the Greek *potamos*, 'river', and may be interpreted as '[settlement on the] river bank' or something similar. This is a plausible etymology, since the city is located in the marshy lowlands near the Adriatic coast, criss-crossed by all sorts of waterways.

Islands in the Adriatic Sea
(Photo: Zoran Knez, 2006; source: Wikimedia Commons)

Magna Graecia

In central and northern Italy, in the lands of the Etruscans and their Ligurian and other Etruscoid relatives, the Greeks were allowed to conduct business and nothing more. But in southern Italy and on the island of Sicily, opportunities for colonization beckoned. This was something of great importance to the Hellenes, whose homeland was plagued by chronic overpopulation. To the south of the land of the Etruscans and on Sicily, the Greeks indeed managed to establish numerous bases, some of which developed into great cities. Thus a Hellenic "New World" emerged in the west, a New World which in respect to people, power, and wealth would eventually compete with the homeland itself; it was to be known as *megalè Hellas* in Greek and *Magna Graecia* in Latin, meaning 'Greater Greece'.

Already in the eighth century BCE, the Hellenes founded a base just to the south of Etruscan territory. The site they selected for this purpose was an island in the Bay of Naples, known today as Ischia, but its original name was *Pithecusa*. It was long believed that this signified 'island of apes', because *pithekos* is Greek for 'ape'; however, there were never any apes on that island. It is now believed that the meaning of the toponym was 'town of jars [*pithoi*]', an allusion to Ischia's role as a warehouse, an emporium where the Greeks stored thousands of amphoras full of oil and wine. The island's present name, Ischia, is derived from the Latin *insula*, 'island', not directly but via a detour through the Vulgar Latin form *iscla*. In any event, *Pithecusa* turned out to be a well-chosen site, because from this island one could trade easily not only with the Etruscans a short distance to the north, along the coast of the Tyrrhenian Sea, but also with the somewhat less civilized Indo-European inhabitants of the adjoining mainland, a mosaic of peoples that included the Latin-speaking Romans. Those populations lived primarily by cattle breeding, and for this reason the Greeks called their country *Italia*, a name in which one can allegedly recognize the word *italos*, 'calf', 'young bull' (Latin: *vitulus*; Italian: *vitello*). This hypothesis may have its charms, but it is entirely off the mark, at least according to Semerano, who proposes an alternative. The word "Italy", he says, is the Latin version of the Greek *Aithalia*, a toponym in which *aithos*, 'smoke' or 'soot', is hiding. *Aithalia* was the name the Greeks gave to Elba because the normally blue sky there was often darkened by the smoke of the numerous forges in which the island's abundant iron ore was processed; in Hellenic eyes, Elba, the island of the Ligurian *Ilvates*, was the 'smoky' or 'sooty' island. However, iron ore and forges were to be found just about everywhere in Italy, and thus the entire country became a 'land of smoke', an *Aithalia,* to the Greeks. (If this is correct, *Italy* is closely related to *Aithiopia*, the 'land of the people with the burned faces', a toponym which we know to be a form of the Greek verb *aithomai*, 'to burn'.) However, the Greek word *aithos* was itself derived from the Usko-Mediterranean *atalu* or *atalya,* originally referring to the 'darkness' associated with a solar eclipse or, more commonly, with the end of the day and therefore also meaning 'sunset' and 'land where the sun sets'. In other words, the term *Italy* can also be interpreted as 'land of the setting sun', which Italy indeed happens to be from the viewpoint of the inhabitants of Greece and the Middle East. If this is correct, we are obviously dealing with an exonym that must originally have been used by the Usko-Mediterranean Pelasgians, the indigenous inhabitants of Greece, and was taken over from them by the Indo-European Hellenes when they settled on the Greek mainland and islands.

The Greeks ensconced themselves in the Bay of Naples, and soon after the founding of Pithecusa other Greek settlements sprang up on the adjoining mainland. The best known of these would turn out to be Naples, *Neapolis* in Greek, meaning 'new city'. Naples happened to be only a stone's throw from Vesuvius, an intimidating volcano with a name of Usko-Mediterranean origin; the root *wasu* signified 'height', 'mountain', and the second part reflects the term *ebbu*, 'shiny'. (The root *wasu* – accompanied by *ilum*, 'upper town' or 'citadel' – is also hidden in the names of some French towns situated on top of a hill, for exemple Vézelay and Vesoul ; and *wasu* can also be recognized in the name of Mount Viso, *monte Viso* or *Monviso* in Italian, one of the highest peaks in the western Alps, situated in the Italian province of Piedmont.) Even closer to this 'shiny' mountain there arose yet another Greek foundation, to be dedicated to Hercules; known as *Herakleon* (*Herculaneum* in Latin, Ercolano in Italian). This town would be buried, together with neighboring Pompeii, by the hot ashes and mud of a terrible eruption of Vesuvius in 79 CE.

By that time the region around Naples had already been ruled for a long time by the Romans, who had named the area *Campania* – an onomastic tip of the hat not to the Hellenic settlers, but to a local Italic tribe, the *Campani*. From the perspective of the inhabitants of the great city on the banks of the Tiber River, *Campania* was a rural and fertile land, and so this toponym – of Italic but not Latin origin, and not related to the Latin *campus,* 'field', as is often claimed – would develop into the binary alternative to *urbs*, 'city'; in Romance languages it would eventually acquire the meaning of 'countryside' – as in the case of the French *la campagne*. In the south of Campania, on the sandy shores of the Bay of Salerno, a Greek foundation was dedicated to Poseidon, the protector of sailors. *Poseidonia* developed into an important sanctuary, with amazing temples that have survived remarkably well until the present. But with the arrival of the Romans, *Poseidonia* was Latinized as "Paestum", and it is by this name that the site has become famous throughout the world. Finally, it also ought to be mentioned that a peninsula between the Bays of Naples and Salerno is known today by the name of its foremost town, Sorrento. That toponym – *Surrentum* in Latin – is of Usko-Mediterranean origin, and contains the same root *sur* as in Tyre/Sur, meaning 'rock', but it also conjures up *saru*, 'high'; the name Sorrento, then, means '[place on the] high rocks', which happens to be an accurate description of the town's picturesque site.

The Temple of Hera in Paestum, dating from ca. 550 BCE
(Photo: Ballista, 2006; source: Wikimedia Commons)

The true western Promised Land of the Greeks was an island, in fact, the biggest island in the Mediterranean Sea; they called it *Trinakria,* 'the island of the three capes', and we now know it as Sicily. Its indigenous population consisted of a number of tribes of which the most important were the *Sikeloi,* or *Siculi* in Latin. It would appear that this was also a Pelasgian, Usko-Mediterranean people. In this name, Semerano sees a variant of the Akkadian *s(a)ikli*, already identified in the name of the Isles of Scilly; in other words, he considers *Sikelo / Siculi* synonymous with *Italy* the ethnonym in which *atalu* hides, likewise meaning 'sunset' or 'west'. The *Sikeloi* too were 'inhabitants of the land of the setting sun', 'westerners'. They were undoubtedly the ones who named the great volcano that looms over the island 'Etna', an oronym in which the Usko-Mediterranean word *attuna*, 'oven', is hidden. It was after the *Sikeloi* that the Hellenes also called the island "Sicily". However, this foreign, incomprehensible name made them think of the figs (*sikè*) and olives (*elia),* produced in great abundance on the island. To the Greeks, then, Sicily was not only the 'island of the three capes', but also the 'island of figs and olives'.

When the Greeks appeared on the Sicilian scene, they found their Phoenician competitors already strongly entrenched on the western extremity of the island, namely, in *emporia* and colonies such as Trapani and Palermo, which controlled the narrows between Sicily and Carthage, the Strait of Sicily. To the Greeks, these names sounded like *Drepanon* and *Panormos*, meaning 'sickle' and 'big harbor', respectively. Such an interpretation seemed to make sense, because Trapani is located on a peninsula in the form of a sickle, and the historical core of Palermo is indeed a fine, large natural harbor. However, these toponyms were in reality indigenous and therefore Usko-Mediterranean, and their meaning was entirely different. Trapani was simply the 'town [*dor*] on the coast or waterfront [*panu*]'.

And the toponym Palermo had a virtually identical meaning, 'settlement or town on the coast' (from *panu* 'coast' and *ramu* or *arammu* 'settlement or town').

Both on the way to Tartessos and during the return journey to Canaan, the Phoenicians had to sail through the waters of the Strait of Sicily, which were therefore off-limits to the Greeks, just like the Strait of Gibraltar; for this same reason the Carthaginians would later maintain an iron grip on western Sicily. (According to the Italian researcher Sergio Frau (2002), the Strait of Sicily was the original site of the Pillars of Hercules that marked the western limit of the Greeks' sphere of activity.) In order to reach the western basin of the Mediterranean Sea, the Greeks therefore had to brave the perilous currents of the narrows called "Scylla and Charybdis" in the *Odyssey*, that is, the Strait of Messina. For the purpose of colonization, moreover, they were confined to the eastern part of Sicily, where around 730 BCE they proceeded to establish a number of bases such as *Naxos* (now Capo Schiso), named after an eponymous island in the Aegean Sea, and *Zankle* (Messina), the harbor that, together with *Reghium* (now Reggio de Calabria) on the other side, controls the passage through "Scylla and Charybdis". Precisely as in the case of the Phoenician *Drepanon*, the shape of the harbor of Messina conjured up a sickle, and 'sickle/ was indeed the meaning of the toponym *Zankle*. This foundation later acquired the name of a city in the Peloponnesus, Messena, where many of the colonists had originated.

Like the Phoenicians, the Greeks preferred to establish their ports of trade on a peninsula or on a little offshore island. The latter was the case on Sicily's eastern coast, where a settlement received the name *Ortygia*, 'island of quails', because the shape of the island conjured up the profile of this type of bird. The quail happened to function as an attribute of the goddess Artemis, the Diana of the Romans, who was for that reason adopted as patron of the city. (Her local temple was not mercilessly razed to the ground by the Christians, as was their deplorable custom once their religion triumphed in the Roman Empire, but was transformed into a church, so that its mighty Doric pillars may still be admired in the interior of the Cathedral, one of the many attractions that make a visit to Syracuse absolutely worthwhile.) The Greek colony of *Ortygia* gradually expanded onto the Sicilian mainland and developed into one of the biggest and most important cities in the Hellenic world; it was henceforth known as Syracuse (*Syrakos*). This was an Usko-Mediterranean name, a combination of *zuruqqu*, 'water' or 'river', and *usu*, 'mouth'. The city and its port are indeed located near the mouth of a river, the Ciane, famous for the clusters of papyrus found on its shores.

On the southern coast of Sicily, perilously close to the Carthaginian sphere of influence, Greek daredevils founded the city of *Selinus* (Italian: Selinunte), whose name was derived from *selinon*, 'wild parsley'. That city was dedicated to the goddess of fertility, Demeter, for whom this herb served as attribute. *Selinus* experienced a period of great prosperity during which magnificent temples were erected, as was the case in neighboring *Akragas* (Agrigento). The latter toponym was of Usko-Mediterranean origin and meant something like 'flooded area' or 'marsh', a reference to the city's location, admittedly on a hill but surrounded by a marshy estuary fed by two rivers. To the Greeks, however, the name sounded like *akra-gè*, 'high land', and today this is still commonly believed to be the meaning of the name. Around 400 BCE, Selinunte was captured and destroyed by the Carthaginians. Its demise was a cause of great rejoicing in its rival city, Segesta, inhabited not by Greeks but by a tribe of indigenous *Sikeloi*. Segesta's name probably reflects its location in the hills to the north of Selinunte and might well derive from Usko-Mediterranean terms closely related to the Akkadian *saqu*, 'high', and *asitu*, 'city', producing the meaning of "Highbury", as one might say in English.[65] Today, virtually nothing is left of this city, except for a theatre and a magnificent solitary temple high on a hill, as the name suggests, overlooking a superb Sicilian landscape.

Sicily remained the scene of conflict and war between Hellenes and Carthaginians, but at the time of the First Punic War the Roman ogre appeared on the scene, eliminated both adversaries, and pocketed the entire island. Already earlier, the Greek possessions in Campania and elsewhere on the Italian mainland had been taken over by the Romans, thus ending the Greek adventure in *Magna Graecia*. The region was gradually Latinized, but today its glorious Hellenic past is conjured up not only by the imposing temples of Paestum, Agrigento, and Selinunte, but also by the numerous toponyms of Greek origin. Of the forgotten pre-Hellenic, Pelasgian / Usko-Mediterranean "deep history" of the island, the names of mighty Etna, of cities such as Syracuse and archaeological sites like Segesta, and of course of Sicily itself, are onomastic witnesses.

Hellas or Greece?

The Greeks called their country Hellas and themselves, Hellenes. "Hellenes" signified 'descendents of Helle', or so the Greeks themselves believed. Helle was a mythological figure, the son of Deukalion – a Greek Noah, the survivor of a primordial flood – and his wife, Pyrrha. Helle was considered to be the mythical ancestor, the "Abraham", of all Hellenes. Among those who find this mythological explanation unsatisfactory, some relate the name "Hellas" to *helios*, 'sun', suggesting that the meaning of the name of the land of the Hellenes, the cradle of the so-called "Greek Miracle", is nothing less than 'land of light'. Some wishful thinking is obviously involved in this interpretation and indeed, the affinity between Hellas and *helios* exists only in the fantasy of the most enthusiastic philhellenes.

"As in the case of most names of lands and peoples, there is no convincing etymology for Hellas and Hellenes'; such, at least, is the laconic and fatalistic judgment reached by the learned *Griechisches Etymologisches Wörterbuch*. This authoritative opinion may well appear to terminate the investigation, were it not for the fact that Semerano has recently drawn attention to the similarity between the term

---

[65] A good French translation would be "Hauteville", which happens to be the name of the Norman dynasty that ruled Sicily and much of Southern Italy during the 11th-12th centuries, and were known there as the *Altavilla*.

Hellas and the Mesopotamian word *ellatu,* meaning 'group of people', 'league', 'clan', or 'federation (of peoples and/or tribes)'. The indigenous Pelasgian inhabitants of Greece presumably used this exonym to refer to the Indo-European migrants who invaded their homeland and who did indeed happen to constitute a loose federation of autonomous yet related tribes such as the Dorians, the Achaeans, the Ionians, etc. Initially, these newcomers appear to have had no common onomastic denominator, but referred to themselves by their specific name, for example, "Dorians" and "Danaeans", as Homer still did. (Incidentally, the ethnonym "Danaeans" – allegedly the descendants of a mythical King of Argos, named Danaos – incorporates in reality the Usko-Mediterranean term *dannu,* 'powerful'; they were the 'powerful people'. The name of the Dorians may well contain the aforementioned root *dur,* 'fortress', giving us the meaning 'people of the fortresses'.) To the Pelasgians, these onomastic niceties were immaterial; to them all of these alien tribes loomed as clearly interrelated interlopers for whom a common onomastic denominator consequently made sense; they were all part of a same "league" or "federation". As time went by, the Indo-European immigrants themselves presumably started to appreciate the usefulness of a common ethnonym, and so they eventually adopted the Pelasgian nomenclature, *Hellas* as well as *Hellenes.* (According to a German specialist in the field, the nomenclature *Hellenes* is first mentioned in a Greek source of approximately 600 BCE [Dihle 1994: 14].)

To this very day, the Greeks have continued to call themselves *Hellenes* and their country *Hellas,* but foreigners speak of "Greeks" and "Greece". The latter terminology appears to have originated in the Greek northwest, in a region known as Epirus, inhabited – like the rest of the Balkan coast of the Adriatic Sea, as we have seen – by the Illyrians, a people who spoke an Usko-Mediterranean language. In that area, the same Indo-European newcomers who were elsewhere called *Hellenes* by the Pelasgians allegedly settled in a place called Graia, and the name of its inhabitants, the *Graikhoi,* was soon used by the Illyrians in the well-known *pars pro toto* manner to refer to the *Hellenes* in general. Furthermore, this nomenclature was "exported" by the Illyrians to regions further west, more in particular to neighboring Italy, so that via the Etruscans and the Romans the appellations "Greeks" and "Greece" eventually penetrated all the languages of the "Western" world. According to a different version of this theory, inhabitants of Graia were involved in the founding of Cumae, one of the very first Hellenic colonies in *Magna Graecia,* so that the Italic peoples, including the Romans, eventually called all Greek colonists *Graeci.* The trouble with both versions of this theory is not only that considerable uncertainty surrounds the identity and location of Graia (which some identify with Tanagra, situated far from Epirus),[66] but also the fact that no etymology is offered for its name either.

According to Semerano, the ethnonym "Greeks" is indeed of Pelasgian origin. But while he leaves open the possibility that the Illyrians were the first to use this name, he offers an entirely different etymology. The Pelasgians in general were presumably far from pleased when Indo-European tribes invaded their homeland. It

---

[66] See e.g. Pausanias (1971.1: 349).

must have come to conflicts with subgroups of the Hellenic league, and so they called these newcomers "Greeks", which simply meant 'enemies'. Semerano indeed claims to recognize in this ethnonym the Usko-Mediterranean root *ger*, denoting hostility and belligerence. In the Akkadian language, for example, *geru* (or *geranu*) meant 'enemy', and *garum* (or *gerum*) was 'to display hostile behavior'; in Hebrew, *ger* meant '[hostile] foreigner' and *gara* signified 'to wage war'. Semerano points to the affinity with the Latin for 'waging war', *gerere bellum*, and the similarity with the French *guerre* and the Basque *gerra* is striking. It is hardly surprising, then, that of the two Pelasgian exonyms the Hellenes themselves adopted the inoffensive "Hellenes" instead of the pejorative "Greeks"! Incidentally, the root *ger* occurs in other exonyms, for example in "Garamants",[67] the name given in Antiquity to a tribe of Berbers who made the Libyan interior unsafe, and also in "Germans", a term that will be discussed shortly.

Let us return to the toponym "Epirus". The Greek word *epeiros* signified 'mainland', and in it we recognize the Pelasgian/Usko-Mediterranean root – *ep(er)u* in Akkadian, meaning 'dust', 'earth', or 'land' – that we already encountered when "Iberia" and "Africa" were dealt with. Epirus was indeed the *mainland* of the Greeks, contrasting dramatically with their many *islands* (or at least with neighboring islands such as Corfu) and with their great peninsula, the Peloponnese, which was in fact regarded by the Greeks as an island, namely, the 'island (*nesos*) of Pelops'. Noteworthy in this respect is the fact that the Greeks also used to differentiate neatly between *nesiotes*, 'denizens of an island', and *epeirotes*, 'inhabitants of the mainland'. As for the etymology of the first part of Peloponnese, the traditional explanation holds that we are dealing with a combination of the Greek terms *pelios*, 'dark', and *ops*, 'eye'; this is supposedly an allusion to the mythical Pelops, a grandchild of Zeus and son of Tantalus. According to Semerano, however, the term *Peloponnesus* includes two Usko-Mediterranean roots, related to the Akkadian terms *bel*, 'lord', also used in the sense of 'god', and *apsi* (or *apsu*), 'deep water', 'sea' a cognate of the English *abyss*; the meaning of "Peloponnese" is therefore 'island of the god of the sea', in other words, 'island of Poseidon'. Poseidon indeed happened to be the Greek version of the oriental god known as Bel or Baal. Furthermore, a connection between the Peloponnese and Poseidon appears in fact to have existed since the earliest of times. The British author Rodney Castleden cites Ephorus, a historian from the fourth century BCE, who then already wrote that "in the olden days" the Peloponnese "seems to have been the dwelling place of Poseidon and the land was considered sacred to him". In his study of Mycenaean Greece, Castleden (2005: 143) also emphasizes that Poseidon was the "chief god" of those Greeks of the Bronze Age, whose heartland happened to be the Peloponnese. The association of the Peloponnese with Poseidon was perhaps originally due to the shape of the peninsula, featuring three long headlands conjuring up his attribute *par excellence*, the trident. In Antiquity, the tip of one of these headlands, Cape Matapan, the southernmost tip of the Peloponnese, was crowned by a temple to Poseidon.

---

[67] The Garamants are mentioned frequently in Nantet (1998), e.g. pp 208ff and 224 ff.

(Photo: M-L Nguyen [2008] of a 418 BCE painting of a drinking vessel from Agrigento; source: Wikimedia Commons)

(Sketch based on a statue in Madrid Archaeological Museum; source; MeyersKonversationlexicon 1880 via Wikimedia Commons)

Two contrasting representations of Poseidon, both with his attribute, the trident

There exists yet another hetero-ethnonym for "Greeks", again with a murky etymology: *Ionians*. Originally, this term appears to have referred to one of the tribes of the Hellenic "league," namely, the one inhabiting the islands of the eastern Aegean Sea and the west coast of Asia Minor; Miletus was the foremost city of this "Ionian Greece". Eventually, however, this nomenclature applied to all Greeks. The Ionian Sea between Italy and Greece is therefore the 'Greek Sea'. This explains why in the west, the Hellenes became known as "Greeks", but in most countries to the east they were called "Ionians". The Egyptians referred to them as *Jawan,* the Hebrews of the Bible knew them as the *Javan,* in Persian they were called *Yauna* and in Hindi *Yavana*. In Buddhist literature, Hellas was known as *Yona*. And *Yunanistan*, 'land of the Ionians', is the name for Greece in the language of the Turks, the unloved neighbors of the Hellenes. As for the etymology of *Ionia[ns]*, Semerano considers this term to be a cognate of the Akkadian *uwanu* (or *ummanu*), meaning 'crowd' or 'people'. It would seem to have been an exonym with a rather pejorative connotation, bestowed on the Greeks by the inhabitants of the Middle East.

A word must also be said about the Aegean Sea. Why was this sea called *Aegean*? Already in Antiquity this was the subject of considerable uncertainty and debate. According to some, a city named "Aegea" or something similar had once flourished on its shores and ruled its waves, bequeathing its name much as Adria had done in the case of the Adriatic Sea. Others believed that Aegea had been a queen of the legendary Amazons, who had perished in the waters of this sea. Greek mythology also knew an Aegeus, a legendary king of Athens. His son, the hero Theseus, departed for Crete in order to slay the Minotaur, but upon his return he forgot to hoist a white sail, as promised, should he succeed in his mission. In the belief that his son had not survived his adventure, father Aegeus threw himself into the waters of the sea, which thus received his name. This is yet another sample of typically Greek mythological etymology, as the Hellenes claimed to recognize the names of mythical heroes in virtually all ancient, Usko-Mediterranean and therefore cryptic topo- or ethnonyms. Considerably more credible is the hypothesis that the term *Aegean* is of Pelasgian/Usko-Mediterranean origin. *Aiges* was a cognate of the Akkadian root *aga'u,* 'water', and meant 'waves', 'waving waters'; in one word, 'sea'. To the indigenous inhabitants of Greece, the Aegean Sea did indeed constitute the waving waters that surrounded their islands and bordered their mainland; it was *the* sea, the sea of seas.

As we know, this sea is sprinkled with islands big and small, of which one particular archipelago is known as the Cyclades. This name is not Pelasgian, but Greek. *Kuklades* means nothing other than 'islands forming a circle [*kuklos*]', and a glance at a map suffices to confirm that this is indeed what they do, more or less. In the middle of that circle lies the islet of Delos, formerly a famous sanctuary dedicated to Apollo. Delos is a toponym of pre-Hellenic origin, or so claims Semerano. He interprets it as a variant of the Akkadian *dalu*, 'cistern', a reference to the way in which the inhabitants used to collect water, because there were never any springs on the island. Even today, visitors to Delos are shown a cistern that dates back to at least the 7th/6th century BCE and whose antiquity is also hinted at by its predicate, "Minoan". To Greek ears, *dalu* sounded like the Greek word for 'visible', *delos*. And so the Hellenes concocted a myth to explain why this was the 'visible island'. According to this story, Delos, in reality a barely distinguishable rock, suddenly became "visible" when Apollo was born there. The ancient Greeks considered this Cycladian Lilliput as the center of their sea, that is, of the Aegean Sea, just as the other famous Apollo sanctuary, Delphi, was considered to be the 'navel', or center, of the inhabited world. (In Delphi, the famous oracle inhabited a kind of chasm in which a spring bubbled out of the ground; the name *Delphi* contains an Usko-Mediterranean root, related to the Akkadian *daltu*, meaning 'opening', 'tunnel'. Our word *delta*, the place where the river "opens up", is a cognate of the root *daltu*.)

The ancient cistern on the island of Delos
(Photo: J Pauwels, 2009)

All non-Cycladian islands of the Aegean Sea are called Sporades. This term means the 'disseminated islands'. *Sporos*, 'seed', is a Greek root we also recognize in 'sperm', 'spore', 'diaspora', 'asparagus', and the French verb *asperger*, 'to sprinkle'. In striking contrast to the geographically disciplined Cycladic archipelago, the Sporades are islands that are scattered most capriciously throughout the Aegean universe. The Greeks who, like Einstein, viewed space and time as inextricable, also used this term to refer to things that are irregularly scattered in time, and this is the origin of 'sporadic' (Urmes 2003: 92, 520).

The world of the Greeks also included the eastern shores of the Aegean Sea, a part of Anatolia known to historians as Ionian Greece. One of the leading cities there was Ephesus, home of the great temple of Artemis, one of the Seven Wonders of the World, originally a sanctuary dedicated to an Anatolian fertility goddess. That city – and its sanctuary - already existed in the Bronze Age, long before the arrival of the Greeks, and it is therefore hardly surprising that its name is not Greek but Usko-Mediterranean. Ephesus originated on a hill overlooking an inlet of the Aegean Sea, and was known as *ker-issa*, 'city [*issa*] on the hill [*ker*]', an expression of which "acropolis" would be a perfect Greek translation; today, that hill is known as Mount Koressos. However, an urban center eventually sprang up near the water, to become known, logically enough, as 'city [*issa*] of the sea [*apsu*]' and this *apsu-issa* was to develop over time into Ephesus. Perhaps it is the resemblance of the *apsu*, 'sea', in Ephesus, with the Usko-Mediterranean word for 'bee', *apu*, as in 'apiculture', that this little animal figured prominently on the coins minted by the city and became also an attribute of the Artemis (or Diana) of Ephesus.[68]

A bee coin from Ephesus of ca. 4th century BCE
(Source: the numismatic collection of the University of Tübingen)

The Greeks swarmed out to the north, to the region of the Black Sea, and to the west, primarily to Italy. The south and east had far less to offer them, mainly because since time immemorial great, powerful, and relatively densely populated empires had been established in Africa and in Asia, such as Pharaonic Egypt, Babylonia, Assyria, and Persia. It was possible to do business there, but for colonial ventures there was hardly any potential. For a long time, the Greeks managed to do no better than to create a number of emporia such as Naukratis, a port in the Nile delta that was authorized by the Pharaoh around 600 BCE in order to promote trade between the

---

[68] "The Coinage of Ephesus", *http://learn.mq.edu.au/webct/RelativeResourceManager/15043963001/ Public%20Files/chapters/chapter02.htm*

two realms. A genuine Greek colonial venture within the Egyptian sphere of influence proved possible only at a respectable distance from the densely populated Nile Valley, namely, further to the west along the Mediterranean coast; around 600 BCE, a Greek colony named Cyrene sprang up there. The site featured a spring known in the local Hamitic language as *q[u]r* ('to bubble up') *enu* ('water' or 'spring'), which sounded in Hellenic ears like *kourè*, 'little girl'. Thus originated the names Cyrene for the city - and Cyrenaïca for the surrounding territory – as well as the belief among the Greeks that the meaning of this toponym was 'little girl'. To the west of this Greek colony, the Sahara touches the coast of the Mediterranean Sea, and the Hellenes called this inhospitable coastal area *Syrtis*, which meant something like 'pile of rocks'; this nomenclature – in which we recognize the Usko-Mediterranean root *sur*, 'rock' – lives on today in the expressions Great and Little Syrte, that is, the bays of Benghazi in Libya and Gabes in Tunisia. Cyrene was situated in that part of the African continent that was known in Egypt as *Leba* or *Libu*, and with their own version of that name – *Lebua* or *Libuë*, 'Libya' – the Greeks referred to Africa, or at least its northern part, inhabited by the Berbers and stretching from the Nile to the Atlas Mountains and the Atlantic Ocean. However, the Hellenes were aware that black people lived further south, and they called them *Nigretoi*, a word that would inspire the Latin terms *niger*, 'black', and *nigretes*, 'negroes'.

The land to the south of Egypt was likewise inhabited by dark-skinned people. As we have seen before, the Greeks and Romans called that region Nubia, and the Greeks also spoke of *Aithiopia*, 'land of the people with sun-burned faces'. But that nomenclature was not very precise, and both "Libya" and "Ethiopia" were used by the Hellenes (and later the Romans) in the familiar *pars pro toto* manner to refer to Africa in general. It was only much later that "Africa" would become the preferred term for the "black continent" in its entirety. And so the terms "Ethiopia" and "Sudan" became available to indicate specific countries to the south of Egypt. Ethiopia was also long known as "Abyssinia", a term that is believed to be the latinized version of the Amharic *habesh*, 'mixed', and to signify 'mixed people'. This was perceived as a somewhat pejorative reference to the ethnic mosaic that has called Ethiopia home since time immemorial, and is therefore no longer used.

The Greeks' relationship with Africa and Asia was revolutionized by the triumphs of Alexander the Great over Persia's Achaemenid state, an empire which had dominated the Middle East in its entirety as well as Egypt for a couple of centuries and which had come close to conquering Greece itself in the early fifth century BCE. Greek colonists settled down in just about all the regions that were pocketed by the Macedonian ruler, and this process involved the founding of numerous new cities. The corresponding nomenclature was dominated, and virtually monopolized, by the young but incredibly successful warlord. In India, he gave a newly founded city – now Jhelum in Pakistan – the name *Bucephala* in honor of his horse, Bucephalos, 'bull's head', that happened to have died there. However, most newly founded cities between the Nile and the Indus received Alexander's own name. No less than seventy Alexandrias are said to have originated at the time, even in the isolated land we now know as Afghanistan, for example the city of Kandahar;

Kandahar is really "Iskandahar", that is, 'city of *Iskander* [i.e. Alexander]'. But the best-known "Alexander cities" were Alexandretta, "little Alexandria," in present-day Turkey, now known as Iskenderun, and or course the great Alexandria in Egypt, *Alexandria ad Aegyptum*, founded in 331 BCE. The latter developed into the greatest and most important commercial and cultural metropolis in the entire Greek *Oikoumene*, and was famous because of its museum, its superb library, and its lighthouse – all of this in addition to the tomb of the Great Alexander himself. Alexandria's lighthouse was named after the little island on which it stood, Pharos. The etymology of that term is shrouded in darkness. However, it is possibly a cognate of the aforementioned *afar*, and therefore also of Africa and Iberia, and in this case its meaning would be 'land surrounded by water', 'island', or 'peninsula'. In any event, the term *pharos* became a synonym for 'lighthouse' in French and in many other languages. The famous Alexandrine beacon, proclaimed to be one of the Seven Wonders of the World, inspired toponyms such as Faro, a port on the Portuguese coast, and Hvar, a Croatian island off the Dalmatian coast, both sites where the Greeks or Romans erected lighthouses that were more or less similar to the prototype in Alexandria.

Second century CE coins from Alexandria featuring the Pharos lighthouse
(Photo: Ginolerhino; source: Wikimedia Commons)

Alexandria functioned as an outpost of Greek civilization in a world in which the Hellenes had hitherto provided preciously little input. Just as Cadiz had earlier been a western outpost of the east, the Hellenic metropolis in the Nile Delta henceforth served as an outpost of the west not only in the south but also in the east, in Africa as well as Asia. In their Alexandrine cockpit, the Greeks assiduously gathered all sorts of information about Africa and Asia, and they continued to do so long after the empire of the Macedonian conqueror had fallen apart and its territorial shards, including Egypt, had been picked up by newcomers such as the Romans and the Parthians. Not coincidentally, then, it was in this city that the great Eratosthenes of Cyrene (280-195 BCE) used to work, namely as director of the famous library; he calculated the circumference of the earth with almost complete accuracy and also coined the term "geography". In comparison to him, that other famous Alexandrine, Ptolemy, who lived in the second century CE, was a lesser geographic god. However, his world map became a mega-hit, and during the Middle Ages he was considered the greatest non-Biblical authority in the realm of geographic knowledge. It would remain that way until Columbus – who trusted him too much – and the other great explorers brought about a revolutionary metamorphosis of the western view of the world.

4

The *Imperium Romanum* and its Neighbors

How Italy became Roman

The glorious city of Rome began extremely modestly as a hamlet on the muddy banks of an unimposing river, the Tiber, in a region called Latium, now known by its Italian name, Lazio. The names Tiber and Latium are of Etruscan origin. Semerano thinks he recognizes in "Latium", just as in "Hellas", a cognate of the Akkadian *ellatu*, 'league'; he claims that, as in the case of the Greeks, the term was originally used by Italy's Usko-Mediterranean population to denote a group of autonomous but internally related Indo-European clans.

Latium was a backward no-man's-land sandwiched between regions inhabited by highly civilized neighbors, the Etruscans to the north in Tuscany, and the Greeks of *Magna Graecia* to the south. Nonetheless, it was the Romans who would eventually control all of Italy and even turn the Mediterranean Sea into their *Mare Nostrum*. To the upstarts of the *urbs Romanorum*, however, the humble beginnings of their city would always remain a source of some embarrassment. Compensation was sought and found in the shape of a grandiose myth, that of Romulus and Remus. These two foundlings, allegedly descendants of the great Trojan hero Aeneas, survived by being suckled by a she-wolf, and as they grew up they founded the city to which Romulus gave his name.

Officially, then, Rome was the 'city of Romulus'. But what are the true origins of the name *Rome*? Most likely, *ruma* or *rumon* was the original Etruscan, i.e. pre-Indo-European name of the Tiber, and its meaning was '[waters that] gnaw [the banks]'; see e.g. Glover (1959:138). Semerano points to the similarity with the Sumerian/Akkadian term *herum*, which refers to the 'gnawing' or 'digging' of the waters in a river bed. Nobody knows precisely when the Indo-European Romans settled that site, but when they did, the term *ruma* made them think of the Latin word *ruma*, '[a mother's] breast', an interpretation that was probably reinforced by the fact that in Rome the Tiber forms a meander in the shape of a female breast, a breast of which the little Tiber Island appears to be the nipple. The original city of Rome, the Rome of Romulus, lay just across the river, and seemed attached to this meander of the Tiber like a baby to a breast. Could it be that this topographic constellation provided inspiration for the myth of the nursing babies, Romulus and Remus? A further possibility is that the name of Rome is derived from another Usko-Mediterranean word, namely *ruma*, meaning 'rock' or 'hill', which would presumably have referred to the Palatine; 'Romulus', supposedly, was 'he who lives on the [Palatine] hill'. As for the toponym Palatine, it is said to reflect the ancient root *b'el*, which referred to a temple – devoted to some deity (*el*) – on an elevated site. Finally, the names Rome, Romulus, and Remus also conjure up the Akkadian *ramu*, 'to found'. There is certainly no shortage of intriguing theories with respect to the name of Rome!

The River Tiber, with the Tiber Island
(17th century engraving by Jacobus Baptist and Lievin Cruyl; source: Pauwels 2006)

The Romans could not match the achievements of the Phoenicians and the Greeks with respect to the discovery of New Worlds, and their geographic knowledge essentially reflected that of the Greeks in the Hellenistic era. Nonetheless, the Romans too have gone down in history as generous dispensers of names of peoples and lands, and this for two reasons. On the one hand, they conquered and colonized vast regions and founded new cities; on the other hand, of all the Indo-European languages, it happened to be their Latin tongue that played a decisive role in the displacement of existing Usko-Mediterranean languages. Ancient topo-, ethno-, hydro-, and oronyms were replaced virtually everywhere by Latinized versions that are still familiar to us today, but whose real meaning escapes us if we try to identify their etymology by means of Latin, Greek, or any other Indo-European language.

Italy itself was Latinized in its entirety at the expense of the neighbors of the Romans, that is, not only the Greeks of Magna Graecia and the Etruscans, but also the Etruscoid nations, the other Indo-European Italic tribes such as the Samnites, and the at least partly Usko-Mediterranean Celts who inhabited the north of the country. Celtic tribes, presumably originating in Gaul, had penetrated Italy in the fifth century BCE and had caused considerable trouble for the Etruscans. In 386 BCE, under the leadership of a certain Brennus, they had even sacked Rome, then settled down between the Alps and the Apennines. This region, previously the homeland of the Raetians, was henceforth known to the Romans as *Gallia Cisalpina*, 'Gaul on this side of the Alps'. The Celts had invaded Italy via the Alpine mountain passes, so it is no coincidence that the name of one of these, the Brenner Pass, keeps alive the memory of Brennus, the legendary Celtic warrior who terrorized Rome. However, it is not certain that this Brennus ever really existed; historians suspect that Brennus was not a proper name, but rather a kind of title used by a number of Celtic leaders; Semerano suggests that its meaning was 'elected leader'.

Panoramic view, from a wide-angle lens, of Pisa's Baptistry, Cathedral and Leaning Tower
(Photo: Patrick Landy, 2008; source: Wikimedia Commons)

On strategically important sites in the land of the Etruscans and throughout *Gallia Cisalpina,* the Romans established army camps and founded new cities, both usually featuring rigid gridiron plans. A city was thus founded on the banks of the Arno River and at the foot of a hill on which an Etruscan settlement, now the picturesque town of Fiesole, was located. It was named *Florentia* after Flor, the goddess of the spring and of flowers, presumably because this event took place in the spring, at the time of the Roman feast of the flowers, the *ludi florales*. The symbol of Florence is still the purple iris, a flower that was considered in Antiquity as the spring flower *par excellence*. At least, such is the conventional etymological wisdom. However, Semerano – who happened to be a Florentine – offers a different theory. The name Florence has nothing to do with flowers, but was derived from *ferentinum*, a word in which we recognize the verb *ferre* ('to bring', 'to carry'); the name alluded to the fact that the city sprang up on land that was deposited – in other words, 'carried' there – by the river. (Antwerp, a toponym which in Flemish ostensibly signifies 'throwing of the hand', has a virtually identical meaning, 'land deposited by the river', in this case by the River Scheldt.)

In the immediate vicinity of the mouth of the Arno, the Romans founded a city they called *Colonia Julia*; later, as an important naval base, it was to become known as *Portus Pisanus,* which eventually led to the city's present name, *Pisa*. This toponym probably reflected the original, Etruscan and therefore Usko-Mediterranean, name of the site; *Pisa* certainly closely resembles the Sumerian term *pisu*, 'mouth of a river'. Incidentally, Semerano is convinced that the same pre-Indo-European root also hides in the name "Bosnia", and in this case the reference is to the estuary of the Neretva River, the major river of that country. The same root also appears to be ensconced in the name of the Italy's Adriatic seaport of Pesaro, situated at the mouth of the Foglia River.

Further north, on the other side of the Apennines, the Romans constructed a road in the beginning of the second century BCE. It was named the *Via Aemilia* in honor of a contemporary consul, Aemilius Lepidus; the region it bisected also received his name and this part of Italy is still known as Emilia. Cities sprang up along the Emilian Way, including *Bononia*, present-day Bologna. However, the name Bologna is not of Roman but of Etruscan origin; this toponym – and similar toponyms, such as Boulogne (also *Bononia*), Bonn (*Bonna*), Regensburg (*Radaspona* in Celtic, *Ratisbonne* in French), and Narbonne – has an Usko-Mediterranean etymological nucleus, signifying 'construction', 'building[s]', in other words, 'city'; its Akkadian and Hebrew versions were *banu* and *banah*, respectively, according to Semerano. In the middle of the land of the Cisalpine Celts, at the foot of the Alps, the Romans also founded a base. On account of its central location in the "plain", i.e. in the Po Valley, and halfway between the Adriatic and Tyrrhenian Seas, it received the name *Medio(p)lanum*: the present-day metropolis of Milan. The region to the west of Milan was the homeland of a Celtic tribe known in Latin as the *Taurini*; there the Romans planted a settlement named after these people, and thus originated the city now known as Turin, *Torino* in Italian.

On the other side of the Po Valley, in the land of a tribe called the *Veneti*, in 181 BCE the Romans erected an army base (*castrum*) that was named – or so some say – after the eagle that adorned the standard of many legions, the *aquila*. Like many other *castra*, this *Aquileia* developed into a prosperous city, mainly because the terminus of the Amber Road moved there from Adria, which struggled in vain against the problem of a receding coastline. However, wealth and prestige would eventually doom *Aquileia*, because they attracted Attila and the Huns, who sacked the city in 452 CE. The surviving – and by now thoroughly Latinized – *Veneti* withdrew to the relative security of a little island that was initially called the 'high bank' (*rivus altus*, Rialto), but was to achieve worldwide fame as the 'city of the Venetians': Venice.

Transalpine Gaul

The Roman wars of conquest served to a large extent to provide employment, in the form of military service, to the peasants of Latium and later of the rest of Italy, whose land was appropriated by Rome's Patrician elite and henceforth worked by slaves. The system of permanent warfare simultaneously provided the steady supply of prisoners of war that was required to maintain the stock of slaves at a high level. The

Roman plebes were compensated to some extent for their expropriation and their military service – at least if they survived it! – with grants of land in the conquered regions, in other words, at the expense of the defeated peoples. *Vae victis*!

As a result of their success in the Punic Wars, the Romans became the masters of southern France. They thus established a foothold in *Gallia Transalpina*, 'Gaul on the other side of the Alps', a region inhabited, just like *Gallia Cisalpina*, by Celtic tribes. There is no consensus with respect to the etymology of the ethnonym "Celts". The Greeks typically postulated an "eponymous", i.e., 'name-giving', mythical patriarch or hero named Galates or something similar. The medieval etymologist Isidorus of Seville, on the other hand, opined that *Gallia* was derived from the Greek word *gala*, 'milk', and that this was a reference to skin of the Celtic people, which was supposedly 'white like milk'. Today there are etymologists who theorize that the ethnonym *Keltoi* is related to the Latin *occultus* and signifies the 'hidden' or 'mysterious' people. A German connoisseur of things Celtic, Alexander Demandt, believes that "Celts" was an auto-ethnonym meaning 'brave people'. However, according to Semerano it was originally an Usko-Mediterranean word, a version of the Akkadian term *kalu*, which referred to the social and territorial "community" of an alien people, and to foreigners in general. The Greek version, *Keltoi*, was virtually synonymous with 'barbarians'; it was not the name of an ethnically and linguistically homogeneous people.[69] Even Germanic tribes were sometimes described as "Celts" (and vice-versa; see e.g. Van Loon [2006: 387])), so the Greeks do not appear to have made a meaningful distinction between Celts and Germans. It was therefore customary to specify which "Celts" one had in mind. For example, the Hellenes spoke of the Celto-Ligurians, the Celto-Scythians, and the Celtiberians. When an alien, barbarian and therefore "Celtic" people invaded Asia Minor a few centuries BCE and settled there, they were labeled as *galtu*, 'terrifying', by the Babylonians, and thus originated the name of the Galatians. These Galatians were defeated by their Greek neighbors, a feat of arms that was commemorated by a word-famous Hellenistic sculpture, the Pergamon Altar, now in Berlin. The surviving barbarian invaders settled in "Galatia", in the vicinity of Ankara, became peaceful denizens of the area and, a few centuries later, established a Christian community to which St Paul was to send one of his epistles. In spite of the similarity between the terms "Galatians" and "Celts", however, it is far from certain that we are dealing here with the same people, in other words, the same "Celts", who were at home in Gaul, as is often suggested (Semerano 2005: 38-39).

Gallia, the Latin version of the Celtic name of the land later known as "France", made the Romans think of *gallus*, 'rooster'. Furthermore, to the Celts of Gaul the rooster happened to be a symbol of bravery; it is for this reason that after the First World War the 'Gallic rooster' (*coq gaulois*) was used to decorate thousands of

---

[69] A recent study of the Celts similarly mentions the possibility that this ethnonym may have been used "as a very general term to refer to a grouping of people who had different ethnicities, languages, etc., but who were lumped together by outsiders, much as we refer to the aboriginal inhabitants of the Americas as 'Indians', or the inhabitants of Australia as 'Aborigines'"; see Collis, (2003: 103).

French war memorials. To the Romans, then, Gaul was the 'land of roosters'. However, in spite of the bravery of Vercingetorix and his Celtic comrades, their homeland was inexorably gobbled up by the Roman Leviathan. Incidentally, Caesar defeated Vercingetorix at a place called Alesia, a cognate of the Akkadian *halsu*, meaning 'fortress'.

The Dying Galatian, in the Capitoline Museum in Rome[70]
(Unknown photographer, 2005; source: Wikimedia Commons from Flickr)

The first region of Gaul to be absorbed by the Roman Empire was the area around the Greek foundation of Marseilles. It was allegedly there that Greeks first used the term *Keltoi* to refer to the indigenous population, possibly borrowing the name from a local tribe. This southern part of France was annexed by Rome in the wake of the Punic Wars; it became a *provincia* of the Roman Empire, and thus originated the toponym "Provence". In the vicinity of Marseilles there was a fortress, a so-called

---

[70] According to *Wikipedia*, "[t]he artistic quality and expressive pathos of [this] statue aroused great admiration among educated classes in the 17th and 18th centuries and was a "must-see" sight on the Grand Tour of Europe undertaken by young men of the day. Byron was one such visitor, commemorating the *Dying Gaul* [sic] in his poem *Childe Harold's Pilgrimage:*

> He leans upon his hand his manly brow
> Consents to death, but conquers agony.
> And his drooped head sinks gradually low –
> And through his side the last drops, ebbing slow
> From the red gash, fall heavy, one by one..."

Note that, while this statue is generally known as *The Dying Gaul* in English, this is in fact a mistranslation of Italian *galate morente* 'dying Galatian'.

oppidum, of the local Gallic tribe, and on this strategically important site the Romans around 120 BCE implanted an army base, a *castellum*, that would later become the capital of Provence. In honor of a general, C Sextius Calvinus, and on account of the presence of warm water springs, the foundation was given the name 'Waters of [Proconsul] Sextius', *Aquae Sextiae*; today the town is known as Aix-en-Provence. In the same general area but a bit further west, near the Rhône, veterans of a Roman legion settled in a place called *Arausio*. It is claimed that this Celtic toponym reflected the name of some Gallic deity, but that is far from certain. However, the Latin version of the name eventually produced the French "Orange", which conjures up oranges, a citrus fruit unknown to the Romans. Many centuries later, a scion of the local princely dynasty, who also happened to control vast landed wealth in regions far to the north of there, would earn fame as "Prince of Orange" and would play an important role in the history of the Low Countries; one of his descendants currently occupies the throne of the Kingdom of the Netherlands, where the "national" color is of course orange.

Willem, Prince of Orange, also known as The Taciturn
(Artist: Michiel Jansz; source: Wikimedia Commons)

Around 50 BCE, Julius Caesar conquered the rest of Gaul. He later wrote an extensive account of this achievement, *De Bello Gallico*, a text that causes more problems for students of the Latin language than Vercingetorix and company ever caused Caesar himself. *Gallia* was carved up by the Romans into a number of administrative regions. An efficient system of roads soon criss-crossed the land, Roman cities took the place of the Celtic hilltop towns or *oppida*, and the Gauls were gradually Latinized. France witnessed the birth of a so-called "Gallo-Roman" civilization, one of the fruits of which is the French language as we now know it. Julius Caesar personally founded a number of cities in Gaul, and populated them with veterans of his army. In 49 BCE *Forum Julii*, 'Julius's Market Square', now called Fréjus, thus originated on the Mediterranean coast to the east of Marseilles. (Further east, in northeastern Italy, an entire region received exactly the same name; it is now called Friuli.) Emperor Augustus later "pacified" the entire mountainous hinterland of the French Riviera, a region now officially referred to as the *Département des Alpes Maritimes*. He celebrated this feat of arms with the erection of a monument that was baptized *Tropea Augusti*. In the shadow of this "trophy" of the great Augustus, an eponymous settlement eventually emerged; today, two millennia later, this *Tropea* is known as La Turbie. The village, located high on a hill offering wonderful views of Monaco and the Mediterranean Sea, is still dominated by the ruins of the Roman monument, now known as the *Trophée des Alpes*. As for the toponym Monaco, *Monoikos* in Greek, Semerano interprets it as a combination of two Ligurian, and therefore Usko-Mediterranean, terms, *mu* ('water') and *nuahu* ('calm', 'stillness'), an allusion to the still waters of the principality's fine natural harbor. In Antiquity, Monaco featured a temple devoted to Melkart/Hercules, worshiped there by sailors seeking the favour of calm waters during their journeys. As for the "pacification" of the Alps by Augustus, an onomastic witness of this achievement still exists on the other side of the French-Italian border, namely Aosta, a city that was originally a camp of legionnaires named Augusta.

The *Trophée des Alpes* at La Turbie
(Photo: Peter Gugereth, 2006; source: Wikimedia Commons)

In another part of the south of Gaul, between the Rhône and the Pyrenees, the Romans founded a city they dedicated to the god of war, Mars, and called *Narbo Martius*: Narbonne. (However, the toponym *Narbo* contained the ancient Usko-Mediterranean root *bona*, "city", so that the Roman name of the city can hardly be said to have originated *ex nihilo*.) Eventually that entire part of Gaul was to receive the name *Gallia Narbonensis*. From there it was possible to travel to Spain via a road across the Pyrenees, whose highest point was the *summus portus*, 'the high mountain pass', now known as the Somport. During the Middle Ages that road would become a branch of the famous pilgrims' route to Compostela; it gained fame as the *Via*

Tolosana, 'the way of Toulouse'. From *Gallia Narbonensis* one could also follow the Garonne River downstream to the Atlantic coast of France. In doing so, one reached a large and important harbor, *Burdigala*, now called Bordeaux. According to Semerano, this toponym combined two Usko-Mediterranean terms. *Burdi* – *burtu* in Akkadian – signified a well, a pond, any body of water, and also a river crossing, which happens to be the meaning of its English cognate, 'ford'. The second part of the Latin version, *gala,* reflected the Usko-Mediterranean *kala,* originally 'dyke', but also 'steep embankment', 'harbor'. The Bordeaux region not only borders the great Ocean Sea; it is also crossed by two mighty rivers, the Garonne and the Dordogne, which converge into an estuary in the shape of a swallow, *hirundo* in Latin, and therefore known as the Gironde. The entire area had an Usko-Mediterranean name of which the etymology is unknown, but whose Latin version, *Aquitania*, recalled the word *aqua*, 'water', so it inevitably acquired the meaning of 'land of the great water' or 'of the many waters'. In Medieval French this name evolved to *l'Aguiane*, *l'Aguienne,* and ultimately *Guyenne.* A propos *water*: within Aquitania, between the waters of the Bay of Biscay and those of the Gironde, there was a peninsula that, centuries later, would witness the construction of countless opulent chateau wineries devoted to the production of Bordeaux *grand crus*; the Romans called this peninsula *Medium Aquae,* '[land] between the waters', and in the course of the centuries this toponym would evolve into Médoc. According to Caesar, the inhabitants of Aquitaine differed ethnically and linguistically from the other Gauls. The Aquitanians appear to have been a branch of the Iberian family, perhaps Basques, or at least a people related to the Basques.

To the north of Provence, on the banks of the Rivers Rhône and Saône, lay what was very likely the single most important Roman city in Gaul, *Lugdunum*, or Lyon. The Romans typically Latinized Celtic toponyms, and did so in this case too. The Celtic city of Lyon was dedicated to the deity of light, *Lug*; known in Latin as *Luxovius,* he was the local version of Hermes (or Mercury) and – according to Caesar – number one in the Gallic pantheon. The cities of Luxeuil in France, Lugo in the Spanish province of Galicia, and (perhaps) Lucca in Italy also bear his name. Like many other Gallic fortified towns, Lyon occupied the top of a hill. The Celtic name for this kind of stronghold was *dunum*, but one also used the composition *appidunum,* 'fortified site on a hill', which may be said to have been the Celtic equivalent of the Greek term *acropolis*; Caesar translated this term into Latin as *oppidum.* However, like many other allegedly Celtic terms, *dunum* – of which 'town' is the English cognate – appears to have a pre-Indo-European, Usko-Mediterranean origin; Semerano points to its affinity to the Akkadian *dannu* – 'mighty', 'strong', and in the case of a settlement, 'stronghold' – and the Sumerian *dun[n]um*, 'fortress'; equally striking is the similarity with the Arabic word for 'city', more specifically 'old town', namely, *madina* (of which the plural is *mudun*). Alongside *dunum* one also frequently used *durum*, which suggests a link with the Semitic *dur, dir* or *dor*, as in the aforementioned *Gadir* of the Phoenicians, now Cadiz, meaning 'walled town' or 'citadel'. In Gaul, numerous fortified sites, preferably located on some high ground, received a name incorporating *dunum* or *dun*, and today we recognize this root in toponyms such as Thuin and (probably) Dinant in French-speaking Belgium, Thun in Switzerland, Daun and Taunus in Germany, and in France, Liverdun near Metz, Issoudun in the Loire Valley, Dinan in Bretagne, Yverdon and Verdun (*Verodunum* or *iber dunum*, 'fortress near the water') and, a little to the north of the latter city and also on the banks of the Meuse River, the small town of Dun. (There is another town called Dun in the Languedoc, and in Burgundy there is a hill named Dun.) Great Britain bristles with *dunums*, including Dundee, Dunbar, Dumbarton, Dumfries, Dunhill, Dunedin, Dunlop, Dunfermline, Edinburgh, Donegall or Dungall, Aberdeen, and the many toponyms that end with the suffixes –don (e.g. Wimbledon) and -down (Blackie 1857: 68-69. On the other side of Europe, *dunums* are also to be found in the Balkan Peninsula, long ago the homeland of the Usko-Mediterranean Illyrians. One example is the city known in Latin as *Singidunum*, which (perhaps) signified 'white stronghold', 'white town'; when the Slavs appeared on the scene, they translated this into their Indo-European language first as *Bialograd* and eventually as *Beograd*, and we say Belgrade. The emphatically white castle in the city's coat of arms underscores the fact that the toponym means 'white city', but precisely what is supposed to be white about it, nobody seems to know. We will later return briefly to the topic of the 'white' in the name of Belgrade.

Two of the many ithyphallic "Herms" of Antiquity[71]
(Photos by Ricardo A Franz (2006) and Lemur12 (2007) of statues in Athens and Dion; source: Wikimedia Commons)

The name *Lugdunum* meant 'Hermes' fortress on the hill', but Lyon was not the only sanctuary dedicated to *Lug* that happened to be located on a high ground. Indeed, not only imposing hills and steep rocks, but also relatively modest hillocks were often used as locus for the worship of Lug/Hermes. However, most privileged in this respect were spectacularly tall and steep rocks, for they evoked the phallus that was frequently associated with Hermes in Greek and Roman iconography – for example in the case of "[ithyphallic] herms", stone pillars with the head of Hermes – and functioned as one of the deity's attributes. When Christianity became the state religion, such sites were turned over to the cult of the Archangel Michael, triumphing over none other than Lucifer, the 'bearer of light'. Examples are the Mont St Michel in Normandy and the steep volcanic peak in Le Puy-en-Velay that is known as the *Aiguille St Michel*, 'St Michael's Needle'.

---

[71] All originally featured his phallus but, in many cases, this was later removed by Christians.

Le Puy-en-Velay, with the *Aiguille St Michel* on the left
(Photo: Patrick Giraud, 2005; source: Wikimedia Commons)

Many other places in Gaul were called *Lugdunum*, for example the modern cities Laon and Loudun in France as well as Leiden in the Netherlands, *Lugdunum Batavorum*. However, two thousand years ago no Gallic (or Britannic) namesake surpassed Lyon in importance. The *Lugdunum* on the confluence of Rhône and Saône happened to be the turntable of Roman traffic in Gaul, and Central France in its entirety was known as *Gallia Lugdunensis*. In those days Lyon was much bigger than Paris and served as the capital not only of *Gallia Lugdunensis*, but of all of Gaul. Lyon, the city of Lug, may be said to have been a 'city of light' long before Paris would appropriate that prestigious epithet.

In the mountains to the east of *Lugdunum*, in the Alps, there lived a Celtic people known to the Romans as the Helvetii. *Helvetia*, 'land of the Helvetians', is now a literary synonym for the federation of cantons that is better known as Switzerland, and on the license plates of Swiss cars one can read "CH", an abbreviation of *Confœderatio Helvetica*, the 'Swiss League'. Semerano sees in this name a combination of two Usko-Mediterranean terms, cognates of the Akkadian *elu*, 'high', and *betu*, 'house', 'place', or 'region', which means that *Helvetia* is the 'high country'. The name "Switzerland" only originated during the Middle Ages. At the very end of the thirteenth century, a rebellion against the Austrian Habsburgs, associated with the legendary William Tell, led to independence and caused the newly independent federation to become known by the name of one of its original members, the centrally located Canton Schwyz, or Switz. As for its etymology, some believe in an affinity with *Schweiss*, 'sweat', *schwitzen*, 'to sweat', and *Sumpf*, 'marsh'. According to this interpretation, Schwyz was originally a damp region, a kind of marsh.

Like *Lugdunum*, *Helvetia* was the Latinized version of a Celtic name. However, in Gaul the Romans also frequently invented purely Latin toponyms. In doing so, they did not display much more originality than the Greeks (with their *Neapolis*) or the Phoenicians (with their *Kart Hadasht*) had done before them. They usually stuck to the Hellenistic tradition of conferring the names of their rulers, particularly emperors such as Augustus, or members of the ruling family. To the north of Lyon an important intersection of Roman roads was thus given the name of Emperor Augustus, *Augustodunum*; this Burgundian city – located on top of a hill, as the suffix *-dunum* suggests – is now known as Autun. A major Roman road connected Autun to Paris, then nothing more than a settlement on a small island in the Seine, now known as the *Ile de la Cité*. In this case too, the Romans simply used the Latin version of the existing Celtic toponym, *Lutetia*. About the etymology of this toponym, the French onomasticians Deroy & Mulon (1992: 368) write the following:

> *Lutetia* is the contracted form of a more ancient version of the name, *Lucotecia*, which was itself based on the Celtic *luco,* 'marsh'. The site of *Lutetia* was indeed very swampy, as Caesar testifies. However, the interpretation of the second element, *–tecia*, is and remains uncertain."[72]

The Romans also acquired the habit of referring to many cities in Gaul (and elsewhere) with the name of the tribe that inhabited the town and the region, and such nicknames often gradually eclipsed the formal name. This too, was the case in the Seine Valley, where *Lutetia* eventually had to give way to the name of the local Celts. *Lutetia,* the city of the *Parisii*, thus became "Paris", and today *Lutèce* is only used occasionally as a literary synonym for the name of the French capital. The name *Parisii* is likewise supposed to be Gallic in origin, but the etymology of the ancient ethnonym to which the City of Lights owes its name is unfortunately shrouded in total darkness.

When Christianity developed roots in Gaul, a certain Dionysius revealed himself to be the most ardent champion of the new religion in the surroundings of Paris. He was martyred on top of a hill that featured a sanctuary of the god of war, Mars, and was therefore known as *Mons Martis*, 'Mountain of Mars'. (According to an alternative hypothesis, the temple was dedicated to Mercury, and the hill was known as *Mons Mercurii,* 'Mount Mercury'.) In the wake of Christianity's ultimate triumph, pagan temples were razed to the ground, and in honor of Dionysius the hill in question was renamed *mons martyri*, 'Martyr's Mountain', or Montmartre in French. (During the French Revolution, an outburst of anticlericalism caused Montmartre to be temporarily named *Mont Marat,* after the demagogue Marat, yet another martyr, because he was assassinated by Charlotte Corday while taking a bath.)

Dionysius – known as *Denis* in French – was decapitated, but when the executioner had done his work, the good saint took his head in his hands and proceeded to walk away, or so the pious legend goes. (Denis was certainly not the only "cephalophoric" saint in the history of the Church; the same story is told about a saintly colleague of his, Miniatus, who lies buried in the fine hilltop sanctuary of San Miniato al Monte, just outside Florence). On a spot that was then generally considered to be the geographic centre of Gaul, called Lendit, Saint Denis finally succumbed, thus symbolically claiming Gaul in its entirety on behalf of Christianity. He was buried there, and inevitably that site – today a bleak suburb of Paris – was renamed after him; a monastery was also founded there, and until the French Revolution it would serve as the mausoleum of the Kings of France. One of them, Louis XVI, involuntarily followed the example of Saint Denis and perished through decapitation, albeit performed in a newfangled way, namely, with the guillotine.

---

[72] Semerano likewise believes that the morpheme *lug,* as in Lutetia, refers to a combination of land and water, in other words, a marsh.

Elsewhere in Gaul, cities were likewise named after their local tribe. In the Loire Valley, for example, the metropolis of the *Turones* received their name, which was to evolve into "Tours"; this toponym has nothing whatsoever to do with the French word *tours*, which happens to mean 'towers'. As for the Loire River, *Liger* in Latin, like many Gallic and other European hydronyms that name is undoubtedly very ancient and almost certainly pre-Indo-European. In *Liger* one can recognize an Usko-Mediterranean root, *leg* or *lig*, referring to still or slowly flowing water and by association also to mud; 'mud' is the meaning of the Semitic term *lihmu*, the related Greek *leimon,* and the Latin *liger,* already mentioned when the topic of the Ligurians was dealt with. The picturesque Loire, then, is nothing other than the 'slow-flowing and/or muddy river'. Similar names, referring to shallow and/or muddy waters, are those of the Ilm which flows through the German city of Weimar; Lake Ilmen in Russia; Lac Leman, as Lake Geneva is called in French; and the Belgian River Leie (Lys in French), whose Latin name was *Legia.*

To the northeast of Paris, a nodal point in Gaul's Roman road system known as *Durocortorum* also acquired the name of its Gallic denizens, the *Remi,* thus eventually becoming known as Reims. Semerano actually interprets the ethnonym *Remi* as a cognate of the Akkadian *ramu*, 'to inhabit', which makes the *Remi* 'the inhabitants' of the place. Reims was the capital of *Gallia Belgica*, or simply *Belgica*, the northernmost part of Gaul, where the majority of people belonged to the great family of Celtic tribes Caesar called the *Belgae*. The British Isles were also home to numerous "Belgic" communities. Some exotic theories have been concocted in an attempt to explain the origin of the ethnonym *Belgae*, but the one proposed by Semerano deserves to be cited here, because it is particularly intriguing. Like the Greek word *pelagos*, 'sea', *Belgae* is derived from an ancient Usko-Mediterranean word, related to the Sumerian *palgu*, the Akkadian *palag*, and the Hebrew *peleg*, 'river', 'water'; its meaning is 'people living near the water', i.e., near a river or near the sea. This description happens to fit perfectly in the case of the *Belgae* tribes of yore, both those of northern Gaul and on the other side of the English Channel.

The Far Side of the Rhine

It is believed that *Gallia Belgica* – a much greater region than present-day Belgium, which takes that name – was also home to people of Germanic origin, in other words, that *Belgica* was bisected by the linguistic frontier that separated Germans from Celts. Like the Greeks before them, the Romans initially did not differentiate much, if at all, between those two ethnic and linguistic families; in the eyes of the representatives of a "superior" civilization, both groups were perceived as equally backward "barbarians". The areas further east, on the other side of the Rhine, were inhabited primarily, though not exclusively, by Germanic peoples in Caesar's time. In particular, the region that had been the heartland of the Celtic Hallstatt Culture between the eighth and the fifth centuries BCE continued to be inhabited by a number of Celtic tribes, such as the *Vindelici* of the Danube Valley.[73] *Belgica* was probably predominantly Celtic, but also partially Germanic. The more one ventured east- or northward, the more Germanic people one found, or so it is supposed. *Belgica,* then, may considered to have been a kind of transition area between Celts and Germans, and a great part of it was also known as *Germania Inferior*, 'Lower Germany'.

Gaul was incorporated into the Roman Empire in its entirety, but the greater part of the land of the Germans escaped that fate. In particular, the Germanic regions to the east of the Rhine and the north of the Danube remained beyond the reach of the Romans, and for many centuries those two rivers would constitute the border of the *Imperium Romanum*. The Romans called the land on the other side *Germania*, and of this Latin toponym the English "Germany" is of course a descendant. However, the term *Germania* was never used by the Germans themselves; it was a hetero-ethnonym, presumably of Celtic origin, that was adopted by the Romans when they conquered Gaul (see e.g. Wolfram 2002: 24-25). The Celtic version of *Germania* was *gair-maon,* and some believe that its meaning was 'fraternal' or 'neighboring people'. This hypothesis seems to be supported by the similarity of the ethnonym with the Latin words *germanus* and *germana* (*hermano/a* in Spanish), meaning 'brother' and 'sister'. The Germans were unquestionably neighbors of the Celts, at least of the Celts of Gaul, but is it possible that Celts considered their Germanic neighbors as brothers and sisters? Possible but unlikely, because relations between Celts and Germans were frequently far from amicable. At the time of Caesar, for example, a bitter territorial conflict pitted certain Gallic and Germanic tribes against each other; in fact, it was that conflict that provided the Roman conqueror with the excuse he needed to proceed with his plan to conquer Gaul.[74]

In any event, Semerano insists that in "Germans" just as in "Greeks" he recognizes the Usko-Mediterranean root *ger(u)*, meaning 'enemy' or at least 'opponent', combined with *ummanu*, 'people', so that the Celtic ethnonym *gair-maon* and its Latin cognate referred to 'hostile men', 'hostile people'. This theory is plausible, especially in light of the fact that it was Germanic invaders who had driven the presumably Usko-Mediterranean Celts from most of the lands to the east of the Rhine, which had been their homeland in the Halstatt Era; we may assume that for this reason the Indo-European Germans were the enemy people *par excellence* from the perspective of the Celts, just as the Indo-European Greeks were from the perspective of the Usko-Mediterranean Pelasgians.

There also exists a theory that *Germanus* was originally a Germanic term, and therefore an auto-ethnonym after all. It is not specified what the meaning of this label was, but allegedly it was used by the different Germanic tribes to emphasize their relatedness. A similar function has been attributed to the name *Suebi.* According to Indo-European-oriented linguists, this word contains the root *swaba*,

---

[73] Halstatt is a town in Austria. The Halstatt Era was followed by the La Tène Era, which lasted from the fifth century BCE to the arrival of the Romans. About the Celts to the east of the Rhine and the Germans to the west of that river, see Carroll (2001: 20).

[74] Demandt (2005: 66); Wolfram (2002: 25); Van Loon (2009: 14).

meaning 'free', 'belonging to our own people' and supposedly related to the Latin possessive pronoun *suus*. The meaning of the ethnonym *Suebi* is thus said to be the 'true people', which also happens to be the meaning of *usko* in languages of Saharan origin. But Semerano begs to differ. He interprets *Suebi* as a cognate of the Akkadian *sab(i)u*, meaning nothing more or less than 'group of people' or 'army', and points to the similarity with the name of the Italic tribe of the Sabines and the German word *Sippe*, 'clan' or 'tribe'. In any event, *Suebi* functioned as a kind of synonym for 'Germans' and was indeed long used to refer to Germans in general. However, while 'Germans' would remain a common onomastic denominator, the meaning of *Suebi* underwent a displacement in the course of time and ended up referring to a specific German tribe, the Swabians, who in the distant past used to migrate far and wide but who eventually settled down primarily in Germany's region of Baden-Württemberg.

Roman soldiers and Germanic captives
(Photos: Martin Bahmann, 2008; source: Wikimedia Commons)

If the Celts of Gaul did indeed consider their Germanic neighbors as dangerous enemies, then it can be said that from the Gauls the Romans inherited not only the pejorative nomenclature but also the hostility itself. Roman experts such as Caesar and Tacitus described the Germans as a warlike and dangerous people. And along the Rhine, the Danube, and the fortified land border – the *limes* – between those two rivers, the Romans constructed defensive military installations. Those forts would gradually develop into cities, and would often be referred to as "colonies". An example is *Colonia Claudia Ara Agrippinensium*, *Colonia* for short, and eventually known as Köln or Cologne. Agrippina was the mother of Emperor Nero; the city was named after her because she was born there while her father, the warlord Germanicus, was undertaking an expedition on the other side of the Rhine. Quite a few colonies received the name of the emperor himself. The city now known as

Augsburg, for example, originated as a foundation dedicated to Emperor Augustus, *Augusta Vindelic(or)um*. On the banks of the Moselle, the tribe of the *Treveri* had had an *oppidum* since time immemorial, and it too was honored with the name of the emperor. *Colonia Augusta Treverorum* – 'Augustus's colony in the land of the *Treveri*' – was to develop into one of the most important Roman cities in Northwest Europe, and it even served for a while as capital of the *Imperium*, or at least as an imperial residence. Today the name of the *Treveri* may be recognized more easily in the French "Trèves" than in the German "Trier". The memory of Trier's glorious Roman past is kept alive by mighty monuments such as the very well-preserved city gate known as *Porta Nigra*, the 'black gate'. The inhabitants of Trier firmly believe that their city is older than Rome herself, and it is generally considered to be the oldest city in Germany.

Descending the meandering Moselle river, Roman, Celtic, or Germanic travelers eventually reached the border town of *Confluentes*, strategically located at the point where the Moselle and the Rhine 'flow together', as the name indicates. That city is now called Koblenz and it lies on the left bank of the Rhine, just like Cologne and numerous other Roman settlements in Germany. On the other side of the river loomed *Germania Magna*, 'Greater Germany', the homeland of Germanic tribes such as the *Saxones*, the Saxons, who were never conquered by Rome. (The etymology of their name will be discussed later on.) Via the Rhine, one could reach the North Sea, called *Mare Germanicum* by the Romans. The Romans also knew the distant Baltic Sea – whence the amber reached Aquileia! – and referred to it as *Mare Suebicum*, which likewise meant the 'German Sea'. Between those two seas stretched the peninsula and islands we now know as the home of the Danish people, Denmark. The Germanic suffix *-mark* was added during the Middle Ages, and referred to a territory along the borders of the German – or "Holy Roman" – Empire. (Austria, for example, was long known in German as the *Ostmark*, the 'eastern march'.) But the term "Danes" is much older, and appears to be of Usko-Mediterranean origin. Semerano points to the similarity of this ethnonym with the already familiar *dunum*, as in *Lugdunum*, and interprets it as 'people of the fortresses'. The term "Baltic" is likewise of Usko-Mediterranean origin and is related, writes Semerano, to the Akkadian *balittu*, 'swamp', 'pond', 'lagoon'. Such a name is indeed rather appropriate for what is essentially the shallow, brackish, and therefore lagoon-like "inner sea" of Europe's north, the non-identical twin of the southern, deep, and salty Mediterranean *mare internum*.

The Romans also knew of a vast land mass that stretched to the north of the Baltic Sea but was hard to reach on account of fog, shoals, and other dangers; it was believed to be a gigantic island, and it was called *Scatinavia or Scadanavia*. This was the Latin version of a Nordic name, *Skadanawyo*, a combination of *skada* 'danger' and *awyo* 'island' meaning 'island of dangers'. "This name seems to have been justified", write the authors of the *Dictionnaire de noms de lieux*, "because of the risks involved for the sailors who crossed from the North Sea to the Baltic via numerous islands and along an extremely indented coastline" (Deroy & Mulon 1992: 437). We would expect Semerano to come up with a different etymology, suggesting an Usko-Mediterranean origin, and he does. The first part of *Scandinavia*, he explains, is related to the Akkadian *sakintu*, meaning 'sediment in water' and also 'shallow water'. And the second part reflected a Semitic term for 'house' or 'settlement', *na'a* in Hebrew. (This *na'a* became *naio* in Greek, as in *naion*, the Greek term for a temple's core, the *cella* or *sanctum sanctorum*, which gave us the term 'nave'.) The meaning of the toponym Scandinavia is therefore 'inhabited land near the shallow water', the latter a reference to the Baltic Sea. Semerano adds that the second part of *Scandinavia* simultaneously recalls an ancient root for 'water', related to the Akkadian *ag(a)u*, that presumably slipped into Gothic and other Indo-European languages as *ahwa*.

About the extreme north of Europe, finally, Rome remained mostly in the dark. It is sometimes said that the Romans knew Iceland, calling it *Thule* or *Ultima Thule*, but it is more likely that this term referred to the high north in general. It is often suggested that *Thule* is related to the Greek *tele*, 'far', 'distant'. Semerano, however, postulates a connection with the Babylonian term *dulu*, 'cosmic disorder', a reference to the cold and darkness associated with that distant part of the world. As for Norway, this toponym has nothing to do with 'north', at least not as far as Semerano is concerned. Instead, he offers an interpretation that fits well with the hypothesis that, after the last Ice Age, Saharan migrants settled even Europe's northernmost reaches and introduced Usko-Mediterranean names that are still very much alive today. As in the case of countless other topo- and hydronyms, *Norge* or *Norvegr* is said to contain a root referring to rivers or water in general, *narum* in Akkadian, and therefore means something like "land of water," "land of rivers," whereby the famous fjords of course come to mind.

Primeval Hydronyms

The Rhine, *Rhenus* in Latin, formed the border between the Roman empire and the world of the Germans. That hydronym was the Latin version of a very ancient indigenous name. Today, the Rhine is associated above all with Germany, and the Germans consider it their "national" river. However, that name is not Germanic at all. The majority of onomasticians believe that "Rhine" is one of those hydronyms that they call "Old European" (*alteuropäisch*) and that are supposed to date back at least to the second millennium BCE,[75] that is, before the arrival in what is today Germany of the Germans and even the Celts. Certain onomasticians are of the opinion that this "Old European" was an Indo-European language, but that is far from certain. It is more likely – and, from our perspective, virtually certain – that these ancient hydronyms were in reality of Usko-Mediterranean origin. In other words, migrants of Saharan origin who arrived in Europe in the "deep past", thousands of years BCE, gave names to rivers big and small, and to other bodies of water, just about everywhere in Europe. These names were later taken over by newcomers, by

---

[75] See *http://en.wikipedia.org/wiki/Old_European_hydronymy*.

Germanic immigrants as well as by Roman conquerors, and they have continued to exist until the present day in some form or other.

In the name *Rhine*, some believe they recognize the Usko-Mediterranean root *ri* or *re*, which means 'to run' or 'to flow [fast]', so that the meaning of that hydronym would be something like 'fast-flowing waters'. This same root may be identified in a large number European hydronyms, not only in northern, but also in southern Europe. The river that crosses Bologna, for example, is called the Reno; *Rhin* is not only the French name of the Rhine, but also the name of a tributary of the Loire; and a river known as the Renne flows through Burgundy. The root *rin* or *ren* is hidden in the names of countless other European rivers, for example in the Arno which flows underneath the Ponte Vecchio in Florence, in a Spanish river called Arno, and in rivers named "Arne" in both France and Germany. The authors of the voluminous and learned *Dictionnaire de noms de lieux* state that these hydronyms are neither of Celtic, nor of Latin, nor of Germanic origin, but are derived from "a pre-Indo-European substrate" (Deroy & Mulon 1992: 30).

Semerano associates the Usko-Mediterranean root *ri* or *re* with two Akkadian terms that designate a body of water, *aranu* and *naru*, and with other Semitic words that have the same meaning, such as Arabic *nahr*. He claims to recognize this root in the names of the Arno in Italy, of the Neretva which flows under the rebuilt Turkish bridge in the Bosnian town of Mostar, and even of rivers with similar names in the north of Europe, such as the Lithuanian Neris, the Narva on the border of Estonia and Russia, and the Nerva, which meanders majestically through St. Petersburg.

Two thousand years ago, the Rhine was not yet the German river *par excellence*. That role was played at the time by the Elbe, which winds its way through the land of the Germans like a kind of long aquatic spine, flowing quite appropriately into the *Mare Germanicum*, the North Sea. It was long believed that the name of this river reflects the Latin *albus* (or *alba*), 'white', so that the Elbe was the 'white river'. Today, however, onomasticians such as Jürgen Udolph of the University of Leipzig no longer subscribe to this theory, and not simply because the muddy Elbe has never been 'white' in any sense of the word. They dismiss the hypothesis of a Latin (and therefore relatively late) origin, and believe instead that we are dealing with a very ancient hydronym of pre-Germanic (*vorgermanisch*) and possibly even pre-Indo-European origin. As far as Semerano is concerned, the word *Elbe* contains the same Usko-Mediterranean root *alb* we have already encountered in *Alps* and in *Albania*, referring to hills, mountains, or any high ground where rivers are said to "rise", and to a combination of water (or ice, or snow) and mountains. This suggests that the meaning of the hydronym *Elbe* might be something like the 'river that flows down from the mountains'.

The root *alb* also appears to be ensconced in all sorts of other hydro- and toponyms just about everywhere in Europe, but primarily in southern France and in Italy. The Aude, a river rising in the Pyrenees and flowing through the province of Languedoc, was called *Albis* in Latin, which also happened to be the Latin name of the Elbe, and *Albula* was the original name of the Tiber. High in the Swiss Alps, in the land of the Raeto-Roman descendants of the Usko-Mediterranean *Raeti* of Antiquity, there is a stream called *Albula* as well as an eponymous mountain pass. The *Colli Albani* are volcanic hills near Rome, whence all sorts of brooks and streams send their waters down to the Tiber. Of the southern French city of *Albi* too, it is believed that the name refers to a combination of a hill and a river, in this case the Tarn. The combination of rocky high ground with a river also characterizes the site of the city of *Avignon*, situated on the banks of the Rhône. Not surprisingly, the root *alp/alv* is hidden in this toponym, albeit in the form *av*, evolved via *alv*, of which one can read in a recent edition of the Michelin Guide to Provence that it is "a pre-Celtic root, simultaneously designating a height and a body of water" (*Guide Vert* 2002: 141). It is possible, and even likely, that *alb* is also concealed in *Alpheios*, the name of a river that descends from the mountains of the Peloponnese into the valley where Olympia is located, and in the name of the fine Syrian city of *Aleppo*, whose site combines a hillock – crowned by an impressive citadel – with a river.

Aleppo citadel
(Photo: Yasemite, 2005; source: Wikimedia Commons)

There are other ancient roots with the significance of 'water', for example *onna*, and this is certainly an Usko-Mediterranean term, related to the Semitic *ayn*, 'spring', 'water'. Its original meaning was probably not just water but any liquid, for example also wine; indeed, Greek *oinos*, 'wine', was also a cognate of Usko-Mediterranean *onna* and/or the Semitic *ayn*, and it in turn gave us the Latin *vinum* and the French *vin*. *Onna* may be identified, for example, in the names of the French rivers Ain and Aisne (*Axona* in Latin), and in Garonne, the 'water' of the 'rocks' (*ker)*; the latter reference is to a river that rises in 'rocky mountains', and these are of course the Pyrenees. Incidentally, *ker*, 'rock', is a root that appears to be hiding in numerous other Old World names, including *Carcassonne*; *Carpentras*; *Carpathians*; the Swiss town of *Chur*; the Austrian region of *Carinthia*; the city of *Corinth*; the island of *Karpathos*, between Rhodes and Crete; *Kerkyra*, the Greek name for the island of Corfu; the French and Italian names for the Matterhorn, *Cervin* and *Cervino*; *Carrara*, name of the famous marble quarries in Tuscany; *Caria*, a rugged, rocky landscape as well as a town (known to the Greeks as Aphrodisias, and now called Geyre in Turkish) in ancient Asia Minor, likewise renowned for its marble; *Garda*, the town on the shores of the lake to which it gave its name, and whose main topographic feature is a high rock; and in geographic terms such as *karst* and *garrigue*.[76]

Other hydronyms based on *onna* are *Seine* and *Saône*. The Celtic name of the Seine was *Isicauna,* a combination of *sawk* (sacred) and *onna*; the Romans turned this into *Sequana*, which was to lead to the French *Seine*. The Saône was also a "sacred river"; its name, *Saucona*, hardly differed from that of the Seine, and it likewise incorporated both *sawk* and *onna*. We can only speculate about the reasons why the inhabitants of Gaul gave the same name to these rivers and considered them sacred. It may have had something to do with the fact that even though these rivers rise not far from each other in the same corner of France, their waters flow in entirely opposite directions, northwestward to the English Channel in the case of the Seine and south towards the Mediterranean in the case of the Saône, thus dramatically bisecting the land of Gaul. Incidentally, the little stream called the Senne, which flows – now underground and therefore invisibly – through Brussels, also used to be a "sacred river", a *sawk onna*. In the twelfth century this body of water was called *Saina* or *Sonna*, and this name is strikingly similar to Seine and Saône. The vast forest to the south of Brussels, from which this river emerged, is called the *Forêt de Soignes* in French and *Zoniënwoud* in Flemish, but in the Middle Ages it was known as *Sonia,* which may be interpreted as 'the forest of the sacred river', 'the sacred forest' (van der Ben 2000: 51).

Onna is at the core of numerous other names of rivers. Sometimes this is rather obvious, as in the case of an Austrian-Bavarian river, the Inn, which was called *Oenus* in Latin. While it is often far from obvious at first sight that *onna* is hiding in a hydronym, the ancient Latin names of rivers may reveal the ancient root referring to water. As examples we can cite the English Avon (*Abona* in the Latin) and the French Marne (*Matrona*), Aisne (*Axona*), and Yonne (*Iscauna*). We also meet *onna* in combination with the already familiar Usko-Mediterranean root *iber*, 'land', in the ancient names of cities situated near water in general, but particularly in a meander of a river, where the land (*iber*) is literally surrounded by water (*onna*). Examples of such toponyms are Verona (*[I]ber-onna*), Bern, Brno, Bregenz (in Austria), Péronne (in northern France), and (probably) Berlin. Obviously because the *(i)ber* in these names suggested the German word *Bär*, 'bear', that animal ended up in the coats of arms of Bern and Berlin, and this in turn suggested that these cities owed their name to the presence of bears, admittedly in a distant past. In similar fashion, some of the numerous German towns whose name contains the Usko-Mediterranean root *iber*,

---

[76] See e.g. *http://fr.wikipedia.org/wiki/Garrigue*.

such as Ebersberg and Ebersbach, are erroneously associated with the wild boar, *Eber* in German.[77] Concerning the common etymology of Verona and Bern, the city of Romeo and Juliet was known to Germans during the Middle Ages as "Bern"; Theodoric, the king of the Ostrogoths, was referred to in the Nibelungen Epic as *Dietrich von Bern,* and this was a reference to Verona since Theodoric never had anything to do with the Swiss city of Bern. The root *iber* can also easily be recognized in the Latin name the Romans gave to the denizens of Verona, *Beruenses*.

Yet another ancient Usko-Mediterranean root referring to bodies of water is *dan, dannu* in Akkadian. Even though its original meaning was 'mighty' or 'powerful' in general, as we have already seen, this term was frequently associated with mighty rivers. The Russian *Don*, known in Antiquity as *Tanais*, is one such 'mighty river', and so is its Scottish eponym, the *Don* of the Aberdeen region. *Dan* also hides in *Dnieper*, in *Dniester*, and – combined with *(h)uppu*, 'river' – in *Danube*. The northern Italian river *Po* is likewise a 'mighty river'. It was known to the Romans as *Padanus*, a name of which *Po* is the short and sweet descendent, but also as *Eridanus*; the latter hydronym combined *dan* with yet another Usko-Mediterranean root meaning 'body of water', *jeor* in Hebrew and *jarru* in Akkadian, so that this name may be interpreted as 'the mighty river'. To be sure, in Antiquity the Po was not the only river known as 'the mighty one'. Mesopotamian sources mention a river called *Ariadan*. And in Antiquity, Athens was bisected by a river, named *Eridanos*, that could on occasion turn into "a gushing torrent that...overflowed its banks after heavy falls of rain".[78] One wonders if the name of the river Jordan might also be a combination of *jeor* and *dan*, and therefore mean 'powerful river'.[79] (Interestingly, a tributary of the Jordan is called the *Dan*.) Finally, the Romans called the Rhône *Rhodanus*, which seems to have been a variant of *Eridanus*; the Rhône certainly deserves to be called 'the mighty river'.

The case of the *Thames* should also be mentioned in this context. This English hydronym incorporates the ancient, pre-Indo-European roots *teme*, 'dark', and *asu*, 'body of water', and two thousand years ago those same roots were already reflected in the names used by Latin authors, namely, Caesar's *Tamesis* and Tacitus's *Tamesa* (cf. the French name for this river, *Tamise*). "For this river the meaning 'dark river' is very appropriate, at least for parts or it", writes Eilert Ekwall, a specialist in the field of English toponyms and hydronyms. Ekwall also suggests that the name of the Flemish town of Temse probably refers to 'dark waters', namely those of the River Scheldt on whose banks the town is located (Ekwall 1928: 405). It is remarkable, moreover, that the *th* in *Thames* is never pronounced like the *th* in *thank*, the *h* was only introduced in the seventeenth century by humanist linguists in an attempt to give

---

[77] See Vennemann (2003: 786-91, 826ff).

[78] *Eridanos, the River of Ancient Athens*, p. 19.

[79] According to the conventional etymology, the hydronym *Jordan* harbors the Hebrew verb *hayarden*, 'to descend', 'to go down'; the river presumably received such a name because during its relatively short course it descends from more than 2,000 meters high in the Lebanon Mountains to almost 400 meters below sea level at the Dead Sea, thus arguably achieving a greater "descent" than any other river.

the spelling of this hydronym a more classical cachet (Cameron 1996: 37); the proper English pronunciation of *Thames* is therefore "temz".

The name *Thames* is wrapped around an Usko-Mediterranean root, related to the Akkadian *damu*, 'dark'. While Semerano finds some merit in this hypothesis, he suggests a different etymology. The Usko-Mediterranean root of "Thames" has nothing to do with *damu*, he says, but with another Akkadian term, *tamu*, meaning 'to turn', combined with *asu*, 'body of water' or 'canal'; the Thames is consequently not the 'dark river' but the 'turning river', the "river with the great meanders' (*il fiume dalle grandi anse*). Semerano does not mention the Belgian town of *Temse*, but we may assume that he would interpret that toponym as '[settlement on the] river bend', an accurate description of the site of the town.

London, too, is a place on a river bend, a town located on a meander of the 'river of the great meanders'. In the name of the British capital we recognize the familiar *dunum*, 'fort' or 'fortified site', a word of which 'town' is the English cognate, as we already know; it is not a coincidence that London is often described in one breath as "London Town". As for the first part of *London*, we are dealing with an Usko-Mediterranean root whose Akkadian version was *lamu* or *lawum*; according to Semerano, it can also be recognized in Italian *landa*, French *lande*, and Old English *laund*; its meaning is obviously 'land', 'territory'. *London*, then, *Londinium* in Latin, was originally something akin to *lamu dunum*, and meant 'fortified site', most likely a reference to the site where the famous Tower of London was later erected.

Semerano mentions another Semitic root that forms the nucleus of a fair number of European hydro- and toponyms, namely, *mus(u)*, which in Akkadian meant 'drainage' or, in an urban context, 'sewer'. We encounter this root on the British Isles, where English toponyms such as Musgrave and Musbury have nothing to do with the Latin *mus*, 'mouse', as is often postulated, but instead refer to the presence of some body of water; in the case of hydronyms in Britain and on the continent, the meaning is nothing other than 'drainage'. The best known of these "drainages" are the *Meuse*, *Mosa* in Latin, the *Moselle* or *Mosella*, the 'lesser Meuse' or 'little drainage' and, on the opposite side of Europe, the *Moskva*, the river that gave its name to a city on its banks: Moscow. 'Drain', or 'trench', or something similar was very likely also the meaning of the name *Moesia*, used by the Romans to refer to the valley of the Danube from Belgrade to the Black Sea, and probably also of *Mysia*, a landscape in the northwest of Asia Minor, on the south coast of the Sea of Marmara.[80]

It is important, finally, to point out that hydronyms such as *Aa*, *Aue* and so forth do indeed signify 'water', are cognate with – but definitely not derived from – the Latin *aqua*. Indeed, such hydronyms are to be found not only on the territory of ancient Gaul but also in areas that were never conquered by the Romans and where Latin was therefore never a vernacular language. The Westphalian town of Bocholt, for example, which lies to the east of the Rhine, is bisected by a stream known as the *Aa*. As in the case of the Latin *aqua* itself, these hydronyms reflect an ancient Usko-

---

[80] Even today, cognates of this ancient *musu* are used in German and in Dutch as a vulgar reference to female genitalia; in this case too, it is generally believed that the meaning is 'mouse'.

Mediterranean root meaning 'water', a root that corresponded to the Akkadian *agu* (or also *aga'u*, *egu*), already mentioned in connection with the Aegean Sea.

Land Surrounded by Water

The British Isles, too, were conquered by the Romans, except some isolated parts of it that were left in peace, for whatever reason, by Caesar, Augustus, and the like. A notable example is Ireland. That island had a Celtic name, *Iveriu,* or *Iberiu*, of which "Erin" is a cognate we are familiar with. An Old English version of *Erin* was *Yra,* but *Yra* was really an ethnonym, meaning 'Irish'. As a corresponding toponym, the English introduced *Yraland* (or *Iraland*), and thus were born the modern English *Ireland* and its international cognates.

In Antiquity, then, the term *Ireland* did not yet exist, but *Iveriu* (or *Iberiu*) and *Erin* did. The Greeks adopted the latter as *Ierne*. To the Romans, on the other hand, *Iveriu/Iberiu* conjured up the Latin *hibernum*, 'winter', and so they baptized Ireland *Hibernia,* or sometimes *Invernia*, meaning 'winterland'. This name belied the fact that Ireland's climate happens to be rather mild. Moreover, the Romans knew lands that were far more "wintery", for example Scandinavia, and it was the aforementioned term *Thule* that in Roman minds evoked the true 'winterland'. *Hibernia* may have sounded like *Iveriu*, but it was obviously an absurd name for an island that was far from 'wintery'. But what was the *real* meaning of *Iveriu*? 'Land of the warriors', say some, fertile country', say others; still others think that the answer to the riddle is 'western land'. Such theories are far from convincing. In contrast, there is no denying the striking similarity of *Iveriu/Iberiu* and *Iberia*, and it is instructive that in Latin one not only used *Hibernia*, but also *Hiberio* and *Iberio*. The latter names do not evoke winter but, like *Iveriu*, appears to reflect the same Usko-Mediterranean root as *Iberia*, referring to 'land', more specifically, 'land surrounded by water'.[81] The Iberian Peninsula is a land surrounded by water, and so is Ireland.

The suggestion that Ireland may have an Usko-Mediterranean name is not that outlandish when one considers that intensive relations had already existed between the Iberian Peninsula on the one side, and the world of the Celts in Gaul and on the British Isles on the other, since the Bronze Age.[82] These relations consisted not only of seaborne trade – for example the famous tin trade – but also of migrations from south to north. The so-called Celtic language and culture of the British Isles and of much of the Western European mainland possibly emerged as the result of the arrival of Usko-Mediterranean people from the south.[83] The culture we refer to as "Celtic"

---

[81] In this respect there is an interesting remark in Deroy & Mulon (1992: 73): "In the beginning of the Roman Empire, the beta of the Greek alphabet was already pronounced like a 'v,' as it would be in Byzantine and in modern Greek."

[82] See the study by Ruiz-Gálvez Priego, *La Europa Atlántica en la Edad del Bronce*.

[83] Semerano (1984: 359) notes in this respect that "the most ancient population of Ireland is supposed to be of Iberian origin"; see also his remark on pp 377-78 about the inhabitants of Ireland in the Neolithic being "*di razza 'iberica' e 'mediterranea', bruna di carnagione e di capelli, di statura piuttosto bassa*".

may well have been a kind of fusion between the cultures and languages of, on the one hand, Usko-Mediterranean people who had already moved there from the south many thousands of years earlier and, on the other hand, Indo-Europeans who joined them some time during the course of the second millennium BCE. With respect to the Iberia of Antiquity, or at least to the peninsula's northern reaches, conventional historiography often cites the "Celtiberians". Of this kind of Iberians it is assumed – without any substantial evidence – that they were Celts or that they were strongly influenced by Celtic neighbors to the north. It would be more useful to postulate the opposite and to look among the Celts for indications of Iberian migrations and influences; perhaps we will then have to reverse our terminology and speak of "Ibero-Celts"! In any event, the toponym *Iveriu* appears to reflect an Usko-Mediterranean origin on the part of the so-called Celtic culture or, at the very least, a potent Usko-Mediterranean linguistic influence on the Celtic world.

English is a language that originated only late, namely, after William the Conqueror and his Norman companions became the masters of England in 1066. In Antiquity, England – just like Wales, Scotland, and Ireland – was inhabited by people we are accustomed to describing as Celts. Already then, the British Isles were known as Albion, which is today a literary synonym for England. This toponym is supposed to be Celtic, but we often hear that it incorporates the Latin word for 'white', *albus/a*. This supposedly alluded to the white cliffs of Dover, which on a clear day may be seen from the other side of the English Channel. According to an alternative theory proposed by Robert Graves, the name Albion refers to the Celtic version of the fertility goddess, Demeter (or Ceres), who was also known as the "white goddess", *Albina*, and to whom the land was allegedly dedicated. As in the case of the Elbe, however, it is extremely doubtful that the supposedly Celtic name *Albion* would reflect a Latin word for 'white', if only because the Romans did not make their appearance in this part of Europe until around 50 BCE. Considering the Iberian connection to the world of the Celts, it is not unthinkable that the Usko-Mediterranean root *alb*, indicating an association of mountains – or high land in general – and water, is concealed in *Albion*. If that is so, then *Albion* is a cognate of the *Albania* that we have encountered before, meaning something like 'high land with many rivers' or 'land in the middle of the water', 'land surrounded by water'; in other words, *Albion* may well be synonymous with *Iberia*.

Remarkably enough, there is yet another synonym for *Albion*, in which – just as in *Iberia* and *Iveriu* – the root *iber* is concealed: *(i)B(e)ritannia*. The Celts who lived on the British Isles, then, were 'the people of the land surrounded by water'. We do not know what they called their country or themselves in their Celtic language, but the corresponding Latin terms used by the Romans were *Britannia* for the land and *Pritani* for the people. Of the latter ethnonym, some believe that it referred to a specific tribe, and with respect to its etymology some exotic theories have been concocted, for example the conjecture that these people painted their bodies and were therefore known to the Celts of the continent as the *Pretani* or 'painted people', which was then Latinized as *Pritani* and *Pritania* or *Britan(n)i* and *Britan(n)ia*. In any event, with the term *Britannia* the Romans undoubtedly referred to the collectivity of England, Scotland, and Wales, because those individual nation-states would only emerge after the fall of the Roman Empire. It was not until 1603, when a member of the Scottish Stuart Dynasty also became King of England as James I, that the old Latin nomenclature was applied in its English version, Britain, to the union of the two countries.

The Romans did not know a "Scotland" – *Caledonia* is what they called this inhospitable region in the north of *Britannia*. This toponym is supposed to reflect the name of a tribe known as the *Caledonii*. According to an alternative theory, it was simply the Latin version of the Celtic *Gaedeldoine,* 'land of the Gaels', *Gael* referring to the local Celtic people and language. Yet another possibility is that *Caledonia* was the Latin version of a Celtic word, *kelidon*, meaning 'forests'. However, like Britain, Caledonia is most likely a toponym of Usko-Mediterranean origin. Semerano explains it as a combination of *kalu,* a root referring to a steep, rocky coast, which will be discussed shortly, and the already familiar *dannu,* 'mighty'; this gives us the not inappropriate meaning of 'land of the mighty cliffs'. (Incidentally, *Kaludon* is also the ancient name of the Greek island of Kalymnos, famous for limestone cliffs that are now a popular destination for rock climbers.) In any event, "Caledonia" would later become a literary synonym for Scotland, just as Albion and Gaul were for England and France. The Romans also sometimes referred to the *Caledonii* tribe as the *Picti,* Picts, meaning the 'painted people', supposedly referring once again to the locals' practice of painting their bodies for battle.

Britannia was the biggest of all the islands inhabited by Celts. On the other side of the sea that separated that island from the continent, however, there was also a "Little Britain". This *Britannia Minor* is now known as Brittany, or *Bretagne*, the Celtic province of France. This toponym, and its Breton equivalent *Breizh*, also hides the Usko-Mediterranean root *iber*. This is hardly surprising, because we know that thousands of years ago already, Brittany maintained close relations with the Iberian Peninsula. Furthermore, Brittany is a land surrounded, though not quite entirely, by water. It is probably not a coincidence that the Gauls called this great peninsula *Armorica*. The meaning of this toponym is 'land [*are*] near the sea [*mor*]' and is therefore virtually synonymous with 'land surrounded by water'. It was only normal that the Romans called the stretch of water between the two Britains – the English Channel – the *Oceanus Britannicus*, which may be interpreted as 'the water between the lands between the water'!

Brittany was home to a number of Celtic tribes, of which one – possibly of "Belgic" origin, like many Celts of *Britannia* – called themselves the *Vindu*. It is commonly accepted that this ethnonym means 'blond people', if only because *gwen,* somewhat similar to *vindu*, is Breton for 'white'. However, there is another etymological possibility. Caesar gave the *Vindu,* whom he mercilessly exterminated because they dared to resist him, the Latin name *Veneti*. And yet, this was a totally different people from the *Veneti* with whom we are already familiar, namely, the Illyrian inhabitants of the coastal regions of the northern Adriatic. The Gallic term *Vindu* had nothing to do with 'white'. It was a cognate of *Veneti,* as was the Greek

Enetoi, and they were all based on an ancient Usko-Mediterranean root meaning 'spring' or 'water', similar to the Mesopotamian *(w)enu* and related to the aforementioned Semitic *ayn*. The ethnonym *Veneti* seems to have been a kind of synonym of *Belgae*, meaning 'people living near the water', 'coastal dwellers'. This label was as appropriate in the case of the *Veneti* of Brittany as in those of the Adriatic Sea, and also in the case of other *Veneti* who, according to classical sources, inhabited the shores of Lake Konstanz, *Lacus Venetus* in Latin, and of the distant Baltic Sea, called *Sinus Venedicus* by Ptolemy, whose southern shores used to be inhabited by (among others) the Wends, an ethnonym that is clearly a cognate of *Veneti*. The area stretching northward from Lake Konstanz to the Danube was inhabited by a Celtic – not Germanic – tribe, the *Vindelici*, whose name was yet another version of *Vindu* or *Veneti*, 'people living near the water'. Their capital was Augsburg, the afore-mentioned *Augusta Vindelic(or)um*; there, too, the name was appropriate, because the city is situated at the confluence of two rivers, the Wertach and the Lech, and close to the site where their waters join those of the Danube.

Augsburg in 1493
(Source: *http://historic-cities.huji.ac.il/germany/augsburg/maps/schedel_1493_XCII_b.jpg*)

Returning to the topic of the *Veneti* of Brittany, their capital was considered by the Romans to be the town called *Venetum (civitas)*, a name that would evolve over the course of many centuries into the present form, *Vannes*. In the Celtic Breton language, *Vannes* is called *Gwened*, a toponym that bears some resemblance to *Vindu*. Vannes, too, is a community of 'shore dwellers', because this quaint Breton town is intersected by two rivers and is located very close to the Bay of Morbihan, viewed by the inhabitants of Brittany as their "inner sea". As for the toponym "Morbihan", *Mor Bihan* is Breton for 'little sea; its binary alternative is *Mor Braz*, 'great sea', that is, the Atlantic Ocean.

The End of the World

The waters separating the supposedly "Celtiberian" inhabitants of Spain from our hypothetical "Ibero-Celts" living on the British Isles, in Brittany, and in the rest of Gaul, were called by the Romans either *Mare Gallicum*, 'Sea of Gaul', or *Mare*

Cantabricum, 'Cantabrian Sea'. We now know this inlet of the Atlantic Ocean as the 'Bay of Biscay', because its southern shores have been inhabited since time immemorial by the Basques. The Basques are a people of Saharan origin, the descendants of those relatively few Iberians who, for whatever reason, were not Latinized by the Romans and managed to continue to speak their Usko-Mediterranean language until the present. They call themselves *Euzkadi*, the 'pure people', meaning 'our own people' – *les gens de chez nous*, as they say in Québec. The Basque language is called *Euskera*, and the Basque country is known as *Euzkal Herria*, 'homeland of the Basque people'. Of this *euski* – probably pronounced as *evski* – the Romans made *Vasci*, and so this land acquired the Latin name *Vasconia* and its inhabitants, the name *Vascones*. This nomenclature eventually made its way into Spanish, as *Vascos* for the people and *Vizcaya* for the country. On account of the Spanish habit of pronouncing the "v" as "b", combined with the international propagation of the Spanish – or, more precisely, Castilian – language, this Spanish terminology slipped into English as *Basque* and *Biscay*. The Bay of Biscay, then, is the 'Bay of the Basques'.

The Basques used to occupy an area considerably bigger than they do today, and to the north of the Pyrenees they extended their reach much beyond the present French-Basque lands around Biarritz and Bayonne. The vast neighboring province of Gascony was originally theirs. Like *Biscay*, the term *Gascony* is also derived from the Latin *Vasconia*, and also means 'Basque Country'. It is no coincidence that the French name of the Bay of Biscay is *Golfe de Gascogne*, 'Gulf of Gascony', because Biscay and Gascony are really synonymous, or at least used to be, before the Gascons adopted the French language. Today, however, the Basque term *Bizkaia* refers to one of the seven provinces of the modern Basque Country, of which three are situated in France and four in Spain; *Bizkaia* is the region around the city of Bilbao.

The Basques were always excellent sailors, at home on the waters of the bay that bears their name and on the Atlantic Ocean in general. In the early sixteenth century, shortly after Columbus' first voyage of discovery, Basque whalers and cod fishermen began to ply their trade in the waters around the island of Newfoundland, as toponyms such as Port-aux-Basques illustrate. The Basques also felt at home in the high mountains of the Pyrenees and their prolongation in northern Spain, the Cantabrian Mountain Range. With respect to the Pyrenees, Herodotus already mentioned *Pyrene*, but he believed that it was a city, and he thought that it was situated in the vicinity of the springs of the Danube. While the Pyrenees had nothing to do with the Danube, they did have an association with springs. In ancient Corinth there was a spring called *Pyrene*, and Semerano draws attention to the affinity of this name with the Akkadian word for 'spring', *buru*, particularly its plural, *burani*. The meaning of the oronym *Pyrenees* is therefore probably 'mountains where the springs [of the rivers] are located'. We have already seen that the term Alps has a nearly identical meaning.

There exists yet another Usko-Mediterranean onomastic combination that refers to the dialectic of mountains and water, namely, *bel-onna*, 'lord [*bel*] of the waters [*onna*]'. It is to this *bel-onna* that numerous mountain tops in the French range of the Vosges owe their name. They are all called *ballons*, 'balls' or 'balloons', and the most famous is the *Ballon d'Alsace*. However, the French onomasticians Louis Deroy and Marianne Mulon correctly indicate that this mountain "is not round, but rather pointed", so that it does not look like a ball or balloon at all. But its German name does. It is *Belchen*, similarly an evolved form of the Usko-Mediterranean *bel-onna*, and this looks and sounds like *Bällchen*, 'little ball'. Hence the erroneous French translation, *ballon*. A couple of mountains located in the Black Forest and in Switzerland are likewise called *Belchen* in German. The meaning of this term is the same as that of the *Ballons* of Alsace, 'lord of the waters'.[84] The name of a town in Germany has the same root as *Pyrenees*, but with the addition of the Latin *mons*, 'mountain', and the German *Bad*, 'spa': *Bad Pyrmont*. These additions were redundant, because the root *pyr* already referred to the combination of mountains and springs. However, this etymological knowledge had undoubtedly been lost for a long time when these additions were introduced, probably during the Middle Ages. At that time *pyr* was interpreted as a form of Peter, and the combination *Pyrmont* was understood as 'St Peter's Mountain', *Petri Mons* in Latin and *Petersberg* in German.

Ruins of the Pyrene Fountain in Corinth
(Photo: J Pauwels, 2006)

Toponyms based on the Usko-Mediterranean roots *alb* and *pyr* may refer not only to springs and rivers as well as other bodies of water, but also to the hills or mountains where those waters "rise". We have seen that *Vindu*, as in *Veneti*, was yet another Usko-Mediterranean root with the meaning of 'water'. Unsurprisingly, this root can also be identified in ancient names of mountains that were perceived as the "mother" of springs, streams and rivers. Examples of such oronyms are Ventoux, an

---

[84] Deroy & Mulon (1992: 45); *http://de.wikipedia.org/wiki/Belchen*.

impressive mountain in the Provence region of southern France, and Mount Damavand, a volcano in Iran of almost 5,000 meters of altitude, featuring numerous thermal springs on its flanks and at its base; the first part of this name appears to be the Sanskrit word for 'house', similar to the Latin *domus*, so that the meaning would be 'house of water'. Other mountains have similar names, for example the Wasserkuppe or 'water peak' in Central Germany.

The prolongation of the Pyrenees in northwestern Spain is called the Cantabrian Mountain Range, and it was to these mountains that the *Mare Cantabricum* of the Romans owed its name. As for the term *Cantabria*, here too we are probably dealing with the already familiar root *iber*, in addition to the root *cant*, which is said to refer to a rock, or to a rocky mountain; presumably it hides not only in *Cantabria* but also in *Cantal*, the name of a region in the French Central Mountain Range (*Massif Central*) and in the name of *Cannes* on the French Riviera, where the old town is located on top of a rocky outcrop.[85] The meaning of *Cantabrian Mountains* is therefore something akin to 'Iberian Rocky Mountains'. However, the root *cant* also appears to have had a more specific meaning, namely, that of rocks or mountains that separate land from water, in other words, that form an "edge" or a "border". It can thus also be argued that the Cantabrians are the 'mountains on the edge of the Iberian Peninsula', the mountains that separate, or form the border between, that peninsula and the Atlantic waters we call the Bay of Biscay. Finally, the root *cant* could also refer to a rocky edge or shore in general, in other words, to a 'water's edge' suitable as anchoring place or harbor. This may well be the reason why the port of Piraeus, nicely sheltered from the sea by relatively steep rocks, was also known in Antiquity as *Kantharos*. And it was probably because a similar harbor on the island of Crete received the name *cant* in the very distant past that the city that sprang up there – officially known as Herakleon, 'city of Heracles' – was until recently generally referred to as *Candia*. (The Venetians, who ruled Crete for many centuries, imported cane sugar from there, a product that thus became known in Europe as 'candy'.[86]) *Cant* also hides in *Alicante*, the name of a port in Spain, and it is the root of the name of the English county of *Kent*, *Cantium* in Latin, the land on the "edge" of the country; situated between the estuary of the Thames, the North Sea, and the English Channel, and featuring the famous white cliffs of Dover, Kent may indeed be said to be England's "water's edge" par excellence. (And Kent's best-known city is of course Canterbury, known in Old English as *Cantwara-byrig*.)

The ancient Usko-Mediterranean root *cant* also provides the key to the etymology of the name of the city of *Ghent* in Belgium, which is very similar to *Kent*. This capital of Medieval Flanders also qualifies as a "water's edge", since it is crisscrossed by two rivers, the Leie and the Scheldt; in addition, *cant* is clearly reflected in the Latin and French versions of the city's name, *Gandavum* and *Gand*, as well as in the Medieval English version, *Gaunt*. (Ghent was indeed the birthplace of John of

---

[85] On Cannes, see Vennemann (2003: 865-66).
[86] The name "Candia" is usually interpreted as a form of the Arabic *El Khandak*, 'ditch', presumably a reference to the moat around the city or its fortress.

Gaunt, son of Edward III.)[87] *Cant* is also the root of *Chantilly*, the name of one of the finest castles in France, associated with lace and whipped cream. It was constructed on a rock emerging from a marshy river valley to the north of Paris. A local tradition explains the name in terms of a purely hypothetical eponymous founder, supposedly a Gallo-Roman, named Cantilius!

But to return to the Basques, they were also excellent warriors, who managed to preserve their independence vis-à-vis the Romans and sometimes served as mercenaries in Roman legions. This militaristic tradition was predestined for longevity. Were d'Artagnan and the Three Musketeers, elite soldiers of the King of France in the time of Cardinal Richelieu, not Gascons? In Rome not only the Basques but the inhabitants of *Hispania* in general had the reputation of being a dangerous, warlike lot. This reputation had an empirical foundation, because already during the Punic Wars the Romans had experienced plenty of trouble with the Spanish mercenaries employed by Hannibal and other Carthaginian warlords. In the end, the Iberian possessions of Carthage did fall into Roman hands, but in Spain this only meant the Mediterranean coast and Andalusia. Like Spain's previous overlords, the Carthaginian West-Phoenicians, the Romans referred to the country by the Phoenician term *Hispania*, rather than the Greek nomenclature *Iberia*. Except in the valleys of rivers such as the *Baetis* (Guadalquivir) and the *Iberus* (Ebro), respective heartlands of the provinces *Hispania Baetica* and *Hispania Tarraconensis* ("Tarragona-Spain"), the Romans for a long time did not have control over the Spanish interior. However, the country's mineral wealth beckoned, and in a series of difficult campaigns Central Spain, too, was gradually conquered. This proved to be the start of a boom in road construction and the founding of cities.

Scipio Africanus set the example after his triumph over Hannibal. In 206 BCE, he established a colony for his veterans in the vicinity of Seville; its name, *Italica,* may have reflected a measure of homesickness, but the colony developed into an important city, where the later emperors Trajan and Hadrian would be born. Caesar's great rival, Pompey, also played a role in the Spanish campaigns, and it was after him that in 75 BCE the city of Pamplona in the land of the Basques was called *Pompaelo*. The name combined "Pompey" with the Basque word *ilun* (or *irun*), 'city'. The Basques themselves actually call Pamplona simply *Iruña,* "the [great] city." (The name of the nearby Spanish border town of Irun has the same meaning.) In the Iberian northwest, the seventh *Gemina* Legion was stationed in order to safeguard the aforementioned gold mines of Las Medulas; this *legion(em)* – and not the *leo* or "lion" featured so prominently in the city's coat of arms – is the key to the etymology of the name of the city of León. Not surprisingly, numerous later foundations received the name of the emperor, for example the city of Saragossa, a toponym in which Emperor Augustus' name is camouflaged under the guise of *Caesar Augustus*. For the "meritorious" veterans of one of this famous emperor's legions, *Emerita Augusta* was founded, the modern city of Merida, where even today many impressive Roman monuments may be admired.

---

[87] See also the remarks on *kant* in Vennemann (2003: 229-30).

Roman theatre at Merida
(Photo: Håken Svensson, 2004; source: Wikimedia Commons)

The Atlantic coasts of Spain and Portugal at the extreme west and northwest of the Iberian Peninsula were to remain distant, little known, and menacing lands to the Romans for a long time, but also finally succumbed to them. In an earlier era, the Greeks had considered the southern part of Spain, the region just beyond the Pillars of Hercules, as the end of the world, but at the time of Roman rulers such as Caesar and Augustus, Gadir and surroundings – the Tartessos of old – had long ceased to be *terra incognita*. Henceforth it was the isolated Iberian regions on the coast of the great, dark Ocean Sea that functioned as the *Far West* of the civilized Mediterranean world. Two specific regions were involved: first, *Lusitania*, the land between the Douro and the Tagus Rivers, inhabited by an Iberian people; second, and most importantly, *Gallaecia*, the modern Spanish province of Galicia, whose name arguably betrays a Celtic connection. Lusitania would later be identified with Portugal, and it is no coincidence that the national epic of this country, written in the sixteenth century by Luis de Camões, is called *Os Lusiados*, 'the Lusitanians'. According to Semerano, the toponym *Lusitania* may be explained as a fusion of *lu*, 'on', and *siddu*, 'side' also in the sense of 'seaside', yielding the meaning of 'land on the coast of the sea or ocean'. The name of the major settlement in that area, situated on the shores of the marshy estuary of the Tagus river, was *alu*, 'settlement' or 'town', on the *sapu* (or *sabu*), 'flood [water]'; the Phoenicians turned this into *Alis Ubbo*, and we now speak of "Lisbon". A seaport further north, favorably and safely situated on the high banks of the Douro River yet very close to the Atlantic, was of great strategic and commercial importance to the Romans, namely, Porto. Porto's original name was *Kale*. The Usko-Mediterranean term *kala* meant 'steep embankment' or 'harbor'; anyone who has been to Porto knows that this name is appropriate in both senses. Under the Romans, *Kale* developed into an important seaport, so it became customary to add the Latin *portus* to its original name. Later, during the Middle Ages, this *Portus Kale* would develop into *Portugal*. Incidentally, *kale* in the sense of 'steep embankment' also hides in *Calais*, the name of a French harbor situated on a stretch of coast featuring impressive cliffs, quite like those of Dover just across the English Channel. *Kale* is also the name of a town in Turkey. It is known for its tombs, carved during Antiquity into a long, rocky cliff that overlooks the Mediterranean shore and is therefore also a 'steep embankment'. Finally, the Usko-Mediterranean *kale* is clearly also the root of the name of one of the capitals of the Assyrian Empire, *Kahlu* (now known as Nimrud), situated on top of a cliff overlooking the Tigris River.

The Romans considered a promontory on Galicia's rocky and dangerous coast in the vicinity of Santiago de Compostela, *Promontorium Celticum*, as the westernmost point of the European mainland, and therefore as *Finis Terrae*, the end of the (inhabited) world. This cape is now known in the Galician language as *Cabo Fisterra*. In reality, it lies somewhat less westerly than the headland called *Cabo da Roca* near Lisbon, but its appearance – like a long finger stuck into the Atlantic – is much more spectacular. Moreover, already centuries before the arrival of the Romans, it was the locus of a sanctuary where pagan pilgrims came from far and wide in order to witness the dramatic daily spectacle of the sun being swallowed by the dark, cold, and turbulent waters of the western Ocean Sea. Roman warlords such as Crassus and Caesar did lead expeditions into this region, but it was only under Augustus that *Lusitania* and *Gallaecia* were finally "pacified", and from then on the Iberian Peninsula in its entirety belonged to the *Imperium Romanum*.

On the northwestern tip of the Iberian Peninsula, there was an ancient seaport that was called *Brigantium* by the Roman conquerors. Very likely, this name was a stylized version of *Iberigantium*, a combination of the same roots we already encountered in *Cantabria*, albeit in reverse order; if so, the meaning of the toponym was '[harbor on] the edge of Iberia'. Today the city is called La Coruña. Here at the western extremity of the Romans' great realm, in *Brigantium*, Roman engineers constructed a lighthouse that was almost as imposing as the *Pharos* of Alexandria, Wonder of the World, and a considerable part of it, the *Torre de Hercules*, subsists even today. This mighty tower, which was indeed dedicated to Hercules, must have loomed like a gigantic pillar, and so the city earned the nickname *columna*, '[city of the] pillar'; in the course of time this mutated into *Corona* or *Coruna*, 'crown', and thus originated the name La Coruña. The lighthouse surveyed the stormy waters of the Atlantic Ocean, then still viewed as the mysterious and awe-inspiring "outer sea", the sea of darkness and death on the wrong side of the Pillars of Hercules. This *mare incognitum* was predestined to be domesticated by sailors from Galicia, *Lusitania*, and other regions of Iberian Peninsula, the *Ishphania* of the Phoenicians. Just as the Phoenicians had discovered in Spain a "New World" full of desirable minerals, the *Nuevo Mundo* on the other side of the Ocean Sea would reveal itself to these Spaniards as an Eldorado full of gold and silver.

Margins of Empire

The Romans established their hegemony over a large part of Central and Eastern Europe. The region of *Pannonia* – roughly the combined territory of modern Austria,

Croatia, and Hungary – was protected against the barbarians of Eastern and North-Eastern Europe by a series of fortresses along the Danube. One of these, situated on the confluence of the Danube and a humble tributary, the Wien (*Vidunia* in Latin), was known as *Vindobona*: Vienna. We already know that *bonum* denoted 'city', and that *vindu* was the root hidden in *Veneti* and referring to people living near a river, a lake, or a sea. *Vindobona* was simply the Latinized version of an Usko-Mediterranean toponym meaning 'city of the people who live on the banks of the rivers' or 'near the confluence of the two rivers'.

Countless people lived along the banks of the seemingly endless Danube, so it comes as no surprise that we encounter the root *vin* in toponyms elsewhere in its valley. An intriguing example is Vinča, the name of a very ancient archaeological site on the banks of the Danube near Belgrade; was it because the name of the inhabitants of that area, like that of the *Vindu/Veneti* of Brittany, was later somehow erroneously associated with "whiteness" (in this case by Slav migrants), that their urban center was baptized Belgrade, the 'white city'? Incidentally, the *win-* in the English toponym *Windsor* also speaks of 'people near the water', in this case of a settlement on a meander of the Thames. Indeed, according to Semerano the suffix *-sor* is a cognate of the Akkadian *saru*, 'to turn', so that in this context it refers to a bend in the river. The same *saru* probably also hides in the name of a tributary of the Moselle, called *Saar* in German and Sarre in French; the *Saar* features numerous meanders, including the famous *Saarschleife*, and therefore deserves to be called 'the winding river'.

Belgrade's coat of arms

In the southeast of Europe, in the already highly urbanized world of the Greeks and their neighbors, there were preciously few opportunities for the Romans to found cities and to bestow names on peoples, although there were some notable exceptions to this general rule. One of these exceptions was Adrianople, the 'city of [Emperor] Hadrian', a name that was to evolve into *Edirne* after the Turkish conquest. Another exception was Constantinople, 'city of [Emperor] Constantine'. The city that had earlier been known as Byzantium became the capital of the Eastern Roman or Byzantine Empire around 330 CE and metamorphosed into the metropolis of the Greek world and the biggest urban center in Europe. To the Romans, Rome had been *the* city, *urbs*. To the Greeks, Constantinople was soon to be *the* city, *Istanpoli,* an expression of which the Turks would later fabricate *Istanbul*, or *Stambul*.

Constantinople was also generally considered to be a "second Rome", and after the fall of Rome herself and of the Western Roman Empire, the term *Rome* was used mostly to refer to the city of Constantine. Arabs and Turks were to regard this Greek city, rather than the Italian Rome, as the true capital of the Roman Empire and of the Christian world. Just like the Arabs, the Turks called Constantinople *Rum,* 'Rome', and its inhabitants the *Rumi,* and they dreamed of conquering this city some day. Sultan Mehmet, "the Conqueror," would realize this dream in 1453. In 1953, five hundred years after the fall of Constantinople, a humorous American song about the city's names became a big hit; the text of "Istanbul" was by Jimmy Kennedy, the music by Nat Simon:

> Istanbul was Constantinople
> Now it's Istanbul, not Constantinople
> Been a long time gone, Constantinople
> Why did Constantinople get the works?
> That's nobody's business but the Turks!

The humor of the lyrics is not appreciated by the Greeks, who have never quite digested the calamity of 1453.

A great portion of Asia had become familiar to the Greeks in the wake of the conquests of Alexander the Great. Alexandria, the city near the mouth of the Nile in Egypt, functioned as an open window through which the Hellenes peered out, not only over Asia but also over Africa. After the Romans took over, they eagerly took advantage of the empirical and theoretical knowledge squirreled by Greek geographers such as Ptolemy, who lived in Alexandria in the second century CE. Moreover, the *Imperium Romanum* established and maintained intensive contacts with countries and peoples in the furthest reaches of Asia. War was frequently waged against Persia's Parthians and their Sassanian successors, and not always successfully; a couple of Roman emperors even ended their careers in Persian captivity. However, via Persia and along caravan routes right across Central Asia, the Romans also traded with the distant Chinese Empire of the Han Dynasty. The most sensational commodity imported from China was silk, so it is hardly surprising that China was known in Rome as 'silk land', *Seres* or *Serica.* And *Sera Metropolis* – 'silk city' – was the name Ptolemy used to refer to the Chinese capital, Changan, now known as Xian. *Sera, Seres,* and *Serica* are supposed to be cognates of a Chinese word for silk, *ssu.* However, Semerano is of the opinion that *Seres* was the Latin version of an ancient Usko-Mediterranean term of Middle Eastern origin, as in the Akkadian *seru,* and had the same meaning as the Chinese term for Japan, '[land of the] rising sun'.

As for Africa, we already know that by this toponym the Romans, like the Phoenicians and the Carthaginians, referred to the hinterland of Carthage. To the west of there, in an area roughly corresponding to present-day Algeria, lay *Numidia.* The inhabitants of that land were Berbers, whose lifestyle was mostly nomadic. The ethnonym "Numidians" was in fact a cognate of the Greek *nomas,* 'nomad', and it is believed that this label was concocted by the Greek colonists of Cyrene, in modern Libya. However, *nomada* already signified 'nomad' in Sumerian, so the term obviously predated the arrival of the Greeks in North Africa.

Further west, the country now known as Morocco was called *Mauritania* by the Romans, meaning 'land of the *Mauri*'. The Romans had adopted this name from the Phoenicians, who used the term *Mahaurim,* 'westerners', to refer to the indiginous inhabitants of the lands to the west of their great colony, Carthage. Centuries later, the dark-skinned denizens of North Africa would be referred to throughout Europe by a cognate of *Mauri*, such as the Spanish *Moros* and the English "Moors", but the term would also acquire the connotation of "Muslims", as we shall see later.

Between the *Africa* of the Romans – the modern nation of Tunisia – and Egypt, the Sahara reached the Mediterranean Sea, except in two relatively small coastal regions blessed with a sufficient annual amount of rainfall as well as a fertile soil. Those two regions were the aforementioned Greek colony of Cyrenaica and, approximately one thousand kilometers farther west, the so-called 'land of three cities' or *Tripolitania.* The latter name was coined by the Greeks and has come to us via the Romans, and yet the inhabitants were not Hellenes, but a mixture of indigenous Berbers and Phoenician colonists. One of these three cities was *Leptis* (or *Lepcis*) *Magna*, whose imposing ruins attract increasing numbers of tourists to Libya. It is likely that the ancient Egyptian name for the entire country, *Leba*, hides in this toponym; if so, *Leptis Magna* might be interpreted as 'the great city of Libya'. A second Tripolitanian city was called *Oea* in Latin, but after the Arab conquest of the area in the seventh century CE, it received a short version of the name Tripolitania, Tripoli, *Tarabulus* in Arabic. However, the nomenclature Tripolitania continued to exist as a label for the entire region and eventually became virtually synonymous for Libya in its entirety, particularly at the time when, from 1911 until 1943, Italy wielded the colonial scepter in the land that is now ruled by Colonel Ghaddafi.

The cosmography of Ptolemy and his learned Alexandrine colleagues was fed by theoretical as well as empirical knowledge. It was a rational image of the world, in which concepts such as symmetry and equilibrium played an important role. The earth floated on the waters of the Ocean, and the continents maintained a perfect equilibrium. In the northern hemisphere, Europe and Asia formed a gigantic land mass. In the south stretched Africa, but nobody knew exactly how big that continent was; however, it was believed to be considerably smaller than the Eurasian combination. Ptolemy consequently theorized that the southern hemisphere had to feature yet another great land mass, probably somewhere to the east of Africa and connected to that continent, just as Asia lay to the east of Europe and was connected to it. The Indian Ocean, then, was not considered to be an ocean, but was seen as another "inner sea" like the Mediterranean; it was called *Indikon Pelagos* in Greek, *Indicum Mare* in Latin. Together, the two southern continents presumably constituted a sufficient counterweight to the great landmass of the north. This fine theory of Ptolemy did not correspond to reality, but there was indeed a *Terra Australis*, a great "southern land" that is now called Australia; it would be discovered many centuries later, long after the Portuguese had rounded the Cape of Good Hope, thus demonstrating that Africa's south was not connected to another continent.

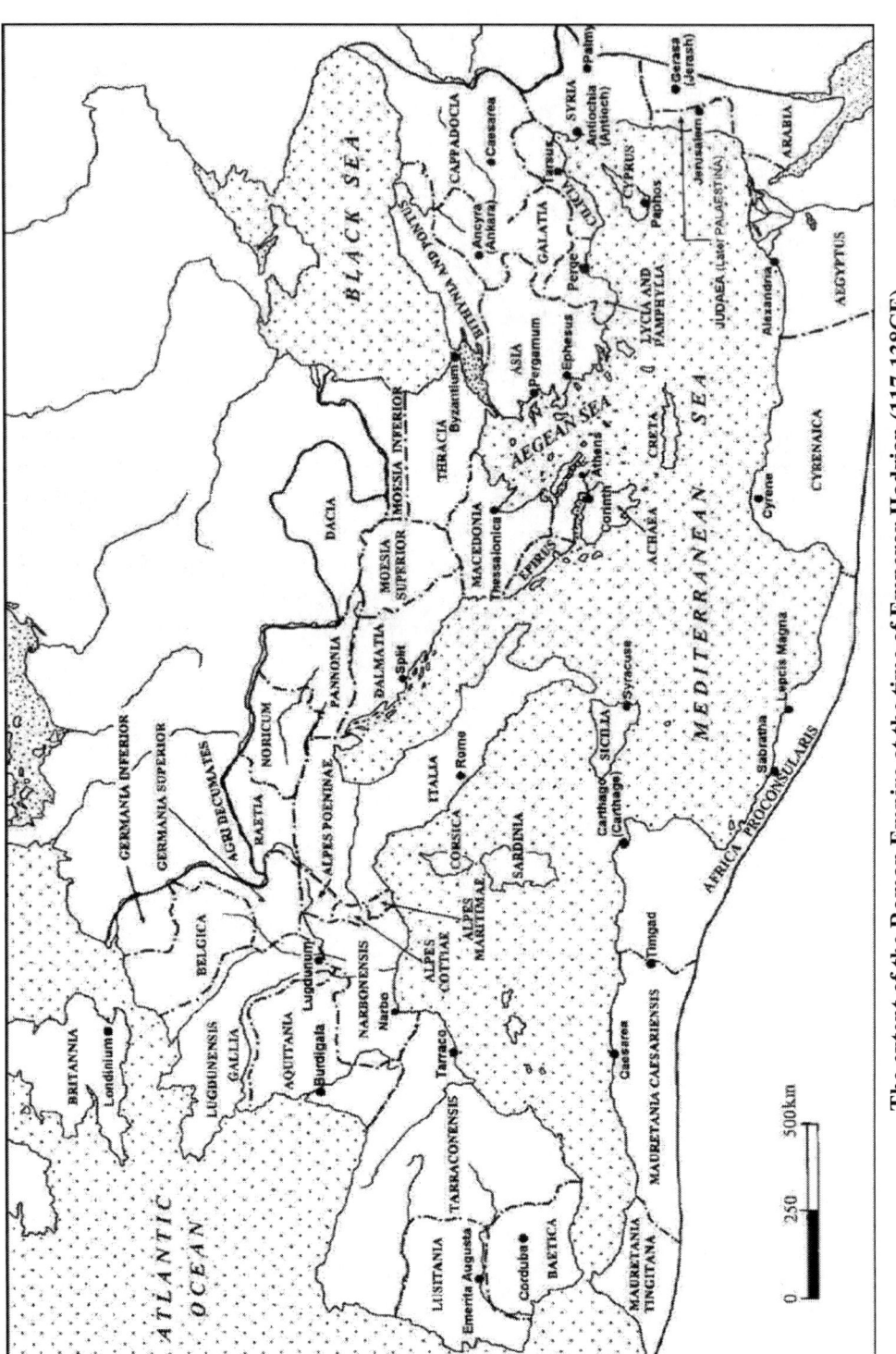

The extent of the Roman Empire at the time of Emperor Hadrian (117-138CE)
(Courtesy of Charles Gates; source: Gates 2003)

5

Barbarian invasions and Dark Ages

Huns and Other Vandals

The fall of the Roman Empire was accompanied by invasions of barbarian tribes, a traumatic development known as the "Great Migrations". Some barbarians appeared suddenly, like a devastating tornado, but disappeared just as quickly from the stage of history without leaving behind any onomastic traces. Such was the case, for example, with the Huns, who wreaked havoc in Gaul and Italy but did not settle there permanently, did not found cities, and did not give names to any towns or regions.

Ruins of the harbour of ancient Aquileia
(Photo: Paolo_1955, 2006; source: *travel.webshots.com*)

Attila's hordes were only indirectly involved in a new foundation, namely, that of Venice. Aquileia, the prosperous terminus of the Amber Road on the Adriatic Sea, was destroyed by the Huns. Surviving *Veneti* fled to an archipelago of little islands situated in a large, sheltered lagoon along the nearby Adriatic coast, and there they founded the city that would bear their name, Venice. The original name of the new settlement was *Rivo Alto* or *Rialto*, 'the high embankment', a name that lives on in that of the Rialto Bridge, which crosses the Grand Canal in the heart of the city of St Mark. With regard to the name "Huns" itself, this Siberian (or "Altaic") ethnonym is of Usko-Mediterranean origin. It is a cognate of the *inu* or *enu* that hides in *Rasenna*, the autoethnonym of the Etruscans, and means 'human beings'. The Huns, then, are simply 'the people'. However, Semerano believes that, for the Chinese, this term may have suggested the verb *yi yun*, 'to move', so that, as far as they were concerned, the Huns were not just 'the people' but a 'people on the move', a 'nomadic people'. As for "Attila", this was actually a Gothic name, or rather a title, meaning 'papa'; the Huns, then, were the people, or more accurately the (ethnically mixed) retinue or *Gefolgschaft*, of 'daddy'.[88]

Vandals pillaging Rome
(19th century engraving by H Leutemann; source: Wikimedia Commons)

The great majority of the invaders were not Asians such as the Huns, but Germanic people, originating from beyond the Rhine and Danube. Those distant ancestors of the present-day Germans were divided into numerous tribes that took turns descending upon the *Imperium Romanum*, either to sack its cities and then move on, or to settle there permanently.[89] The Vandals opted for the first course of action and thus caused so much damage – at least according to an old but uncertain

---
[88] On the close relations between Huns and Goths, see Christian (1998: 226-32).
[89] That great political-social-economic consequence of the Germanic invasions of the Roman Empire, namely, the emergence of the feudal system, has been described brilliantly by Perry Anderson (1996) in *Passages from Antiquity to Feudalism*

tradition – that now, well over a thousand years later, their name continues to be associated with senseless destruction, with "vandalism". They raped and pillaged their way through Gaul, dwelt for quite some time in Spain, and then crossed to North Africa where they took Carthage; hence, they traversed the Mediterranean, dispersed in Italy, and thus evaporated in the smoke of history. This rather inglorious end of the Vandals' adventure is understandable in light of the fact that the so-called "Great Migrations" frequently involved only relatively small groups of migrants, who did not exterminate or drive away the existing population but simply settled among them as the new lords of the land. In the case of such "elite invasions", the newcomers often ended up being absorbed by the host people, even when they sometimes managed to foist their language (and/or their religion and other forms of culture) onto the natives.

Campaigning Goths, according to 3rd and 4th century Roman descriptions
(C H Yonge, 1880; source: Wikimedia Commons)

Another infamous Germanic tribe was the Goths, who probably came from Scandinavia. Their original homeland may well have been the island in the Baltic Sea that still bears their name, Gotland. The etymology of this ethnonym is uncertain but Semerano suggests that it may derive from elements meaning 'people' (*ga'u* in Akkadian, *goy* in Hebrew) and either 'fortresses' (*dunum*) or 'mighty' (*danu*), i.e. 'people of the fortresses' or 'mighty people'. The Goths settled temporarily in Gaul, later to be known as France. There they adopted a hedonistic lifestyle, almost certainly at the expense of the autochthonous Gallo-Roman inhabitants, and this gave rise to the (originally German) expression "living like the Goths in France", which was eventually transformed into "living like God in France". In France, "Goth" and "Gothic" would long remain bywords for all things German. When, at the end of the eighteenth century, medieval architecture was widely denigrated in favor of Neo-Classicism, French snobs repudiated their own cathedrals, at least semantically, by branding them "Gothic", thus blaming the Germans for those medieval monstrosities. And during the First World War the term *les Goths* served as a term of abuse that was only marginally less pejorative than *les boches*.

Among the Goths, the Ostrogoths were distinguished from the Visigoths. The name "Ostrogoths" is widely believed to mean 'eastern Goths'. According to an alternative interpretation, however, the prefix *ostro-* reflected the Germanic word *austr*, related to Latin *lustrum* and English *luster*, which produces the meaning of 'shiny Goths'. But how could such a name have originated? Perhaps the 'shine' of *ostro* referred to the shining light of dawn, in other words the east, so that we are dealing with 'eastern' Goths after all. The Ostrogoths did indeed spend a lot of time in eastern lands, for example in the Pontic Steppes of southern Russia, and they were therefore also known as the "Goths of the Steppe". In that part of the world they put an end to the centuries-old rule of the Scythians, and they also made life miserable for their Byzantine neighbors. Then they concluded a "strategic partnership" with the Huns, and accompanied the latter when they wreaked havoc on Western Europe.

The Ostrogoths ended up in Italy, where in 493, under the leadership of Theodoric the Great, the aforementioned *Dietrich von Bern,* they founded a kingdom with Ravenna as capital. (The toponym Ravenna appears to be Usko-Mediterranean; its meaning was 'settlement [*rawum*] near the water [*onna*]'.) The name of Theodoric, whose remarkable mausoleum is one of the many tourist attractions in Ravenna, was *Thiudareiks* in Gothic, and meant 'king [*reiks*, as in *rex*] of the people [*thiuda*]'. A half century later Italy was reconquered by the Byzantines, who thereby put an end to the Ostrogothic saga.

As for the Visigoths, according to conventional wisdom they were the "western" Goths, but here too, there is dissent. According to Dietmar Urmes (2003: 430), the Gothic word *wisu* supposedly had the same meaning as its English cognate *wise*, and could also mean 'good'. This suggests that the Visigoths might have been perceived as "good guys", presumably in comparison to the Ostrogoths. This tribe invaded Italy from the Balkan Peninsula, sacked Rome in 410 CE, and then settled down in the southwest of Gaul, where Toulouse functioned as their capital. There they were challenged by the Franks, who, under the leadership of Clovis, appeared determined to transform all of Gaul into a Frankish realm. The Visigoths were beaten badly by Clovis, so they sought salvation further southward, across the Pyrenees. In Spain they had better luck: they founded a kingdom that would survive until in 711 CE the Arabs suddenly appeared on the scene and overran the Iberian Peninsula.

The capital of Visigothic, "Palaeochristian" Spain was the venerable old Roman city of *Toletum*, Toledo. Toledo's name was of Iberian origin. At its core is an Usko-Mediterranean root, *dol* or *tol*, meaning 'hill', 'height'. And indeed, Toledo is situated – rather magnificently, it should be added – on top of a hill that is embraced by a meander of the Tagus River, as one can see in a number of paintings by El Greco, who lived and worked there for many years. Numerous other European toponyms incorporate the pre-Indo-European root *dol* or *tol,* for example Toul, Dol-en-Bretagne, and Toulouse, that other former Visigothic capital, whose name combines *tol* with *apsu*, 'water', giving us 'hill overlooking the water', that is, the Garonne River.

The Franks, under Clovis, defeat the Visigoths
(19th century fresco in the Panthéon (Paris) by an unknown artist; source Wikimedia Commons)

The Burgundians were yet another Germanic tribe that crossed the Rhine in order to settle in Gaul, more precisely in that part of Eastern France that still bears their name, Burgundy. The Burgundians – some claim that the ethnonym's meaning was 'big' or 'strong men' – had been displaced from their own homeland by the invasion of Attila and his Huns, an event that took place in 436 CE and constitutes the historical nucleus of the Nibelungen Saga. Another Germanic tribe, the Langobards or Lombards, penetrated Italy in 568 CE and founded a state in the Po Valley, where the province of Lombardy – the area around Milan – owes its name to them. A bit further south, the Byzantines had entrenched themselves in Ravenna after ousting Theodoric's Goths, and so this region, in sharp contrast to Lombardy, remained "Roman", i.e., continued to belong to the *Romanitas* instead of being engulfed by the spreading oil slick of the *Barbaritas*; that part of Italy therefore became known as

Romania, and today it is called Romagna. Mussolini, who like the Byzantines dreamed of restoring the Roman Empire in all its glory, was born in this province.

El Greco's View of Toledo
(Photo of a painting dating from ca. 1596-1600; source: Wikimedia Commons)

During the great migrations that accompanied the fall of the Roman Empire, other Germans, namely the Saxons and the Angles, crossed the North Sea and settled on the British Isles. According to the etymologist Dietmar Urmes, the name of the Saxons incorporates the ancient Germanic word *sax,* 'dagger' or 'short sword', so the *Sahsnotas* or Saxons were the S*chwertleute,* 'bearers of swords'. In analogous fashion, the ethnonym *Angles* is sometimes said to derive from the verb 'to angle', i.e., to fish with hook and line, suggesting that the Angles had originally been a tribe of fishermen. This interpretation smacks of "folk etymology", almost as much, in fact, as the spurious legend which holds that the Angles earned their name because a medieval pope, impressed by their physical beauty, compared them to angels, *angeli* in Latin. Regardless of the meaning of their name, the Angles bequeathed it to a great part of the Celtic Albion of yore, the Romans' *Britannia,* which thus became known as England. Another onomastic tip of the hat to the Angles is of course the toponym "East Anglia". The memory of the Saxon settlements survives in the place-names Sussex, Essex, Wessex, and Middlesex – respectively the south, east, west, and middle of the land occupied by Saxon immigrants.

The Jutes were yet another tribe that participated in the Germanic migration to Britain, but most of them remained behind in the Germanic homeland, where the Danish province of Jutland still bears their name. Germanic tribes were not the only ones heading for *Britannia* at the time; *Caledonia*, the non-Romanized north, became *Scotland* on account of being invaded by Celts coming from Ireland known as the *Scoti*. In this ethnonym Semerano identifies a cognate of the Akkadian *saqu(tu)*, 'high[land]', also recognized in "Damascus", suggesting the interpretation 'inhabitants of the highlands'.

Gaul was overrun by all sorts of German men and women, among their number not only the aforementioned Goths and Burgundians, but also the Franks. The latter were actually a kind of league of different tribes, for example the Salians (or Salian Franks); collectively they called themselves the *vrancken*, i.e., the 'free' or 'brave' people. The homeland of the Frankish tribes was the land between the Rhine and the Weser, a region that is called *Francia* on a late-Roman map, the *Tabula Peutingeriana*. However, after the Franks had conquered all of Gaul, at the expense not only of the Romans but also of Germanic competitors such as the Visigoths, the term *Francia* was increasingly used by chroniclers to refer to the new state, stamped out of the Gallic ground by Frankish warlords such as Clovis; thus originated the term *France*. France, in one of history's manifold ironies, turns out to have a Germanic name!

Other Frankish tribes remained behind in Germany and gave their name to the "Franconia" region around Nuremberg, which is now part of the German *Land* of Bavaria *(Bayern)*. The name of the Bavarian "free state" *(Freistaat)*, as that member of the German federation labels itself, and of its beer-loving, *Lederhosen*-wearing denizens, is particularly interesting. An ancient cognate of "Bavarians" is "Bayuwars", which means 'people of Baioheim', and "Baioheim" is Bohemia, *Böhmen* in German, in other words, the land we now know as the Czech Republic. Two thousand years ago this was the homeland of the Boyars, a Celtic tribe, and it was they who gave their name to the region, *Boihemium,* 'land of the Boyars'. (According to Semerano, that ethnonym contains an Usko-Mediterranean root, related to the Akkadian *ba'u*, 'to walk', which suggests 'people on the move', in other words, 'nomads'.) Already in the first century CE, however, these people were driven from their land by a Germanic tribe, the Marcomanni, whose name meant 'people living near the border'. The name *Boihemium* was henceforth associated with its new Germanic inhabitants. Ptolemy, for example, called them the *Baiochaimoi,* and in Latin they were known as the *Baioarii,* which evolved to "Bayuwars" and eventually to "Bavaria" and "Bavarians". During the Great Migrations, the Marcomanni/Bayuwars moved to the land that is now called Bavaria. The vacuum they left behind was filled by Slavs, and so Bohemia became a Slavic outpost within a predominantly Germanic realm.

The Bayuwars were one of the Germanic tribes that did not take advantage of the implosion of the Roman Empire to seek fortune on the other side of the Rhine or the Danube, but stayed behind in *Germania Magna*. Germany was and remained the homeland of numerous Germanic tribes, not only the Bayuwars but also the Thuringians and (the majority of) the Saxons who inhabited regions further to the north, regions whose modern names – Thuringia, Saxony, and Lower Saxony – reflect those ethnic identities even today.

To the west of the land of the Bayuwars, on the banks of the Upper Rhine, lived the Alamanni. This entity was not really a tribe but a "collective contingent" (as Maureen Carroll, an authority on Ancient Germany, writes) of all sorts of Germans who had settled near the border of the Roman Empire in order to trade or look for work, for example as mercenaries. Eventually they did form a genuine tribe, and their crossing of the Rhine in the middle of the third century CE played a crucial role in this "ethnogenesis".[90] Considered as "Alamannic" today are the ethnicity and language of the people living in the Black Forest, the northern part of Switzerland, and also of Alsace, the region to the west of the Rhine that is now part of France. Because in the past the Alsatian Rhine often flooded its valley, settlements and towns mostly sprang up on the banks of its less dangerous tributaries, such as the Ill. As an example we can cite a city whose favorable location near the confluence of the Ill and the Rhine and on an intersection of major overland roads caused it to be called *Stratiburgum*, 'city of trade routes': Strasbourg. Another well-known town on the banks of the Ill is Colmar. In Roman times, this was the location of a country estate that, like all such *latifundia*, had a large dovecote, a *columbarium*, and it is from this Latin term that the toponym "Colmar" was derived. As for the name "Alsace", it is commonly accepted that it refers to the Alamanni who settled on the banks of the River Ill which, running parallel to the Rhine, bisects the region; Alsace and Alsatians were the land and the people straddling, or "sitting on", the Ill.

From the perspective of the Gauls, the region inhabited by the Alamanni was where the land of the Germanic people began. And so, in accordance with the well-known *pars pro toto* principle, they gave to all of *Germania* the name of the Germanic tribe that was most familiar to them; it is for this reason that Germany is known in French as *l'Allemagne*, 'land of the Alamanni'.

Deutsch versus Welsch

The Germans, naturally, did not call their homeland 'land of the Alamanni', and neither did they use a cognate of the Latin term *Germania*, which, as "Germany", was to slide from Latin into the English language. The Germanic people of Antiquity appear to have referred to themselves primarily by the name of their specific tribe, rather than by a general label. Some time during the "Dark Ages", however, a common onomastic denominator did emerge. The Franks, Saxons, etc., henceforth called themselves – and their language – *deutsch* (or *teutsch*) and their land *Deutschland*. *Deutschland* signifies nothing other than 'land of the people', that is, 'land of the German people'. However, the term *deutsch* itself cannot be said to be 24-carat

---

[90] Carroll (2001: 114); Postel (2004: 64ff., especially p 75).

German since, if we may believe Semerano, it is merely the Germanic form of a very ancient, pre-Indo-European word. Its Akkadian form was *tapputu*, meaning 'community', but *deutsch* is more easily recognized in the Illyrian and Old Irish cognates, respectively *teuta* and *tuath*, 'people'. It was with the latter meaning that the term slipped into the Indo-European languages, and thus were born the German forms, first *deuda* and *thiota,* and then *deutsch*. In any event, *deutsch* became the Germans' own name for themselves and also for the German language. This term was to enter English as *Teuton(ic)* and Medieval Latin as *theodiscus.* Medieval Latin texts referred to all Germanic peoples and all Germanic dialects with the label *theodiscus*; today, *theodiscus* still lives on as the Italian word for 'German', *tedesco*.

The German language as we know it today was standardized only at a late stage, namely during the sixteenth century, via the medium of Luther's translation of the Bible. During the Middle Ages, the Germanic peoples spoke many different dialects, of which some would develop separate identities, such as Swiss German, or even become a totally new language. The latter was the case with a number of so-called "Low German" dialects that were spoken in the northwest of the land of the Germans, in the Netherlands, and in the northern part of Belgium. These dialects happened to be the predecessors of the language English speakers know as "Dutch", but Dutch speakers call it *nederlands,* 'Netherlandic'. For a long time, Dutch / Netherlandic was not considered to be a separate language, but a form of *deutsch* in general, and of Low German in particular; for this reason, the speakers of Dutch / Netherlandic would call their tongue not only *nederlands*, but also, at least until the nineteenth century, *nederduits*, which may be translated as 'Low German'. As far as the inhabitants of the British Isles were concerned, the land and the language of the Germanic people, those who called themselves *deutsch*, started just across the North Sea, in the Low Countries, and it was there that the English speakers became acquainted with the term *deutsch* and turned it into *Dutch*. They continued to use this term to refer to their closest Germanic neighbors – the people of Holland, Flanders, etc. – even though the latter's Low German dialect gradually evolved into a separate Germanic language, eventually to be called *nederlands*, 'Netherlandic', by the people who speak it. In order to refer to the language of Germany proper, English speakers therefore started to use the term "German". Understandably, the fact that the English term *Dutch* and the German term *deutsch* are homonyms but not synonyms was to be the cause of considerable confusion. For example, when members of a German Protestant sect settled in Pennsylvania and identified themselves as *deutsch*, the English-speaking Americans assumed that these newcomers were Dutch; as a result of this, the local (German) Mennonites are still known as the "Pennsylvania Dutch".

When the smoke generated by the Great Migrations finally cleared, a linguistic border appeared to bisect the western part of Europe. It separated the inhabitants of northern and eastern regions who called themselves *deutsch* and spoke a Germanic language – not only German itself but also the language eventually known as "Dutch" – from people to the west and the south who spoke a Romance tongue, that is, one of the numerous languages descended from Latin, such as French and Italian. In the Germanic areas, where the auto-ethnonym was *deutsch*, one also used an onomastic common denominator to denote all the speakers of Romance languages: *welsch, wels, welf, walsch,* or *Waals,* with the latter being the Dutch / Netherlandic variant. This term was derived from an Indo-European word for "foreigner," and was clearly also related to *gallisch,* German for "Gallic" or "Celtic" in general; the French translation of the German term *welsch* (and its variants) is in fact *gallois.* From the perspective of the speakers of Germanic languages, *welsch* (or *welf,* etc.) referred primarily to the inhabitants of the nearby land of Gaul, but not exclusively, because the Italians too qualified as *welsch,* as foreigners speaking a Romance idiom. At the time of the conflict between Popes and German Emperors, champions of the papal cause in Germany were called *Welfen,* meaning 'Italians'. The term migrated to Italy to be used there in the form of *Guelfa,* likewise denoting papal supporters; the label used for Italian sympathizers of the Emperor, on the other hand, was inspired by the name of the family castle of the imperial Hohenstaufen Dynasty, Waiblingen, which was distorted in Italian as *Ghibellini,* 'Ghibellines'.

Every Germanic region near the linguistic border had its own version of the Germanic label for speakers of a Romance language. As far as the Austrians were concerned, the *Welser* were the Italians. In the lands of the former Habsburg Empire, not only in the modern state of Austria but also in the Czech Republic, for example, many inns patronized by Italians received names such as *Welser Hof, Welscher Hof, Walscher Hof,* etc. Even today, Austrians occasionally refer to Italy as *Welschland.*

Some Germanic people lived in the Balkans, and they too had neighbors who spoke a Romance language, namely the Romanians; the Germans called this region 'land of *Welsch* people', but the local version was *Wallachei,* "Wallachia". In Switzerland, the German inhabitants had French-speaking neighbors whom they called *Welsschweizer*. They are still there today, and live in *la Suisse Romande* or *la Romandie,* in and around cities such as Geneva and Lausanne. The Francophone Swiss actually use German terminology when they refer to their own language as *welche.*

Further north, the linguistic border runs right through Belgium. The locals there who speak a Romance language are known to their Germanic compatriots, the Flemings, as *Walen,* 'Walloons', and their land, as "Wallonia". The French-speaking Belgians now also use this terminology but, like the Swiss *welche,* 'Walloon' and 'Wallonia' are terms of Germanic origin. Before this Germanic nomenclature was adopted, the part of Belgium where the inhabitants speak a language of Latin origin was called *le roman pays,* 'the romance land', a term that closely resembles *la Suisse Romande.* The term *Wallonia* was "invented" in the 1840s by the poet François-Joseph Grandgagnage and became common currency only at the end of the nineteenth century (Van Istendael 1989: 135).

The Germanic term *welsch* (and its variants) originally signified 'Gallic' and referred to the Celts of Gaul who, due to many centuries of Roman occupation, gradually became "Gallo-Romans" and, eventually, the French as we know them today. The meaning of *welsch* was thus displaced in the course of time, denoting first 'speakers of a Celtic language', and then 'speakers of a Romance language'. However, with the label *welsch* one also continued to refer to foreigners in general.

(Authors such as Isaac Taylor (1893: 42) and Kenneth Cameron (1996: 44) note in this respect that the meaning of "walnut" is nothing other than a 'foreign nut'.)

Italy shown as *Welschland* on a German map of the world in the form of a clover leaf
(Designed by Heinrich Bunting of Magdeburg, 1582; source: *http//:strangemaps.wordpress.com/*)

During the Great Migrations, Germanic migrants such as the Angles and the Saxons settled on the British Isles, as already indicated. These German newcomers used their own version of *welsch, Wahl* – plural: *Wealas* – to refer to the native Celts. The part of Britain's "Celtic Fringe" that is called *Cymru,* 'land of the [or our] comrades', by its inhabitants, thus became known as "Wales". (The name *Cymru* survives, however, in English toponyms such as Cumberland.) To the southwest, there was a peninsula that was called *kernou*, the 'horn', by the Celts on account of its shape; the term *kernou* thus also acquired the meaning of 'peninsula'. The inhabitants of that area were referred to as the *Kernow* (*Cornovi* in Latin), the 'people of the horn' or, more prosaically, the 'inhabitants of the peninsula'. The Germanic, Anglo-Saxon immigrants on the British Isles spoke of the region of the *Wealas* in *Kernow*, and this *Kernow-Wealas* eventually spawned the toponym *Cornwall*.

Magyars and Slavs

To the west, the land of the Germanic *Deutsch* bordered on the realm of the Roman *Welsch,* that is, of people who spoke a Romance language. To the east of the Romans' *Germania Magna*, on the other hand, lay a vast region inhabited by a different kind of non-*Deutsch* foreigners. The vast expanses of Eastern Europe were home, *inter alia*, to the Magyar people, a league of ten tribes who called themselves *On-Ogur*, 'ten arrows'. Because the Magyars were often confused with the Huns, an "h" was prefixed to this exotic ethnonym in Western Europe, thus giving birth to the name *Hungary*. The Hungarians are related to the Turks, Finns, and Estonians; they all originated in Central Asia, and together their languages constitute the so-called Finno-Ugric language family. In the ninth and tenth centuries, the still nomadic Magyars undertook a series of raids throughout Europe, as Attila's Huns had done earlier. However, they were finally crushed by the German Emperor Otto I in 955 CE on the banks of a Bavarian river, the Lech, in the vicinity of Augsburg, whereupon they settled permanently in the great valley of the Danube to the east of Vienna. There, in the heart of the land the Romans had known as *Pannonia*, in the *puszta*, the topographic zone of Europe that is most similar to the steppes of Central Asia, a nation thus emerged that is called *Magyarorszag* by the Hungarians and Hungary by everyone else.

The above is a synopsis of the conventional story about Hungary, its people, and their language, but competing, heterodox theories also exist. According to one of them, which happens to fit very well within the framework of this study, the Asiatic origin of the Magyars and their relatedness to Finns and Turks within a non-Indo-European, so-called Finno-Ugric family of languages, is a myth invented by Austrian scholars during the nineteenth century for political or ideological reasons. Instead, an ethnic affinity is postulated between the Magyars of Antiquity and the Sumerians.[91] The Magyars, then, presumably already settled in their part of Europe many thousands of years ago, and their language – allegedly similar not only to Sumerian, but also to Etruscan - may very well qualify as Usko-Mediterranean. Adopting a similar position, Semerano declares the Hungarians' auto-ethnonym to be a combination of cognates of the Akkadian *madu* ('mass' or 'people') and *gerru* ('caravan', 'expedition'); in other words, the Magyars are 'the nomadic people', 'the people on the move'.

In contrast to the Magyars, who are speakers of a language that is conventionally classified as Finno-Ugric but may possibly qualify as Usko-Mediterranean, and is certainly non-Indo-European, the majority of Eastern Europeans were (and are) of Indo-European origin, like the Germans. The vast Eastern European interior, for example, is the homeland of the great ethnic family of the Slavs. Those people called themselves *Sloveninu*, which meant 'those who can speak', 'those who speak a [i.e., our] language'. (*Slovo* is Slavic for 'word'.) This *Sloveninu* is recognized easily in the name of a small Eastern European country, *Slovenia*. (However, some Slovenians prefer to believe that the name of their country is a cognate of the aforementioned *Veneti*, whom they consider to have been a proto-Slav ethnicity.[92]) *Sloveninu* also produced both the Greek ethnonym *Sklavenos* and its Latin cognate,

---

[91] See e.g. the book by Sandor Nagy (1973). For an overview of the many theories with respect to the Hungarians, see *http://groups.msn.com/AncientWisdomCulturesPeople/magyars.msn*
[92] "Identifications of Veneti as Slavs", *http://en.wikipedia.org/wiki/Vistula_Veneti*

Sclav(en)us, as well as their variants in many other languages. Conversely, the Slavs considered speakers of other languages as 'dumb' or 'incomprehensible' people; precisely this is the meaning of the Slavic words for Germans, *Nemesti, Nemec,* or *Nymiec*. The term *Nemesti* is essentially the Slavic equivalent of the Berber term *Iguinawen,* the Greco-Latin "barbarian", and the Germanic *wels(ch)*.

Hungarians entering the Carpathian basin, 9th century CE
(Anonymous painting of 1360; source: Wikimedia Commons)

An alternative theory, proposed by the German linguist Heinrich Kunstmann, deserves to be mentioned here. He claims that in Old Slavic the meaning of *Slavs* was 'belonging to the whole' (*zum Ganzen, zu allen gehörend*), that is, 'belonging to the/our community'. As for the Slav word for Germans, *Nemesti* or similar, he claims it to be related to the Latin *nemo* and the Old German *nioman*, 'nobody', and to mean not 'dumb' but the opposite of "Slav" itself, namely, 'not belonging to the/our community' (*keiner von allen, keiner von uns*) (Kunstmann 1996: 24, 47). His explanation for "Croatia" (*Hrvatska*) is that it is derived from *hrva*, "very likely an exonym used by an Iranian people to refer to Slavs". *Serbia* and *Serbs* are also supposed to be derived from an Iranian root, *sarvah,* meaning 'all' or 'inclusive', that is, 'belonging to our community or people' (1996: 38-39). Kunstmann does not explain, however, when, where and how the Croats and Serbs are supposed to have taken over this nomenclature from Iranians.

The linguistic border between the Germans and the Romance *Welsch* in the west has changed but little since the era of the Great Migrations; on the other hand, the one between the worlds of the Germans and the Slavs has in fact fluctuated dramatically as a result of conquests, colonization, wars, and deportations. At the time of the Great Migrations, Slavic tribes pushed far westward, thus in a sense forcing

Germanic tribes to cross the borders of the Roman Empire. In the fifth century CE, for example, Slavic migrants drove the Germanic inhabitants from a Central European region where, hundreds of years earlier, the Celtic tribe of the Boyars had lived, namely, "Bohemia" (as indicated in the discussion of the origins of the Bavarians earlier). This land was henceforth also referred to by the name of the Slav newcomers, who called themselves *Ceske,* 'Czechs'. And so Bohemia became the land of the Czechs, a western outpost of the presumably "eastern" Slavs.

It is hardly surprising that in Western Europe the term *Bohemian* became associated with foreign people, an incomprehensible language, and a strange way of life. All these things are conjured up by the French term *bohémien,* popularized by the book of Henri Murger, published in 1851, that served as the libretto for Puccini's famous opera, *La Bohème.* Bohemians became a byword for strange people in general, and in particular for gypsies; the latter admittedly did not come from Bohemia, but their appearance and nomadic lifestyle also differed greatly from that of the sedentary inhabitants of the western part of Europe. To the Germans too, the term Bohemian (böhmisch) evoked a nearby yet strange people, and it had a vaguely pejorative connotation. It was in this sense that the German President, Hindenburg, a Prussian aristocrat, dismissed Hitler as "a Bohemian corporal", (*ein böhmischer Gefreite*), because the later *Führer* was born in the small town of Braunau, situated within the boundaries of Austria yet very close to the Czech border.

In the southern reaches of the land of Bohemia, the Slavic population first formed a genuine state in the beginning of the ninth century CE; historians refer to this entity as the "Empire of Greater Moravia", Moravia is a region within the Czech Republic, a nation that Germans in the past often called in one breath *Böhmen und Mähren,* 'Bohemia-and-Moravia'. The capital of Moravia is Brno, whose name has the same etymology as Verona and Bern; Brno, too, is situated on the meander of a river. It was during the ninth century that missionaries from Constantinople converted the Slavs of the Moravian Empire – as well as the Serbians, Russians, etc. – to the Eastern/Byzantine version of Christianity. They simultaneously introduced into these regions a new version of the Greek alphabet that proved practical for the hitherto unwritten Slavic languages. The latter achievement was the work of two monks who were to ascend into the historical heavens as the "apostles of the Slavs", the brothers Constantine and Michael from Thessalonika. Michael was also known as Methodius, and Constantine as Cyrillus, and it is after the latter that the new alphabet was called "Cyrillic". Cyrillic was to survive in Serbia and Russia, but not in Bohemia or Moravia. The reason for this is that during the Middle Ages the Germans launched a counter-offensive against their Slavic (and other) neighbors in Central and Eastern Europe. A couple of centuries of Germanic *Drang nach Osten* caused the Roman version of Christianity to displace Greek Orthodoxy within the borders of the now defunct Moravian Empire; Latin replaced Greek as the language of the liturgy, and the Cyrillic alphabet, closely associated with the Greek Orthodox Church, likewise fell victim to this development. The border between Latin and Greek Christianity shifted further eastward, namely, between the lands of the Catholic Croatians and the Orthodox Serbians.

6

In the name of Allah

The Desert between Petra and Arabia Felix

As seen from a "Western" perspective, the Arabs are a Semitic people that for many centuries quietly minded its own business in a vast but sandy and backward bailiwick of the Middle East. We know them primarily as nomadic inhabitants of the steppe, or of the desert, as "Bedouins". This is not a coincidence, because the latter term is derived from the Arabic word for steppe, *badija*, and in Arabic, Bedouins are known as *badawi*. However, not all Arabs are nomads, and this has been so since the very distant past. The Arab family also included many sedentary inhabitants of oases and cities, people who earned their living as farmers, artisans, artists, officials in temples and palaces, intellectuals, and – last but by no means least – merchants. The latter had been familiar since time immemorial with the caravan and seaborne trade that linked their own land not only with Persia, India, China, and the rest of Asia, but also with Europe and Africa. Even so, the archetypical Western association of Arabs with the desert is not entirely unjustified. Indeed, *arabah* supposedly means 'steppe' or 'desert', and so the *Arabi* are the 'inhabitants of the steppe or of the desert'. Already in Ancient Mesopotamia, the term *arbu* signified 'desert', and the label "Arab" - first mentioned in Assyrian sources dating from approximately 1,000 BCE - referred to inhabitants of the desert. According to an alternative and ultimately more convincing theory, however, the meaning of the Arab word *arab* is really 'those who speak an understandable language'; its binary opposite is *ajam*, 'those who speak an unintelligible language'. The term *arab* was exported from the Arabian heartland to neighboring Mesopotamia, where it was associated with the arid homeland of the people to whom it referred, and so it happened that *arab* and its cognates acquired the meaning of desert and of inhabitants of the desert.

In the seventh century CE, the Arabs suddenly stormed onto the stage of history in spectacular fashion. They had been motivated and armed spiritually by the Prophet Mohammed, a merchant from Mecca, with a new monotheistic religion that was strongly influenced by both Judaism and Christianity. This religion became known as "Islam", which is generally interpreted as meaning 'submission to the will of God'. (*Islam* has the same trisyllabic S-L-M Semitic root as the words *Muslim* and *salaam*, 'peace', familiar from the Arab greeting *salaam aleikum* and its Hebrew equivalent, *shalom*.) Within a century of the death of the Prophet, the *Dar Al Islam*, the 'House of Islam', stretched from Morocco to the frontiers of China. This, more or less, is what we can read in our history books, and for the Arab people the emergence of Islam was indeed an epochal event, without which their language and culture would never have been able to spread so far and wide. However, it is also often assumed that all Arabs are Muslims, and vice-versa. The former is basically true, except for some statistically unimportant exceptions; the latter is entirely mistaken, because the predominantly Muslim Turks and Iranians, for example, are not only not Arabs, they are not even classified as Semitic peoples or, put more accurately, speakers of a Semitic language. Another caveat is in order: the Arabs were already important actors in terms of world history long before Mohammed.

The so-called Treasury at Petra on a painting by David Roberts
(Lithograph: David Roberts, 1830s; source: Roberts 1842)

It has already been mentioned that the domestication of the camel around the end of the second millennium BCE made it possible to travel back and forth between Mesopotamia and Egypt via the Arabian and Syrian deserts. This was a window of opportunity of which the pre-Islamic Arabs knew how to take advantage, and it is since that time that Arabs have been associated with camels. The northern regions of the immense Arab Peninsula were privileged in this respect on account of their location on the direct route between Egypt and Mesopotamia, and it was primarily their inhabitants who profited from the new possibilities. Their fortunate number included the Nabataeans, a tribe whose homeland was in the modern state of Jordan. According to Martin Bernal, *nabat* is the Semitic root for 'spring', 'oasis'; the Nabataeans were the 'oasis dwellers'. The settlement that functioned as their capital was called *Rekem* in their Semitic language, and meant 'red sandstone'. That name alluded to the spectacular mass of red rocks that characterize the site and provided the construction material for handsome temples and other buildings. In Arabic itself, *Rekem* would later be known as *Sala*, meaning 'rock', and we now know this town – and its well-preserved and rightly world-famous ruins – by its Greco-Roman name, *Petra*, a direct translation of *Sala*. (The name of the Apostle Peter likewise signified 'rock'; Peter was the 'rock', according to the Bible, upon which Christ intended to build his church.) Greeks and Romans called the area around Petra *Arabia Petraea*, 'rocky Arabia'.

The Nabataean merchants traded along the Silk Road as far as the Chinese Empire of the Han Dynasty, where their city was known as *Wutan,* the 'rose-colored city'. But Petra was also involved in another type of long-distance trade, namely, commerce with the denizens of the southern part of the Arab Peninsula. The Romans called that area *Arabia Felix* ('Happy Arabia'), thus differentiating it neatly from both *Arabia Petraea* and *Arabia Deserta*, the vast desert in the interior of the Arab Peninsula. It was the place of origin of frankincense, the combustible resin of a local tree, a mysterious product that was in great demand because it was used during worship rituals in the temples of Babylonia, Egypt, Palestine, Greece, Rome, and elsewhere. Myrrh, another type of resin, used in embalming and as an ingredient of perfumes and incense, was also imported from the south of the Arab Peninsula and resold by the Nabataeans in the markets of the Middle East and Egypt.

The Arabian south now features the states of Oman and Yemen. The toponym Oman is very ancient, and was already mentioned by Pliny and Ptolemy, but its etymology is unfortunately a question mark. As for Yemen, it is worthwhile citing the explanation offered in the *Dictionnaire des noms de lieux*:

> The name [Yemen]...has for centuries been used to designate the region of southern Arabia in general. To the Semitic peoples of Antiquity, who oriented themselves by facing the east, the regions situated to their right were not only those we call the south, but also those which, as they saw things, were associated with happiness, prosperity, and wealth. In the Semitic languages, the root *y[e]m[e]n* happens to mean precisely 'right, right hand' and is loaded with these connotations. The Arab name *al-Yemen* thus refers to the right, the south, the fortunate land. In light of this, one understands why in Roman Antiquity southern Arabia was called *Arabia Felix* (Deroy & Mulon 1992: 521).[93]

The onomastic counterpart of Yemen, 'the right', is the part of the Middle East that was to the left (and north) of those who witnessed the rising of the sun in the sanctuary of Mecca, namely, Syria and surrounding territories such as Jordan and Lebanon. In Arabic, this region is often referred to as *Al Sham*, 'the left', or *Bilad al Sham*, 'land of the left hand'. (But the term *Al Sham* is sometimes also used to refer to the foremost city of that region, Damascus.) As lands situated on the right, in

---

[93] See also Urmes (2003: 137).

other words, to the south, were traditionally associated with happiness, lands situated to the left, that is, to the north, were similarly associated with unhappiness.[94]

In "Happy Arabia", states already emerged at a very early stage – states that have gone down in legend as Punt, Ophir, and Saba. However, it is possible that all or some of these names referred to African lands such as Sudan, Ethiopia, and Somalia. The Egyptian Middle Empire (2250-1750 BCE) engaged in commerce with the southern land of "Punt", which could have been either Yemen or Somalia. According to the Bible, King Solomon, who supposedly ruled in the tenth century BCE, sent ships via the Red Sea to a region known as Ophir in order to fetch ivory, gold, and similar luxury goods. He himself enjoyed the pleasure of a visit from the Queen of Sheba (or Saba), a country that is traditionally identified as Yemen, although many believe the queen was Ethiopian.

The Queen of Sheba
(Drawing by an unknown artist, ca. 1595; source: Wikimedia Commons)

As for the Red Sea, it received that name on account of the great masses of red algae (*trichodesmium erythraeum*) that are found in it, but nobody appears to know when, where, or by whom this name was first used. In any event, the Ancient Greeks already mentioned the "Eritrean" or "Red" Sea, *erythros pontos* or *erythra thalassa;* the Romans followed the Hellenic example and spoke of *mare rubrum*. The name of the African statelet Eritrea, situated in that part of the world, simply means 'land on the Red Sea'. *Arabia Felix* itself traded with Ethiopia and other parts of Eastern Africa via the *Bab Al Mandab*, 'Gate of Sighs', the strait between the Arab Peninsula and Africa that was so named because for centuries it witnessed the importation of slaves from Africa who realized that they would never again see their homeland. The export commodity of choice in that neighborhood would later be coffee, the roasted bean of a local shrub that was predestined to flourish in Columbia, Brazil, and elsewhere in the New World. Muza, or Mocha, was the name of the most important

---

[94] *http://en.wikipedia.org/wiki/Bilad_al-Sham*. The term *Sham* has nothing in common with the Biblical name Cham, one of the sons of Noah.

Yemenite harbor from which this product was shipped, and so it happened that in Europe the term "mocha" became a synonym for fine coffee.

The caravan route between Petra and Yemen crossed a region that is known in Arabic as *Hedjaz*, 'corridor'; it is indeed a narrow strip of land between the shores of the Red Sea and the gargantuan desert in the interior of the Arab Peninsula, an inhospitable land known since time immemorial as *Rub al Khali*, the 'empty quarter'. For a long time, Petra functioned as the Arab crossroads of the great trade routes in the Middle East, but in pre-Islamic times other Arab cities also enjoyed eras of great commercial prosperity. There was a remarkable example favorably situated along a caravan route through the Syrian Desert, half way between the Levantine coast and Mesopotamia, between the ancient heartlands of the Phoenicians and the Babylonians. It was an oasis with countless palm trees and became known, and eventually internationally famous, as Palmyra, 'city of palm trees'. This was an exonym of Greek origin; the locals, speaking Aramaic, a Semitic language, called their city *Tadmor*, which meant approximately the same thing, namely, 'city of dates' or 'city of date palms'. Palmyra's fame spread as far as China, where the city of palms was known as *Chieh-lan*, 'date city'. In the third century CE, Palmyra played an important role as a kind of buffer state between the mighty empires of the Romans on the one hand and the Sassanian Persians on the other. Under leaders such as Odenathus, Palmyra took the side of Rome and fought valiantly against the Persians. Arabs thus began to play an important role even in Rome itself, and in 244 CE an Arab named Philip even became emperor. However, shortly thereafter the legendary Queen Zenobia came to power in Palmyra, and she turned her armies against the Romans and fought them as far away as Egypt and Asia Minor with temporary success. But her luck eventually ran out and in 272 CE Emperor Aurelian took her city and put an end to the career of the Palmyrene Cleopatra.

An ancient avenue among the ruins of Palmyra
(Photo: Zeledi, 2005; source: Wikimedia Commons)

An Arab Far West

The Arabs already played a considerable role in world history long before Mohammed. However, it was his new teaching, Islam, that revealed itself to be the dynamo of an unprecedented expansion of the Arabs' religion, language, and culture in general. Mohammed was a merchant from Mecca, an ancient city that had functioned since time immemorial as a trading post as well as a centre of pilgrimage, focused on the worship of a small cubical shrine called *Kaaba*, meaning 'cube'; the eastern corner of the *Kaaba* featured - and still features - the famous Black Stone, believed to be a meteorite. Not surprisingly, the name Mecca is based on the root *mkrb*, 'sanctuary' (Rodinson 1994). Initially, Mohammed did not have much success with his monotheistic teachings in Mecca, but he was welcomed with open arms in the neighboring town of Jathrib, usually referred to as Medina, 'the city'; Medina is now known as *Medina an-Nabi*, 'city of the Prophet'.

After the death of Mohammed in 632, his followers took only a few years to conquer the entire Middle East at the expense of the Byzantines and the Sassanian Persians. They captured Jerusalem already in 638 CE, quite notably without any bloodshed. *Al Quds,* 'the sacred', was what the Arabs called that city, because it was there that, in a vision, Mohammed had risen to heaven from a rock where later the magnificent "Dome of the Rock" mosque would be built. After Mecca and Medina, Jerusalem ranks as the holiest city in the world of Islam.

Mecca in 1850
(Artist: unknown; source: Wikimedia Commons)

Around the same time, Damascus, capital of the former Roman and then Byzantine province of Syria, fell into Arab hands. Palestine and Syria were thus quickly integrated into the Arab-Muslim orbit. Islam revealed itself to be a tolerant religion, so that Christian as well as Jewish communities just about everywhere in the

Middle East survived and have continued to exist until the present. Even so, the new religion preached by Mohammed gradually became the faith of the vast majority of the population, and Arabic replaced Aramaic as the region's leading language.

Egypt had previously been a province of the Byzantine Empire, dominated by Greeks. The majority of the population there were Christians who had adopted a special liturgy that the Greeks called *Coptic*, 'Egyptian'. Here too, the triumphant arrival of the Arabs in the year 639 CE meant that the majority of the Egyptians converted, sooner or later, to the Islamic religion, even though even today many Coptic communities subsist in the country, and that Arabic replaced the hitherto leading language, in this case Greek. The Arabs set up a camp of tents while besieging a key Byzantine fortress near the site of ancient Memphis. This settlement was to become permanent and, known as *Al Fustat*, 'the tent', revealed itself to be the embryo of a new Egyptian capital; it is now referred to as "Old Cairo". Fustat's site, just south of the Nile Delta, was far more functional for east-west travel - and thus for staying in touch with Arabia and for conquering North Africa – than that of Alexandria, the old Byzantine capital and Egypt's window on the Mediterranean, a city that is separated from regions further east by the delta. As far as the Arabs were concerned, furthermore, Alexandria was too closely associated with Egypt's former rulers, the Byzantine Greeks, and with their religion, Christianity. Egypt as a whole became known as *Misr al-Fustat*, meaning something akin to 'Settlement of the Tent', but today it is customary to use just *Misr*. This is a very ancient term of Mesopotamian origin. In Akkadian, *misru* was the dual form of the word for 'land' or 'territory', i.e. meaning specifically 'two lands' or 'two territories'. In Babylonia it was used to refer to the Pharaonic empire, the union of Lower and Upper Egypt, as the 'double land'. This terminology was adopted by virtually all other orientals, including the Assyrians, Hittites, Phoenicians, Hebrews, and Arabs, who continue to use it (Deroy & Mulon 1992: 152-53).

A sketch of Cairo in the 19th century
(Artist: David Roberts; source: Roberts 1842)

In the tenth century, Egypt was conquered by a Shiite dynasty from Tunisia called the Fatimids because they considered themselves to be descendants of Fatima, the Prophet's daughter. In order to celebrate their victory over their rivals, they founded a city on the banks of the Nile in 969 CE, virtually next door to Fustat, and named it 'city of victory', *Al-Qahirat,* known to non-Arabs as Cairo. According to an alternative etymology, the city was founded when the planet Mars, *Al Qahir* in Arabic, stood high in the heavens, which was seen as a favorable omen.

To the south of Egypt commenced the lands inhabited by black peoples. Probably inspired by Ancient Greek nomenclature, the Arabs called it 'land of the dark-skinned people', *Bilad as Sudan*. The Arabs also called black people *Zanj,* and with this label they often referred to both the land and people of East Africa, which is why this part of the Dark Continent was sometimes called "Azania" in Europe. The Arab term *Zanj* is at the core of toponyms such as Zanzibar, 'land of blacks'.[95]

Arab merchants were interested primarily in the coastal regions of East Africa. They called that area *sahel,* 'the coast', and its population *sawahil,* 'people of the coast'. The *lingua franca* which emerged in that part of the world as a result of intensive trade between Arabs and Africans – essentially a Bantu language larded with numerous Arab loan words – thus received the name "Swahili". The Europeans would eventually take over this Arab terminology and, somewhat tautologically, they started to speak of the "Swahili Coast". Along that coast, Arabs lived and did business for hundreds of years. One of their most important centres was Mzizima, 'the healthy city', but in 1866 the local sultan gave it a new name, Dar es Salaam, 'house of peace'. Dar es Salaam is today the capital city of Tanzania.

From Egypt, the Arab conquerors pushed farther west along the Mediterranean coast and through the Libyan Desert, eventually reaching the fertile region of Northwest Africa. They called that land Al Djazair, 'the island', because it is surrounded by three seas, namely, the Mediterranean, the Atlantic Ocean, and the great "sand sea" of the Sahara. The meaning of that term has narrowed over time, and today Al Djazair is the Arab name of the country we call "Algeria". Originally, however, "the island" consisted of Tunisia and Morocco as well as Algeria. From the perspective of the Arab Peninsula, Al Djazair lay in a remote western part of the world, so to the Arabs it was a kind of "Far West". Consequently, that distant land was also known as Al Maghreb, 'the west', 'land of the setting sun'. (We recognize here the same Semitic root as in the Phoenician word *Mahaurim,* 'westerners', which produced the terms *Mauri* and Moors.) In Arabic, the onomastic companion of Al Maghreb, 'sunset' or 'the west', is Al Mashreq, 'sunrise' or 'the east', a term used to refer to the Arab lands situated to the east of Egypt and to the north of the Arabian peninsula. Ensconced in Al Mashreq is the Arabic root meaning 'east', namely *sharq*, which we will meet again when discussing the term "Saracen". Incidentally, Egypt is seen as a special case, a "land in the middle", belonging to neither Al Maghreb nor Al Mashreq.

---

[95] The *-bar* of this toponym is almost certainly a cognate of Usko-Mediterranean *iber* discussed earlier.

Maghreb is a term that even today refers to Northwest Africa in general; in Arabic, however, that toponym now serves as the name of the kingdom of Morocco. The name *Morocco*, used in English and other Western languages, originally referred to the city of Marrakech, founded in the eleventh century. Marrakech is a Berber name, said to mean something like 'get out of here!' This strange nomenclature is allegedly an allusion to the inhospitable nature of this place at the time before the introduction of a system of irrigation permitted horticulture and thus also the emergence of a city that developed into the great and handsome metropolis of Northwest Africa. Coincidentally, the Arab version of the name, *Marrukush*, means 'the beautifully decorated one', in other words, the 'handsome city'. On account of the fame of that city, the entire country was associated with Marrakech and thus ended up with the same name. In Europe, the name *Morocco* first surfaced in an Italian document of the year 1138 CE. Although in Arabic the country is usually referred to as *Al Maghreb*, as already mentioned, the name *Marrakech* is sometimes used as a synonym for the official name.

"La ville de Maroc" (Marrakech)
(Artist: A de Bérard: source: Charton 1860-61)

The biggest and best-known city of Morocco is *Dar Al Baida,* but in the Western world everyone speaks of "Casablanca". The meaning of the Arab as well as the "western" – in reality Spanish - version is 'White House'. That name originated when in 1570 CE the Portuguese captured what was then a fishing port with a handful of little white houses, and called it *Casa Branca.* The Portuguese remained for nearly two centuries, and during that time the toponym gained international acceptance. Eventually, however, it was primarily Spanish merchants who went there to do business, and as a result Europe and the rest of the world adopted their version of the name, with the Spanish *blanca* instead of the Portuguese *branca*.

The capital of the country is not Casablanca but Rabat, an Arab toponym meaning 'castle' or, more precisely, 'fortified monastery'. When towards the end of the eleventh century the Spanish Christians took Toledo from the Arabs, the bad tidings hit Islamic Morocco like a bombshell, and soon a counter-offensive was organized. Many devoted Muslims assembled in castles that also doubled as a kind of monastery and, using these strongholds as bases, waged holy war again vigorously – and rather successfully – in Spain. *Rabat* (or *ribat*) is the Arab word for such a castle / monastery, and *Al Murabitun* is the name of its inhabitants. These "Almoravids", as they became known in Spain, made life particularly miserable for the Spanish crusaders. It comes as no surprise, therefore, that the Christian side quickly followed the Muslim example. Thus originated the orders of the "fighting monks", such as the Knights Templar, the Knights of St. John (also known as Knights of Malta), the German or Teutonic Order and, in Spain itself, the Orders of Santiago and of Calatrava. In the Muslim camp, the "dynasty" of the Almoravids was succeeded by that of the Almohads (*Al Muwahhidun)*, the 'true believers in one God'. The name purported to underscore the fact that these Muslims considered themselves genuine monotheists, in contrast to the Christians, whose religion – featuring a Trinity, a Virgin Mary, and countless saints – was viewed as a kind of polytheism masquerading as monotheism.

Rabat in the 19th century
(Artist: A de Bérard; source: Charton 1860-61)

As had been the case with Egypt, the Maghreb too was conquered by the Arabs at the expense of the Byzantines. The foremost Byzantine stronghold in that region was Carthage, and it would take a long time before the Arabs could lay their hands on that city. In the meantime, they settled down not far from there, in Kairwan, a site whose name – 'caravan' – betrays that it was originally a modest but strategically well-located caravan station, a so-called caravanserai. After Carthage was finally conquered the city of Tunis arose there, but for Arabs, Kairwan has remained an extremely important center to this very day; on account of its ancient mosque, for example, constructed already in the seventh century, Kairwan ranks as one of the holiest cities in the 'House of Islam'. As far as Tunis is concerned, the capital of Tunisia is a predominantly modern city, but its historical core is a fortress that was probably founded by local Berbers even before the arrival of the Phoenicians. "Tunis" is nothing other than the Arabic version of the Greco-Roman *Tynes* or *Tunes,* itself derived from the familiar Usko-Mediterranean term *dunum*. In 146 BCE, Tunis was razed to the ground by the Romans just like Carthage, but it was on its ruins, and not those of Carthage, that the Arabs founded the new city that was predestined to surpass Kairwan and to develop into the most important harbor of that part of North Africa. Tunis became the capital of the province the Romans called *Africa*, a name the Arabs turned into *Ifriqyia*; and just as the term *Africa* would eventually refer to an entire continent, the city gave its name to the central part of North Africa: Tunisia. Incidentally, in Arabic the name of the country is exactly the same as that of the city, namely, *Tunus*.

The Kairwan mosque[96]
(Photo: unknown; source: www.sacredsites.com)

The Arabs did not destroy the great library of Alexandria, as an ancient legend has it. Instead, they carefully preserved and studied the manuscripts they found there, and so it was that they adopted many cosmographic concepts from the Ancient Greeks. When one of their leaders, known as Oqba, reached the Atlantic Ocean in

---

[96] For information and illustrations concerning the colonnade, see p. 58.

the vicinity of the Pillars of Hercules, he knew that the Ancients had associated that part of the world with the saying *Nec plus Ultra,* 'there is nothing beyond'. And so he rode his horse into the Atlantic's salty surf, invoking Allah as witness that he was unable to go on conquering land. But Tariq, a converted Berber rather than an Arab, knew better. In North Africa, the memory was still alive of the arrival of the Vandals who, at the time of the disintegration of the Western Roman Empire, had invaded their land from Spain. Since that time, the Visigoths had settled in Spain, but even so the latter country remained known in North Africa as *Vandalia,* 'land of the Vandals'. It has been theorized that the Arabs turned that word into *Al Andalus,* 'Andalusia', but this hypothesis is the subject of much controversy. In the year 711 CE, Tariq and a small Arab/Berber army crossed from Africa to Europe at the site that had been known for centuries as the Pillars of Hercules. He made his landfall at the foot of the high and steep rock formerly known as Calpe, but now renamed by the Arabs *Jabal Tarik,* 'rock [or mountain] of Tariq', and this gave us the familiar toponym *Gibraltar.* The other Pillar of Hercules, the mountain on the African side of the Strait of Gibraltar, situated near the Spanish exclave Ceuta and earlier known as Abila, was renamed *Jabal Musa,* 'Mount Musa', in honor of Tariq's commander, Musa ('Moses').

Tariq crushed the army of the Spanish Visigoths in the vicinity of Jerez, captured their capital, Toledo, and in a very short time managed to conquer nearly the entire Iberian Peninsula, including its extreme southwest. That region, which stretched even further west than the Moroccan coast reached by Musa, was henceforth known in Arabic as *Al Gharb,* 'the west' in the sense of the 'extreme west', the 'western end of the world'; that part of Portugal is today known as the Algarve. (*Gharb* has the same familiar old root, meaning 'sunset', as Europe: *ereb.*) The Romans had always considered the Iberian west coast as the extremity of the European continent, as *Finis Terrae,* and *Al Gharb* was simply the Arab version of this ancient Latin term. Along the coast between Gibraltar and the Algarve, on the so-called Costa de la Luz in the vicinity of Cadiz, there is a headland the Arabs called the 'western point', *Taraf al-Gharb*; tourists sipping Sangria or Sherry on a local terrace there can survey the stretch of Atlantic waters where in 1805 Nelson wiped out a French fleet, a victory that caused a few acres in the heart of London to be named "Trafalgar Square".

The success of the Arabs in Spain was facilitated by the fact that a segment of the Visigoth nobility opted to collaborate with the invaders rather than to take up the cause of their own king, Roderick (Spanish: Rodrigo). As a result of this, the estates of the fallen Roderick and his followers were divided amongst the Arab conquerors and the Visigoth Quislings according to an ancient Germanic custom known in Gothic as *landeluth,* a term that might be loosely translated as 'land lottery', 'drawing of lots for the land'. The Arabs turned this into *Al Andaluth* or *Al Andalus,* and it is with this term that they started to refer to the conquered Iberian lands. It is increasingly believed that this is the correct etymology of the toponym *Andalusia.*

The Arab conquests did not peter out at the Pyrenees but, as is generally known, their progress was checked on account of a defeat inflicted on them in 732 CE, somewhere between Tours and Poitiers, by the Frankish warlord Charles Martel. In Spain itself, meanwhile, Christians resisted successfully in the mountainous north. An Arab army was ambushed and destroyed in 722 CE near the village of Covadonga, in Asturia, a region in the Cantabrian Mountains. This proved to be the beginning of the so-called *Reconquista*, the 're-conquest', by the Christians, of the Iberian Peninsula. It was a war that lasted almost eight centuries, ending only in 1492 CE with the fall of the last Arab city in Spain, Granada. Asturia, then, revealed itself to be the cradle of a Christian kingdom that would later be known as Léon and, later still, as Castile; it is for this reason that, even today, the Crown Prince of Spain bears the title of "Prince of Asturia". The name "Asturia" was already known in the Roman era. The *Asturi* were a local Iberian tribe, but their name seems to have originated as a toponym, combining two Usko-Mediterranean terms, *as(i)tu*, 'city' or 'territory', and *hurru*, 'mines'. 'Land of mines' was, and continues to be, a most appropriate name for the mineral-rich province of Asturia, whose population contains a high percentage of coal miners.

Further east, in the Pyrenees, other Christian principalities emerged around the same time, including Navarra and Aragon. The Aragon is a tributary of the Ebro River, and its name – containing *onna*, an Usko-Mediterranean root referring to water – was bestowed on a small kingdom that originated in its valley. Navarra is a toponym of Basque origin featuring the term *naba* or *nawu*, 'valley [or plateau] in the mountains', and meaning something like the 'high country', 'mountain meadow'. This label probably reflected the contrast, within the land of the Basques, between the mountainous interior and the coast, between the land of the Basque cattle breeders and that of the Basque fishermen.

Interior of the Great Mosque at Córdoba
(Photo: Hans Peter Schaefer, 2002; source Wikimedia Commons)

During the many hundreds of years of the Reconquista, the term *Hispania* was used to refer to the northern, Christian part of the Iberian Peninsula, while *Andalusia* alluded to the southern, Muslim part. *Al Andalus* experienced its Golden Age in the tenth century under the Spanish branch of the dynasty of the Umayyads, who had earlier ruled in Damascus. Their capital, *Kurtuba*, or Cordoba, was one of the biggest cities in Europe. In Cordoba, Christians and Jews lived harmoniously together with the Muslim majority, and this tolerance and collaboration, primarily in the field of science and art, produced one of the most brilliant civilizations, not only of the Middle Ages but of world history. Other great cities of *Al Andalus* were Seville, Toledo, Valencia, and Lisbon. Granada had been home since time immemorial to an important Jewish community, and to the Arabs this city was known as *Gharnat al Yahud*, the 'pomegranate of the Jews'. As Granada meant 'pomegranate', this fruit inevitably became the symbol of the city. With the conquest of Granada in 1492 CE the Reconquista chapter was closed, and ever since that time a pomegranate adorns the middle base of the coat of arms of the Spanish kingdom. Granada was the capital of the dynasty of the Nasrids, and their palace was the enchanting Alhambra, an Arab term meaning the 'red palace'.

The population of Andalusia consisted of people who had called the Iberian Peninsula home since the time of the Tartessians, Phoenicians, and Romans, but also of newcomers, either Arabs who had migrated to their "Far West," or North African Berbers who had converted to Islam and joined Tariq on his daring Vandalian venture. As far as the Spanish Christians were concerned, they all came from North Africa, from the region that had been known since the time of the Roman Empire as *Mauretania*, the land of the *Mauri*. Muslim Spaniards – and gradually Muslims in general – thus became known as *moros*, as "Moors". This term conjured up not only a commitment to the Islamic faith but also a dark skin color, not necessarily black but certainly darker than that of the white denizens of "Christendom", as Europe was then still generally called. (When Europe would later become acquainted with the truly black inhabitants of West Africa, they would call them "blackamoors" [Kiernan 1972: 203].) For hundreds of years, North African "Moors" – Moors from "Barbary", that is, such as Barbarossa and Dragut – would make the south of Christian Europe unsafe and force the people, especially in Italy and southern France, to withdraw to walled towns and villages; these would be situated preferably on hilltops at a respectful distance from the coast, which was raided regularly by fast sloops from Algiers, the Moroccan port of Salé, and other Moorish pirates' dens. In the eighth and ninth centuries, those dreaded pirates even established a foothold in Provence, namely, in a mountainous and forested region of the interior that is still known as Les Maures. We have seen earlier that the Latin term *Mauri,* which has given us *Moors*, descended from the Phoenician word *Mahaurim*, meaning "westerners". It is a remarkable irony of history that a word used centuries ago by easterners to refer to westerners would eventually be used by westerners to refer to easterners.

In the footsteps of Alexander the Great

Following the death of the Prophet, the Arabs disseminated from their peninsula not only to the west, to Al Maghreb, but also to the east. This occurred primarily at the expense of the Persian Empire of the Sassanians and their Zoroastrian state religion. Mesopotamia was Arabized and Islamized virtually in its entirety; as a result, the population of the modern state of Iraq is predominantly Arab and almost one hundred percent Muslim. In very little time, a site in the vicinity of ancient Babylon developed into the great political, religious, and cultural Arab metropolis of the region: Baghdad. This was a Sassanian-Persian name meaning 'gift [*dad*] of God [*bagh*]'. Under Abbasid caliphs such as Harun Al Rashid, Baghdad revealed itself as the legendary city of the famous poet Omar Khayyam, of the fairy tales of the One Thousand And One Nights, and of Ali Baba and the Forty Thieves. These caliphs ruled, at least in theory, over the entire "House of Islam".

The bridge of boats, Baghdad
(Artist: M E Flandin; source: Charton 1860-61)

As for the modern state of Iraq, it only appeared on the scene after the First World War. All sorts of more-or-less exotic theories attempt to explain the origin and meaning of the name *Iraq*, but a major problem is presented by the fact that it is not clear whether the toponym is of a very ancient or a more recent vintage, nor if it is of Mesopotamian, Persian, or Arab origin. If it is Arab, its meaning may well be 'root' or 'land with deep roots'. But it is uncertain whether this is a reference to this country's deep historical roots or to its two great rivers that penetrate like roots into the interior of the Asian mainland. More convincing is the hypothesis that the term *Iraq* was coined at the time of the Arab conquest of Mesopotamia and Persia. At that time, the Arabs began to differentiate between *Iraq Arabi*, 'region of the speakers of our [Arab] language', and neighboring Iran, known to Arabs as *Iraq Ajemi*, 'land of those who speak an unintelligible language', namely, Indo-European Iranian or Farsi.

In the Abbasid era, Baghdad also functioned as a nexus of international trade routes. Via India, Arab merchants even reached faraway China, known in Arabic as *Al Sin*. Business was carried on in the port city of Guangzhou, which the Arabs sometimes called *Khanfu*, sometimes also *Sin al Sin*, 'China's China'. The Portuguese – and afterwards all Westerners – were to refer to this great seaport as *Cantão*, 'Canton', because they confused the city with the province, whose name is Guangdong. The name "Guangzhou" actually means 'capital [*zhou*] of the province [*Guang*]'. Commercially and culturally, the Arab world and China were also connected by an overland route across Central Asia that had already been in use at the time of the Romans: the famed Silk Road. It led from the Chinese capital Xian, then known as Changan, 'city of eternal peace', to Baghdad, whose nickname in the era of the Abbasid Caliphate was *Medinat as Salaam*, 'city of peace'. The existing trade infrastructure along a seemingly endless string of cities and caravanserais facilitated the expansion of the Arab language, culture, and religion. Conversely, the success of Islam and of the Arab way of life in general promoted trade between the Middle and the Far East. Islam itself did indeed serve as a kind of ideology that encouraged and facilitated trade, and this was one of the reasons why the religion introduced by Mohammed could grow deep roots in the entire area from Iran to China.[97]

Tang soldiers at Xian gate
(Photo: J Pauwels, 2007)

In the 640s, the conquering Arabs also pushed north from Mesopotamia to the Caucasus, but in this mountainous region the population appeared to be far less receptive to the message of Mohammed and to Arab culture in general. Armenia and Georgia had been Christian since approximately 300 CE, and have remained so until the present day. Islam only acquired a foothold here at a late stage, namely, when the

---

[97] This theme is the subject of a book by Lucas Catherine, *Ik wist niet dat de wereld zo klein was*.

Islamized Turks invaded in the eleventh century; this event drove many Georgian and Armenian Christians from their land and led to the emergence of a Muslim state inhabited by a Turkic people, Azerbaijan. The name Azerbaijan means 'garden of fire', and alludes to the fire columns that dot the landscape there, the result of the spontaneous combustion of bitumen. Before the arrival of Islam, these "eternal fires" used to be worshipped by the devotees of the Zoroastrian religion, who were therefore also known as 'fire worshipers'. (In the Iranian city of Yazd, one can visit one of their "fire temples" even today.) Thus there emerged in the Caucasus a bitter hostility between the Christian Armenians and Georgians on the one side, and the Muslim Turks, Azeris, etc., on the other, a hostility that continues to haunt that part of the world.

In the middle of the seventh century CE, the Arabs conquered and Islamized Persia, hitherto ruled by the Sassanians. That country featured many flourishing cities with melodious Persian names. Shiraz, for example, was known on account of its gardens and vineyards; the name is supposed to mean 'city of wine' or 'city of vineyards'. It was there that the grape variety now known all over the world as *Shiraz* or *Syrah* was developed. Viticulture already had a thousand-year old tradition in Shiraz, and it is possible that the great reputation of its wine had induced the Phoenicians to export *Shiraz* vines to Spain in order to establish a vineyard there for the benefit of their colonists. And so a Phoenician version of Persia's "wine city" emerged at a stone's throw from Gadir, in the form of a town known today as Jerez. Indeed, in earlier times this Andalusian city used to be called Shiraz, a fact that lends an unexpected air of authenticity to the English version of the name, *sherry*. However, the arrival of Islam brought about the end of viticulture in the Persian city of Shiraz, because consumption of alcohol was forbidden by Mohammed.

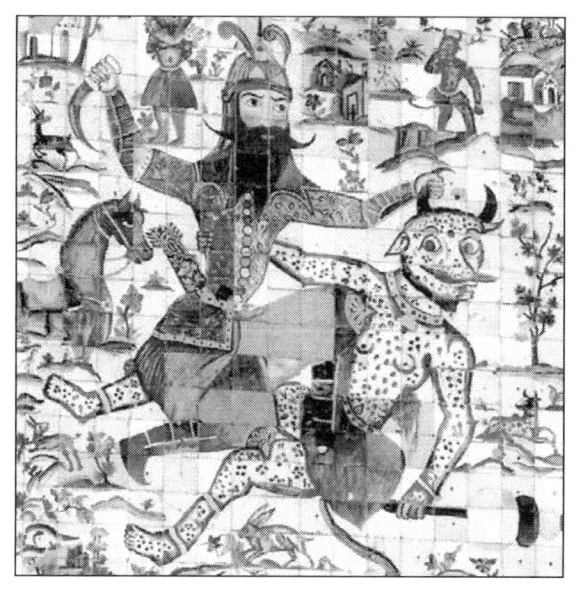

Mural at the Karim Khan citadel, Shiraz, depicting the force of good overcoming evil
(Photo: Zereshk, 2007; source Wikimedia Commons)

Isphahan was another famous Persian city, but it originated only in the Sassanian era as an army camp. The toponym is totally unromantic, and means 'army' or 'armory', but in spite of this Isphahan is considered today to be the most beautiful city in the country. As for the modern capital, Teheran, it too developed into an important centre at a late stage. Its name signifies 'low-lying and warm site', a reference to its location in a valley with a mild climate; this in contrast to the mountains of the nearby Alborz Range, also sometimes called Elburz. This oronym appears to contain the same Usko-Mediterranean root *alb* - referring to the combination of mountains and water, snow and/or ice - that we already met in names such as Alps and Albania.[98]

Iran's highest mountain, Damavand, in the Alborz Range
(Photo: Arad Mojtahedi, 2006; source: Wikimedia Commons)

Having pocketed Persia, the Arabs pushed southward to India. Arabs had been familiar with that country for centuries, and like the Persians, Greeks, and Romans, they too associated this land with its great river, the Indus. The Arab name for the Indus was Sind, and that was also the name they gave to the regions to the west of the Indus, roughly the area of modern-day Pakistan; the rest of the subcontinent, stretching to the east of the Indus, was referred to by the Arabs as Hind. Via the Arab Sea, Arab merchants had traded since time immemorial with India, and the legendary figure of Sinbad personified the brave Arab adventurers who sought their fortune on the "Seven Seas" between the Middle East and East Africa on the one hand and the

---

[98] *http://fr.wikipedia.org/wiki/Elbrous.*

Indian subcontinent on the other. With the advent of Islam, however, trade ceased to suffice. The desire to conquer and thus to aggrandize the "House of Islam" now obsessed the Arabs, and soon the fighters for Allah followed the footsteps of the Great Alexander to the banks of the Indus.

In 711 CE – remarkably enough, the same year that Tariq crossed into Spain – Sind fell into Arab hands, and so Islam began to develop roots in the subcontinent. The Arabs also conquered large parts of Hind, but India beyond the Indus could never be Islamized to the same extent. This region remained grosso modo faithful to its Hindu religion or, to put it more accurately, to the numerous belief systems for which we use the collective label of "Hinduism", such as Brahmanism, Jainism, etc. This remained so even when in the sixteenth century Islamized Mongols – the "Moguls" – founded a great empire that was to survive until the British colonized it in 1858. When the British withdrew from India after the Second World War, the reality of newly gained independence reflected the old religious contrasts, and two new states appeared on the subcontinental scene: first, predominantly Hindu India with its Muslim minority, and second, the exclusively Muslim state of Pakistan. The name *Pakistan* was formed from the initials of the three great Muslim provinces of India's northwest – Punjab, Kashmir, and Sind – together with *stan*, 'land'. Not coincidentally the result, Pakistan, has a meaning in Urdu, the language of the Muslims of the Subcontinent: 'land of the pure'.

The mountains, deserts, and oases of Central Asia

Starting from its Persian base, Islam likewise made spectacular progress in Central Asia, a region that had been known in Antiquity as *Transoxania*, the 'land on the far side of the Oxus'. With a total length of 2,400 kilometers, the Oxus, now called the Amu-Darya, is the longest river in Central Asia. Its sources are to be found in the high Pamirs, and on the way to its mouth, formerly in the Caspian Sea but now in Lake Aral, it flows between two deserts, the Kizil Kum or 'Red Sands' and the Kara Kum or 'Black Sands'. Its original name appears to have been *us(s)u*, 'arrow', a Mesopotamian and therefore Usko-Mediterranean term whose Greek cognate, oxus, meant 'fast'; the Oxus, then, was the 'fast river', the 'arrow', the river that was 'fast like an arrow'.

A synonym for Central Asia is "Turkestan", because that region – and not the modern state of Turkey – happens to be the cradle of the linguistic and ethnic family of the Turks. The language of this people is neither Semitic (like Arabic) nor Indo-European (like Iranian); it is a Finno-Ugric idiom, related – at least according to the Finno-Ugric theory – to Finnish and Hungarian. The original name of the Turks was *Türük*, the 'mighty people'. In the language of their Chinese neighbors, however, this sounded like *Tu-kue*, meaning 'helmet', and this somehow sparked a legend holding that the Turks owe their name to the supposedly helmet-shaped Altai Mountains of the Turkish heartland. In reality, *Altai* (*Altyn-Yish* in Turkish) means something very different, namely, 'golden mountains'. However, according to

Semerano, this oronym is not of Turkish but of Usko-Mediterranean origin; he considers it to be a cognate of the Akkadian *alitu*, 'height' or 'mountain'. People of Saharan origin, and therefore speakers of idioms that may be said to belong to the Usko-Mediterranean (or at least Dené-Caucasian) family of languages, did indeed migrate as far as Central Asia, and – as we now know – via the Bering Strait into the Americas, where the language of the Apaches, for example, belongs to the Dené-Caucasian family.[99] According to Semerano, the ethnonyms of the Huns, the Ainu, the aboriginals of Japan, and of the North-American Inuit or Eskimos, all share the same Usko-Mediterranean root referring to 'human beings'. And we have seen that this root, *inu* or *enu*, also hides in Rasenna, the auto-ethnonym of the Etruscans. It should therefore not come as a surprise that these migrants left onomastic tracks even in the far eastern reaches of the Eurasian land mass. Thus Siberia – *Sibir* in Russian – appears to be an Usko-Mediterranean name, meaning 'land of water' or 'land of rivers and/or lakes'. Semerano comes to this conclusion by noting the similarity with the Akkadian root *beru* or *buru*, 'well', 'pool', 'pond', or any 'body of water'. And in the name of the Siberian city of Omsk he claims to recognize a cognate of the Akkadian term *ammu*, 'swamp'.

In Turkish and Iranian, *stan* means 'land', and so *Turkestan* is the 'Land of the Turks'. This land is an enormous region, stretching from the shores of the Caspian Sea to the wilds of Mongolia. Today it comprises the territories of the states of Kazakhstan, Uzbekistan, Kirghizia (or Kyrgyzstan), and Turkmenistan, all of them inhabited predominantly by people of Turkic origin. The Uzbek people only originated at the end of the Middle Ages as an ethnic fusion of Turks, Iranians, and Mongols; the ethnonym *Uzbek* actually means the 'independent people'. As for Turkmenistan, that country received its name in the fifteenth century from non-Turkic neighbors, the Tajiks. Turkmenistan is a variant of *Türkmanand*, 'similar to Turks', and this name was inspired by the fact that its people are a slightly Mongolized European type, somewhat less Turkic than the Kirghizians and the Kazakhs. The inhabitants of Tajikistan, on the other hand, are of Iranian origin, and their Afghan neighbors call them *Parsivan*, 'Persian-speakers'. The Persian term *taj* means 'crown', and so the Tajiks are the 'crowned people'. (Incidentally, the term *taj* is also featured in Taj Mahal, the name of a world-famous monument in India, which means 'crown palace'.)

As in the Middle East, the landscape of Central Asia is characterized by mountain ranges, deserts, and oases, and at one time its population consisted primarily of nomads. It is therefore hardly surprising that here, too, the seeds of Mohammed's message fell onto fertile soil and so the Arab conquerors made good headway in spite of enormous distances that needed to be covered. The great cities of Samarkand and Bokhara were captured, and already in 715 CE Kashgar (or Kashi), today the westernmost city in China, was reached. The Chinese Empire itself was now within reach, war was inevitable, and in 751 the Arabs destroyed a Chinese army in a battle

---

[99] "The languages belonging to Dené-Caucasian are spoken from the Pyrenees to the Rockies" (Wells 2002: 171).

fought on the banks of the Talas River. The result was that Islam could penetrate deep into China, or at least deep into the western part of that gargantuan country.

That region, whose landscape also alternates between mountains and deserts, was known at one time as Chinese *Turkestan*, because it was, and is, inhabited predominantly by a Turkic people, the Uighurs. That ethnonym means 'union' or 'alliance', and it refers to a federation of eastern Turkic tribes. The heartland of the Uighurs is the Tarim Basin. In the very middle of this huge area stretches the great desert known as the Taklamakan. According to popular etymology, that name means something like "you can enter it, but you can never leave it"! It has also been argued - just about equally unconvincingly – that the toponym is an old Uighur word meaning 'vine', which would be an allusion to the fact that this area, or at least the edge of the desert, is very suitable for viticulture.

The Tarim Basin is surrounded by mountains, such as the Himalayas in the south. This oronym is of Indian origin; in Sanskrit, *hima alaja* means 'house of snow', 'snowy abode'. In 1865 the highest peak in that range, and in the entire world, received the name of the British Surveyor-General in India in the 1860s, Sir George Everest. And yet, there was no shortage of indigenous names. In ancient Sanskrit, for example, the mountain was called *Devgiri*, 'holy mountain', the Nepalese use another Sanskrit term, *Sagarmatha*, 'the head of the sky', and in Tibet they talk about *Chomolungma*, 'the mother of the universe'. Other mountain ranges in the same area include the Pamirs or 'cold steppe meadows' to the east of the Himalayas, and the Tien-Shan, the 'heavenly mountains', to the north. In the course of time, the oases of the Tarim witnessed the birth of a number of cities, for example, Urumqi, a toponym meaning 'beautiful meadow'. As for the Tien-Shan, in the fifteenth century those mountains became the birthplace of a people – a fusion of Indo-Europeans and Turkic-Mongolians – that we now know as the Kirghizians, and today they have a country of their own, Kyrgyzstan. Its territory consists mostly of steppe, so it is no coincidence that the name of the Kirghizians means simply 'inhabitants [*ghiz*] of the steppe [*kir*]'. Incidentally, the Chinese term for mountains, *shan*, encountered in Tien-Shan, may be recognized in toponyms such as the name of the Chinese province of Shandong (or Shantung), 'mountains of the east', and of the province of Shanxi, 'mountains of the west'.

In the Tarim Basin, the Chinese had to make room for the Arabs and for Islam, but later they were able to reconquer that part of Central Asia, and it was incorporated into the Chinese Empire as Xinjiang (or Sinkiang), 'new [*sin*] border province [*kiang*]'. Even so, the denizens of the region have remained predominantly Muslim until the present. The Islamization of the Chinese Far West happened at the expense of religions that had been at home there before, particularly Buddhism. Even today, surviving statues of the Buddha and ruins of pagodas in the surroundings of Kashgar and elsewhere in Xinjiang silently bear witness to the time, long ago, when Buddhism had untold devotees there. Not only the Uighurs converted en masse to Islam, but also their neighbors – and Turkic relatives – in that part of Asia, the Kazakhs, whose name means 'free people' in Old Turkish. Expert opinion is divided with respect to the question whether the ethnonyms "Kazakhs" and "Cossacks" share the same root or not; some etymologists are convinced that they do, while others believe the similarity is purely coincidental. Here is a comment offered by the French version of Wikipedia:

> The Kazakhs, a Turco-Mongol people of Central Asia, should not be confused with the Cossacks, who are essentially Slavic. However, the two names may have a common origin in the Turkish language (...) The Turkish term *qazaq* supposedly means 'free' or 'on the run'; it applies equally well to the Cossacks, who fled their original homeland in order to be able to live freely in the outlying areas of the Russian empire, as to the Kazakhs, an independent and nomadic people (*http://fr.wikipedia.org/wiki/Kazakhs*).

It was the Kazakhs who fabricated the name of Lake Aral. In their language, *aral* means 'island', and with this term they referred to that great but shallow interior sea because it featured thousands of little islands; Lake Aral, then, is the 'lake of islands'. However, it is also possible that the Kazakhs considered that big lake as a kind of "island" of water within the gigantic "sea of land" of Asia's interior. The land of the Kazakhs was never occupied by the Chinese, but it was eventually swallowed up by the Czarist Empire, and after the Russian Revolution it became a Soviet republic within the USSR. At present the Kazakhs have their own country, Kazakhstan, while in Sinkiang separatist Uighurs agitate, hitherto unsuccessfully, for an independent homeland; if that ever materializes, it will undoubtedly be called Uiguristan.

Beyond the World of Islam: China and its neighbors

In Central Asia, Islam developed deep roots among the Uighurs and Kazakhs, but not further east in *Mughulistan*, that is, in the land of the Mongols or 'brave people', ethnic relatives of the Turks. Instead, this nomadic people was to invade the Islamic Middle East a few times during the Middle Ages, dominate all of Central Asia for a while, and even threaten Christian Europe. On the other hand, some European Christians saw the Mongols as potential allies in the struggle against the "Mohammedan heresy", Islam.

Genghis Khan
(14th century CE representation by an unknown artist; source: Wikimedia Commons)

In the thirteenth century the Mongols produced a great leader, Genghis Khan. The meaning of his title, *Khan,* was exactly that, 'leader' or 'commander'; "Genghis Khan" signified 'General Khan', 'king', or even 'emperor' of all Mongols. He ruled from the "capital" of Mongolia, in reality not much more than a sprawling camp of tents, named Karakorum. *Kara* meant 'black', and *korum* was an ancient word of Mesopotamian origin; initially, it referred to a walled town, a citadel, but eventually it acquired the meaning of walled (or at least protected) 'trade center' or 'abode of merchants'.[100] In other words, *Karakorum* was the 'black trade center'. It was Genghis Khan who, in 1258, captured and laid waste to Baghdad, thus dealing a mortal blow to the once mighty Abbasid Caliphate. His grandson, Kublai Khan, also accomplished earth-shaking deeds, but in areas further east; under his leadership the Mongols invaded China, where they established the Yuan Dynasty. This Mongol Dynasty was to rule the Middle Kingdom between 1279 and 1368 from a new capital, Peking. "Peking" is the correct spelling according to the older Wade-Giles method of transcribing Chinese; today, however, the Pinyin method is preferred, and its spells the name of the capital as "Beijing". In any event the meaning is the same, namely, 'northern capital', in Mandarin. Peking/Beijing was indeed situated in the extreme north of the Chinese Empire at the time, as is illustrated by the fact that the Great Wall, which separated the Middle Kingdom from its boreal neighbors, can easily be visited from the Chinese capital on a day trip. The Far East features quite a few cities whose name means 'capital': Nanking is the China's 'southern capital'; Kyoto means 'capital of capitals', while Tokyo is the 'eastern capital' of Japan; and Seoul is the 'capital' of Korea.

The Mongols attacking Baghdad, 1258
(Artist: unknown; source: Bibliothèque Nationale de Paris via Wikimedia Commons)

---

[100] See e.g. Klinger (2007: 32) and Schwertheim (2005: 16-17). More on Karakorum can be found in Christian (1998: 418-19).

The Mongols called China *Cathay*, 'land of the Khatan [or Khitan]'. The Khatan were an ethnic relation of the Mongols, a tribe that held power in a swath of northern China in the tenth and eleventh centuries. It was at the time of the Mongol Yuan Dynasty that Marco Polo claimed to have traveled to the land of "Cathay" and to have actually visited the court of Kublai Khan (but see below). Later, at the end of the fourteenth century, the Mongols experienced yet another moment of glory under Timur the Lame, also known as Timur Lenk or Tamerlane, who selected the ancient city of Samarkand, in present-day Uzbekistan, as capital of his immense empire. That city had been known to the ancient Greeks as *Marakanda*. Its name, like other toponyms in Central and Far Eastern Asia, appears to be of Usko-Mediterranean origin; it contains the same root, *cant,* as in Cantabria, Kent, Ghent, etc.

The Registan, ancient centre of the city of Samarkand
(Photo: Steve Evans, 2005; source: Flickr via Wikimedia Commons)

At that time the Mongols, or at least those inhabiting that part of Central Asia, had already been Islamized and Arabized to a great extent, and it was a descendent of Timur, Babar, who shortly thereafter established the Islamic Mogul Empire in India. In predominantly Muslim Central Asia and in the Middle East, the sedentarization of the Mongol nomads was gradually but irrevocably accompanied by their Islamization. (In similar fashion, the sedentarization of the nomadic Slavs and Magyars in Europe went hand-in-hand with their conversion to Christianity, the dominant and indeed hegemonic religion that proved to be eminently functional in the pre-industrial, feudal society of Medieval Europe; it was not a coincidence that the end of feudalism and the Industrial Revolution would be accompanied in Europe by a considerable de-Christianization.)

The Mongols also made it all the way to Europe, where they raped and pillaged primarily in Russia. In Christendom, the Mongols also became known as the

"Tatars", a term that was originally only used to refer to a specific influential tribe within the great and heterogeneous Mongol family. King Louis IX of France, better known as Saint Louis, supposedly drew attention to the similarity of that ethnonym to the Greek word *tartaros,* 'underworld' or 'hell', and so the term "Tartars" became a synonym for the "hellish" Mongols in general. In the south of Russia, in the Volga Valley, a separate Mongol state emerged in the course of the thirteenth century, that is, after the death of Genghis Khan: the so-called Khanate of Kipchak. This entity became known in Europe as the Golden Horde, a name that is allegedly due to the fact that the Kipchak Khan resided in a gold-colored tent. Warriors of the Golden Horde constructed a fortress, a *kerim,* on a large and strategically important peninsula of the Black Sea that has been known ever since as the Crimea. The Crimean Tartars remained at home on that peninsula until Stalin, who suspected them of pro-German sympathy, had them deported to the interior of Asia during the Second World War.

To the east of the homeland of the Mongols lay the gigantic country that is called "China" by the rest of the world, but not by the Chinese themselves. In Mandarin, the leading language of that country, *guo* is the word for 'country'. Domestically, China has always been known as *Zhong Guo* (or *Chung Kuo* if one uses the Wade-Giles, rather than the Pinyin, method of transcription), and this means 'Land of the Middle', 'Middle Kingdom', 'Middle Empire'. As far as the Chinese themselves are concerned, their country is the land at the center of the world, the empire around which the rest of the world revolves.

Some of the many thousands of life-size figures in the Terracotta Army, dating from 210 BCE
(Photo: Maros, 2007; source: Wikimedia Commons)

The Chinese call themselves Han, meaning the 'humans', 'the people'. Han is the Chinese equivalent of *deutsch*, and China might well be called "Hanland", just as the land of the Germans is called *Deutschland*. However, there are millions of people in China who, in ethnic and linguistic respects, cannot be classified as Chinese, for example Mongols; in China, these are referred to as non-Han ethnic "minorities". Han, then, means something like 'Chinese people', but this name was also given to, and possibly deliberately adopted, by an important imperial dynasty, namely, the one that ruled from approximately 200 BCE until 200 CE. The Han Empire was a contemporary of the Roman Empire, and commercial and even diplomatic relations between the two were carried on via Central Asia as well as by sea. The very first dynasty to rule over all of China, however, was the immediate predecessor of the Han, namely, the Chin (or Qin) Dynasty, in power from 221 until 206 BCE. The so-called "First Emperor of Chin" (*Qin-Shihuang*) is generally regarded as the founder of the Chinese Empire; he was also the builder of the original Great Wall, symbol *par excellence* of the country. An idea of the power and wealth of that great ruler is conveyed even today by the thousands of terracotta soldiers and horses that were found in a mausoleum in the vicinity of the old imperial capital, Xian or Changan. It is most likely from *Changan* that the word *Xanadu* was derived, even though S T Coleridge, who used it in a poem he wrote in 1816, actually had in mind the abode of the Mongol Emperor Kublai Khan:

> *In Xanadu did Kubla Khan*
> *A stately pleasure dome decree:*
> *Where Alph, the sacred river, ran*
> *Through caverns measureless to man*
> *Down to a sunless sea.*

The fame of Changan – simultaneously a point of departure and arrival of the Silk Road – radiated far and wide, and thus the entire country became internationally known as the "Land of Chin", "China". In the Roman Empire, China was referred to as *Seres* or *Serica*, 'silk land', and Changan, as *Sera Metropolis*.[101] However, towards the end of the first century CE the term *Thina* surfaced in a travel account, the *Periplus Maris Erythraei*, and in the form of *China* this toponym gradually eclipsed all other names referring to the Middle Empire. A notable exception was provided in the late Middle Ages, when the term "Cathay" – *Cataya* in Latin – was temporarily fashionable and was used, for example, by Marco Polo. The reason for this was that the Mongol Khans of the Yuan Dynasty were in power in China during the thirteenth and fourteenth centuries. They had made it a habit to call China *Cathay*, as we have seen. The term *Cathay* was Mongolian in origin and was predestined to be fashionable only as long as the Mongols were on the move. When the Khans lost power in China in favor of an indigenous dynasty, China was soon called *China* once again in Europe, but in Mongolia itself, and also in Russia, a

---

[101] See chapter 4 for more information about this.

country that would be dominated by Mongols for a long time, China has been called *Kita* – in other words, *Cathay* – until the present.

In the ocean to the east of China, there lies an archipelago that has been inhabited since time immemorial by a people that is very different from the Chinese, namely, the Japanese. In the course of time, however, the latter have adopted a great deal of Chinese culture, including the name of their own country. To the inhabitants of the Middle Empire, this land was *Riben Guo*, the 'land of the rising sun'. The Japanese themselves took over this nomenclature and took to calling their country *Nihon* in their own language, a term of which *Nippon* is the more familiar modern version. This toponym combines the roots *ni,* 'sun', and *hon,* 'origin'. In the Japanese Kanji system of writing, which happens to be of Chinese origin, the word Nippon is represented by the same character as in Chinese and is thus legible also to the Chinese; but while the Japanese pronounce the word as *Nippon*, the Chinese read it as *Riben Guo*. According to some Sinologists, it is possible that this Chinese name for Japan also inspired the term that was popularized in Europe thanks mainly to Marco Polo: *Zipangu*, from which the familiar Western form *Japan* is supposed to be a descendent. Other Chinese language specialists, however, are of the opinion that the term *Japan* originated in a different manner. In the south of China, and particularly in the country's most important seaports, such as Guangzhou ("Canton"), the leading language is not Mandarin Chinese but Cantonese. In the latter language, the character for 'land of the rising sun' is pronounced as *Jihpen-Kuo* or *Jipang-Kuo,* and it is this term that Marco Polo allegedly turned into *Zipangu*. If it is correct, this etymology provides grist to the mill of supporters of the relatively recent theory which holds that Marco Polo was never in China at all, but gathered information about that country during a long stay in the Middle East, probably in Arab and Persian harbors that traded with Canton and distant China in general. Marco Polo claimed to have been a high-ranking functionary at the court of the Great Khan in Beijing, but this is highly questionable, if only because in order to become such a "mandarin", one had to pass exams that proved to be incredibly difficult even for the brightest Chinese. Furthermore, as a mandarin, Marco Polo would certainly not have picked up Cantonese, but rather Mandarin terminology, so he would have come to know Japan not as *Jipang-Kuo* but as *Riben Guo*. If – as it is now increasingly suspected – he gathered his information about Japan and China in Persian and/or Arab seaports, then such Chinese terms as he would have become familiar with would undoubtedly have been of the Cantonese rather than Mandarin variety since Arab trade with China had for centuries been primarily conducted at Guangzhou/Canton. (However, the *lingua franca* of the seaborne trade between the Middle East, India, and southern China at that time was not Cantonese but probably some form of Arabic, while earlier it may have been Malay (Baker 1996).

The suspicion that Marco Polo never personally visited China is also reinforced by the fact that in his travel account he never mentions the Great Wall. If he had lived in Beijing, as he said he did, then he would most certainly have become acquainted with this immense construction and would have mentioned it in his book; but if Cantonese sailors and merchants served as his sources, they would not have been able to tell him much, if anything at all, about a wall which, no matter how impressive, happened to be located far inland and played no role whatsoever in their busy lives. In defense of Marco Polo, however, it should be mentioned that some Sinologists consider it possible that *Zipangu* could have been derived from the Mandarin term *Riben Guo*, since we do not know how *Riben Guo* was pronounced at the time of Marco Polo, when in the great palace in Beijing the throne was occupied by a Mongol Khan.

The Great Wall of China
(Photo: Herbert Ponting, 1907; source: Wikimedia Commons)

7

The Saga of the Vikings

The Emigrants

In the ninth and tenth centuries, Western Europe was tormented by burly, blond barbarians who raided its coasts and river valleys, raping and pillaging and victimizing primarily the monasteries and churches where in those Dark Ages wealth happened to be concentrated. Those intruders arrived on speedy longships, also known as "drakkars", not only from the land now known as Norway but also from Denmark and Sweden, i.e., from the entire northern part of Europe where one thousand years ago the leading language was Old Norse, the linguistic ancestor of the modern Germanic tongues of these "Nordic" countries; because of that, they were all referred to as "Norsemen". In any event, their visits to Western Europe were inevitably accompanied by murder, rape, and plunder. Untiringly, the monks intoned a special litany: "from the fury of the Norsemen, oh Lord, deliver us"! But alas, their efforts proved utterly futile in the face of all this Nordic violence.

Viking dragon ship depicted on the Bayeux Tapestry
(Unknown artist; source: *www.ushistoryimages.com/viking-ships.shtm*)

In our history books, the Norsemen are also referred to as "Vikings". This is how they called themselves and is how they were known in their own homeland, where the bulk of the population subsisted on a primitive and therefore rather unproductive form of agriculture. The result was, as in Ancient Greece, a quasi-permanent form of overpopulation, whereby those who had no prospects at home opted to undertake raids in faraway countries. For this reason they were called "those who leave the homeland". The latter is indeed the meaning of "Viking", a term that reflects the ancient Germanic root *vik*, used as a suffix in numerous German, Dutch, and English toponyms such as "Greenwich". In other words, our Norsemen were the "emigrants", "those who left the village" in order to seek their fortune abroad, either temporarily, by raiding for loot, or permanently, by settling in foreign lands. In Western Europe they were mostly interested in raiding, but on the Atlantic coast of France, near the mouth of the Seine, they did in fact settle permanently. This region thus acquired the name Normandy, 'land of the Norsemen'. Its capital, however, the city of Rouen, located on the banks of the Seine just about half way between Paris and the English Channel, has a very ancient name of Usko-Mediterranean origin. In the Latin version of the name, *Ratomagus*, Semerano recognizes a combination of cognates of the Akkadian terms *ratum*, 'river', and *makanu*, 'dwelling place', giving us the meaning 'settlement on the river bank'.

Danes about to invade England
(Painting by an unknown artist thought to date from the 9th or 10th century CE; source: Wikimedia Commons)

The British Isles were also a favorite target for Viking raids, but here too a number of toponyms of Nordic origin indicate that Scandinavians occasionally settled down permanently. The name of the Irish capital, Dublin, for example, is derived from the Old Norse *Dubh Linn* (or *Lind*), meaning 'borough [in the original sense of fortified settlement] on the dark water'. (The Liffey River, which bisects Dublin, was evidently also a 'dark water', like the Thames is believed by some to be.) The archipelago of the Hebrides, situated to the west of Scotland, likewise owes its name to the Norsemen. The Old Norse term *Havbredey* signifies 'islands at the end of the sea', and this ancient toponym was already taken over by the Greeks and Romans of Antiquity; Ptolemy called this archipelago the *Hebudes*. As for the Faroes, these islands (*öer*) received their names from the Vikings who settled there in order to devote themselves to the uncharacteristically peaceful activity of sheep (*faer*) rearing.

The raids of the Vikings forced the feudal authorities of many regions to erect forts or "boroughs" in vulnerable or strategically important sites. The term *borough* and its French and Dutch/German cognates *bourg* and *burg* referred to virtually the same kind of forts or fortified towns the Celts had called *dunum*; the Romans had called them *oppidum*, but sometimes also *castellum*. A string of such *burgs* were thus founded by the Count of Flanders along the North Sea coast of his domain in the ninth century, including the town now known as Bruges or, to use the Flemish nomenclature, Brugge. This toponym has nothing to do with a bridge (*brug* in Flemish) as is often opined, but is simply the evolved version of *burg*, 'borough'. During the era of the Vikings, boroughs such as Bruges/Brugge likewise emerged throughout England, a historical fact that is reflected onomastically in the many toponyms ending with the suffix *borough*.

Norsemen landing in Iceland
(Artist: Oscar Werneland; source: Guerber [1909] via Wikimedia Commons)

In other parts of the world, where opportunities for plunder were limited or non-existent, permanent emigration sometimes turned out to be an interesting option to the Scandinavian adventurers. This was the case, for example, on the other side of the Atlantic Ocean. Vikings from present-day Norway had already started to explore the turbulent waters of the North Sea and the North Atlantic at an early stage. Thus they became acquainted with islands such as the Orkneys, and this knowledge had filtered down to the Romans, who called these islands the Orcades. This was a toponym of Usko-Mediterranean origin, meaning something akin to "high [*arku*] islands," probably an allusion to their location to the north of Scotland. The modern name is likely a combination of this ancient *arku* with the Norse *ey*, "island". In the ninth century, a large island was discovered further northwest; on account of its cold climate it was first called "snow land" (*Snjoland*) and then "Iceland" (*Island*). Although these names conjured up an inhospitable region, Vikings did settle down there, and in particular in a settlement that received the name Reykjavik, which meant "bay of smoke"; this was an allusion to the steam generated by the numerous volcanic hot-water springs that are to be found in that area. Thus a Scandinavian bridgehead emerged in the middle of the North Atlantic, a bridgehead from which further explorations could be undertaken in that boreal and icy part of the world.

Around the year 985, an expedition led by Erik the Red reached a huge island further to the west. The climate there revealed itself to be even more rigorous than in Iceland, but Erik imagined that he could entice pioneers to come to it by concocting the euphemistic name "Greenland". This, at least, is the conventional explanation for that most inappropriate of toponyms. However, an interesting and more plausible alternative is available. The name Greenland has nothing to do with the color green, but was inspired by Greek mythology and cosmography, or Ancient myth and geography in general, of which even the denizens of the northern lands must have heard echoes. The Atlantic Ocean was often associated by the Hellenes with Cronos, king of the Titans, the son of Gaia (the earth) and Uranus (the sky) and father of Zeus. The Atlantic was therefore also known to the Greeks as the 'sea of Cronos' or 'Cronian Sea'. The Romans knew Cronos as Saturn, but they too often referred to the Atlantic as *Mare Cronium*. In honor of this mythological figure, the Greeks also gave the name *Cronia* to an island in the northern part of the ocean. Perhaps this was a vague allusion to Iceland, but that island was later referred to by the Romans exclusively with the term *Thule*. The term *Cronia* thus shifted to denote other islands whose existence in the North Atlantic waters was suspected, and must therefore have come to mind for onomastic purposes when Erik the Red made his discovery; he may have even sincerely believed that he had arrived on the legendary 'island of Cronos'. In any event, Erik came up with the name *Cronland*. It was the clumsy translation of this Norse term into Medieval Latin, *Groenlandia,* that was to cause the fallacious but now familiar association with the color green.

**Statue of Leif Ericsson,
Trondheim, Norway**
(Source: *http://www.cksinfo.com/clipart/people/
famouspeople/explorers/leif-Ericson.png*)

Distant Vinland

A certain Bjarni Herjolfsson as well as the son of Erik the Red, Leif Ericsson, both attempted a leap from Greenland to areas even further west, and thus they were to make a landfall on the American continent around the year 1,000 CE, five centuries before Columbus. In the "New World", as one would say later, those brave Vikings discovered an inhospitable coastal region they called *Helluland*, that is, 'land of flat stones'. This was possibly Baffin Island or, more probably, the north of Labrador, a Canadian region that is part of the North American mainland. Labrador does indeed feature a coastal region with many big, flat stones that may well have been the *Helluland* of the Vikings.

L'Anse aux Meadows, site of a Viking settlement at the northern tip of Newfoundland
(Photo: Carib, 2002; source: Wikimedia Commons)

Somewhat less unattractive to the Norsemen, there loomed a low-lying coast bordered by forests in the south of Labrador that was called *Markland,* 'land of forests'. However, when they eventually founded a settlement, it was in yet another region, to which they gave the fascinating name "Vinland". Since that toponym suggests that it was a territory situated southerly enough to permit viticulture, it was long believed that Vinland was perhaps in Massachusetts, or even Virginia. (It was not really necessary to look that far south, because cultivation of the vine is possible quite a bit further north; today, wine is produced in the Canadian province of Nova Scotia.) However, it is now known with certainty that Vinland referred to the cold and rocky northern coast of the island of Newfoundland. On a site now known as L'Anse aux Meadows, archaeologists have indeed located the remains of a Viking settlement. In that northern latitude, there can admittedly be no question of viticulture, and yet it is certain that this site is the Vinland of a thousand years ago.

In reality, the prefix *vin* has nothing to do with wine, but is an Old Norse word for 'meadow', and even now in Norway there are more than one thousand toponyms in which *vin,* in the sense of 'meadow', appears. Vinland, then, means 'land of meadows'.

Such an appellation is plausible, because the Norse pioneers subsisted primarily by cattle rearing. Consequently, they were always and everywhere searching for meadows for their cows, which they took along on their boats. There are no meadows on Baffin Island or in Labrador, and this explains why no settlements arose there. After a long exploration through a world of rocks and forests, hostile to their cattle and therefore to themselves, the Vikings finally found what they were looking for on the island of Newfoundland, and so we can understand that they named that land after the green meadows their cows needed so desperately. Can it be a coincidence, also, that the modern half-French, half-English name of Vinland, L'Anse aux Meadows, means 'bay of meadows'?

The Vikings were unable to hang on to their Vinland for very long, probably no more than about ten years. Perhaps the meadows did not suffice in quantity or quality for their cattle. They also experienced serious problems with the indigenous population, pejoratively referred to by the Scandinavian colonists as *Skraelings,* which meant 'wild men', 'ugly people', or something to that effect. These *Skraelings* were the ancestors of the Beothuks, the natives whom the Europeans would later – around 1500 – encounter in Newfoundland, and whose name meant nothing other than 'people'. The Vinland Vikings probably also came into contact with Eskimos, a people that is now referred to in Canada by its auto-ethnonym, *Inuit,* also meaning 'people'; the term *Eskimo* – 'eaters of raw meat' – was a pejorative label the Europeans took over from the "Indian" neighbors of the Inuit. What name did the Skraelings give to the Vinland Vikings? The answer to that question is shrouded in a cloud thicker than Newfoundland fog.

Finally, it should be mentioned here that a large island named Vinland is depicted in the *Mare Oceanum,* to the west of Greenland, on the famous Vinland Map, a *mappa mundi* which also shows Europe, Africa, and Asia. This document first surfaced in 1957 and is now preserved at Yale University. It supposedly dates back to the 15th century, but its authenticity is disputed. If it is indeed authentic, it would be the first map to display a part of the New World.

In the land of the Rus

The Norsemen also tried their luck in the east. To them, this meant the other side of the Baltic Sea, and the Vikings who were involved in this Herculean enterprise were predominantly Swedes. Sweden – *Sverige* in Swedish – is a modern state that was formed by the union of the aforementioned Gothic inhabitants of the island of Gotland and the southern Swedish province now known as *Götaland,* with the tribe of the *Svear* in the Swedish interior; the result was the 'kingdom of the Swedes', *Svea-Rike, Sverige* for short.

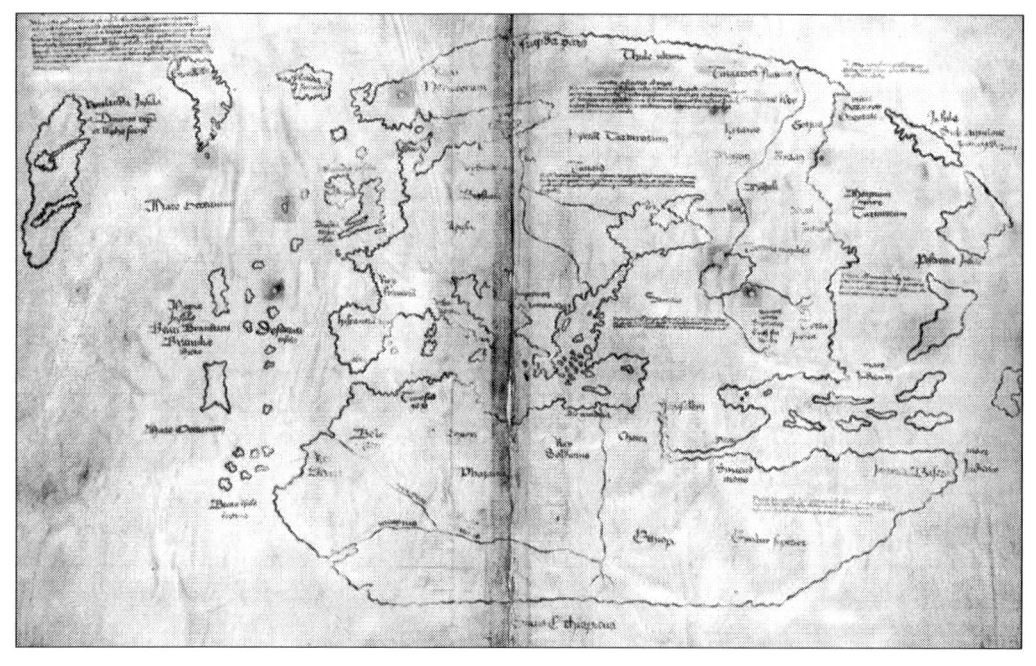

The Vinland Map
(Source: Yale University Press via Wikimedia Commons)

The Swedes arrived in Eastern Europe with their famous drakkars, equipped with one single mast up which a great sail was hoisted if the wind came from the right direction; if the latter was not the case, the crew would row. *Rodr* was the Old Norse word for this tough kind of labor, and the Swedish Vikings therefore called themselves the *Rodsmenn*, the 'rowers'. This term soon became *Ruotsi* on the other side of the Baltic Sea, in the supposedly Finno-Ugric language of the ancestors of the modern Finns, Estonians, and other "Finnic" peoples who had already lived there for thousands of years and continue to represent the great majority of the population there in spite of the immigration of Slavic tribes. Even today, Sweden is called *Ruotsalein*, 'land of the rowers', in Finnish and Estonian. *Rodr, Rodsmenn, Ruotsi*: this nomenclature was to produce the ethnonym *Rus*, "Russian", and the toponym "Russia". A gigantic European region – known in Antiquity as *Scythia* and/or *Sarmatia* – was thus saddled with the name, or rather the nickname, of a people that was not really from there, but that was predestined to play a very important role in its history.

An alternative etymology is offered by the German linguist Heinrich Kunstmann. He postulates a historical migration of Illyrians from the Dalmatian coast to the interior of Eastern Europe, whereby the term *Rus* arose as a corruption of the name of the town of origin of the migrants, Ragusa or Rausa, today known as Dubrovnik. A very similar south-north migration by inhabitants of the Illyrian town of Apollonia, colloquially known as *Opolini*, allegedly produced the nomenclature "Poles" and "Poland" (Kunstmann 1996 144-45, 199 ff.). The conventional view is that *Poland* is derived from the Slav *pole*, 'field' or 'plain', so that the Poles are the 'inhabitants of the plains'. Semerano believes in a much older origin; he suggests that the name contains an Usko-Mediterranean root related to the Akkadian *palasu* and the Latin *palus*, 'marsh'. Its meaning would therefore be 'land of marshes', an allusion to the Masurian lakes and other ponds and marshes that are sprinkled liberally across the Polish plain. Incidentally, the name of the city of Gdansk – Danzig in German – is alleged to be a combination of *gada*, 'bank', and *onna* or *ayn*, 'water', and therefore means something like 'settlement on the waterfront' or 'city on the river bank'. As for the land between Poland and Russia, now known as Lithuania, its name is no mystery, at least as far as Semerano is concerned. He sees it as a combination of Usko-Mediterranean terms related to the Akkadian words *litum*, 'land', and *agu*, 'water', meaning something like 'waterland'. The fact that the basin of the River Niemen and its countless tributaries accounts for more than 70 percent of the total surface of that country, strengthens the credibility of Semerano's hypothesis.

The Swedish Vikings did not reconnoiter the other side of the Baltic Sea for their pleasure, but rather to do business. They were attracted by the lure of interesting products that were to be found there and for which a great demand existed in the homeland of the Vikings as well as in foreign markets. As examples we can cite furs, honey, beeswax (used by the monks of Christian Europe to manufacture candles), and of course also amber, a commodity that had already mesmerized the Ancient Greeks. Furthermore, our rowers soon learned that via the great rivers that intersect Russia's huge land mass, one could go trading as far as the distant shores of the Black and Caspian Seas, where spices and all sorts of other exotic oriental goods were offered for sale by Arab, Persian, Turkish, and Byzantine merchants. An important trade route – a Medieval version of the Amber Road of Antiquity – thus developed between Scandinavia and the Baltic Sea on the one side, and the Black, Caspian, and even Mediterranean seas on the other. Some Vikings undertook that long voyage from the Baltic to Constantinople and then returned to their Nordic homeland, while others settled permanently in emporia they themselves founded along that trade route; they were predestined to be assimilated in the course of time, by the indigenous Finno-Ugric, Baltic, or Slavic populations.

In the Norsemen's own country, a settlement was usually surrounded by a kind of palisade, and was therefore known in their Germanic language as a *gardr* or *gaard*, a root that survives in English terms such as 'garden' and 'orchard', both originally referring to an enclosed area. Numerous emporia were founded by the Swedish Vikings between the Baltic and the Black seas, and these would later develop into important Russian cities, thus received a name ending with *gardr* or *gaard*. This suffix produced the Slavic word *gorod*, meaning 'city'. The land on the other side of the Baltic Sea was soon teeming with settlements, so much so that the area became known as *Gardariki*, the 'region of cities'. Just as the Phoenicians and the Greeks had earlier founded a *Kart Hadasht* and a *Neapolis*, the Vikings also boasted a "new city" in their trans-Baltic "New World", namely, Novgorod. Ironically, Novgorod is today regarded as the oldest city in Russia. Originally, that settlement of Swedish "rowers" was situated on an island in the Volkhov river, and was therefore also known as *Holmgard*, 'island city', or also simply as *Gardar*, '*the* city'. As the settlement increased in importance, thus outgrowing the island, it was transferred to the river's bank and was henceforth referred to as *Novgorod*, the 'new city'. This name spread far and wide; on a Venetian map of the fifteenth century, it is shown in an Italian version, as *Nuovo Grado*.

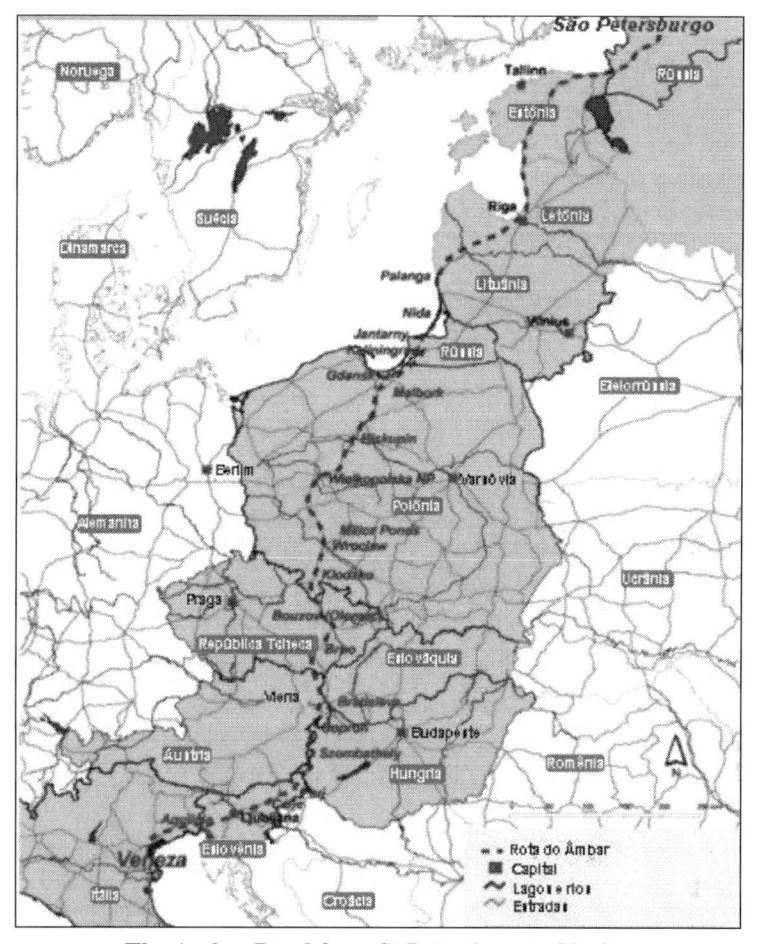

The Amber Road from St Petersburg to Venice
(Adapted from *Bild* Bernsteinstrasse by Bonas, 2006; source: Wikimedia Commons)

The Swedes also adopted many existing local toponyms of Finnic, Baltic, and Slavic origin. The other side of the Gulf of Bothnia, for example, was the homeland of the Finns, a non-Indo-European, so-called Finno-Ugric people whose land was called the *Finnmark*, in other words, the 'Finn border land'. This region, where many Swedish emigrants settled, was later to be known as Finland. The ethnonym *Finn* is supposed to mean 'inhabitants of the marshes', 'denizens of the fens'. But as in the case of that other Finno-Ugric people, the Magyars, some experts postulate Usko-Mediterranean antecedents and/or connections of the Finns with the Semitic Middle East. Semerano is convinced that the ethnonym *Finns* contains the same Usko-Mediterranean root as the Old Irish *fine*, 'tribe', the Akkadian *bin(n)u*, 'son' or 'descendent', and the Hebrew *bene*, 'people'. And he identifies the Finnish auto-ethnonym, *Suomi*, as a cognate of the Babylonian terms *samhu*, 'league', and *summuhu*, 'being united by an oath'. Helsinki is supposed to contain a root related to the Akkadian *halsu*, 'fortress'. As for Finland's Nomads, the Lapps, the name by which they are universally known – in reality a hetero-ethnonym – conjures up for Semerano the Usko-Mediterranean term *lab(i)u*, 'to roam'. In other words, the Lapps are the 'roamers', the 'nomads'. He also maintains that their auto-ethnonym, *Sahme*, means 'people' (*sabu[m]*) living near the 'water' (*me* or *mu*).

Sweden and Finland are separated by the Bothnian Gulf. To the inhabitants of these countries, this was not the "upper" part, as we would see things, but the "lower" part, the "bottom", of the Baltic Sea, and that is the meaning of that hydronym. Archaic peoples were indeed inclined to view the south as "above" and the north as "below", and it is not very long ago that cartographers placed the south on top and the north at the bottom of their maps. The southern shores of the Gulf of Finland is where the *Eistir* lived, another Finno-Ugric people whose homeland is known as *Eistland*, "Estland". A specific tribe of the Estonians was referred to as the *Refalir* and their foremost settlement was *Revala* or *Reval*, a name that was to be used until well into the twentieth century, primarily by the Germans, as a synonym for Tallinn, now the capital of Estonia. The name *Tallinn* originated in 1219, when Danish crusaders invaded the land of the pagan Estonians and built a castle they called *Tanlinn*, 'borough of the Danes'. It is during this campaign that a red flag with a white cross is supposed to have descended from the heavens; this flag, the *Danebrog*, is Denmark's national emblem and is reputed to be the oldest national flag in the world.

Varangians in the Imperial City

In the interior of Eastern Europe, the Vikings came into contact with people of Slavic origin. It is not known what these natives called themselves but, as already mentioned, they gradually acquired the nickname of the Scandinavian immigrants themselves and became known as the "Rus". The immense territory of these people, known in Antiquity as Scythia and/or Sarmatia, was henceforth known as "Russia". The Swedes were interested primarily in the most important trade route between the Baltic and the Black seas, the route that led via the Dnieper river valley to Constantinople and was called by them *Austvegr*, the 'eastern road'. Novgorod constituted the northern terminus of this road, and another important Viking emporium could be found at its halfway point, *Koenugard* or 'boat city'; in the Slavic language of the indigenous population, Old Russian, this became *Kijangorod*, which would develop into *Kiev*. Novgorod was the center of a region known as the 'northern Rus', and Kiev that of the 'southern Rus'.

Via the Dnieper, the Vikings reached the Black Sea, and hence they followed the Bosporus to the southernmost terminus of the *Austvegr*, Constantinople. The metropolis of the Byzantine Empire was then – around the year 1,000 – by far the greatest, wealthiest, and most beautiful city in Europe. The Vikings called this city *Tsargard*, the 'imperial city', or *Miklagard*, the 'great city' – a virtually literal translation of the colloquial Greek name, *Istanpoli*, '*the* city'. They were known there as "Varangians", an appellation that contained the old Germanic root *war,* meaning 'oath'. The Varangians were 'fellows of the oath' because they undertook long and dangerous voyages collectively, in groups of adventurers who had solemnly sworn to assist, and be loyal to, each other. Semerano, however, disagrees with this conventional etymology and suggests instead that this ethnonym contains an Usko-Mediterranean root related to the Akkadian *(w)arahu*, 'to attack', so that the original meaning of the term *Varangians* was the 'aggressors'. He also views *Rus* as a cognate of the Semitic term *rasu* or *ros*, 'head' or 'chieftain', claiming that this term was originally used in the Middle East to describe the Scythian inhabitants of the Pontic steppes.

Varangian guards ca. 1100
(Skylitzis Chronicle of ca. 1100; source: Wikipedia Commons)

In Constantinople, the men from the north did wonderful business in markets teeming with spices and other exotic goods they could resell in their homeland and elsewhere in Europe for good money; their example continues to be followed even today by Russian and Polish entrepreneurs who flock to Istanbul's Grand Bazaar to buy all sorts of goods. Particularly big, strong, and brave Vikings could also find employment in the bodyguard of the Byzantine emperors, who happened not to trust their own people and preferred to surround themselves with Norse mercenaries. On the walls of the great Aya Sophia Church, members of this "Varangian Guard" scribbled notes in their typical Runic writing, and many of these graffiti are still there today. As far as the Byzantines were concerned, the distant north or northeast of Europe was the land of the Varangians, and the Baltic Sea was known to them as the Varangian Sea.

The most important product traded by the Vikings, not only to the Byzantine Empire, but also to their own homeland, to the rest of Europe, and to the markets of the Middle East, were not the familiar fruits of the boreal forests – furs, wax, and honey – but slaves, as the British historian Perry Anderson (1996) has emphasized in his masterful study of the transition from Antiquity to the Middle Ages. Serving as slaves were people kidnapped by the Norsemen just about everywhere in the immense interior of Eastern Europe, where the majority of the population consisted of Slavs. In the Roman Empire, slaves – *servi* in Latin – could be either white or black, and had all sorts of ethnic and linguistic backgrounds; the famous Spartacus, for example, was a Thracian. However, when in the tenth century the Vikings came to monopolize the slave trade, virtually all unfree people came from Eastern Europe, and henceforth slaves were without exception members of the Slavic group within the Indo-European ethnic/linguistic family. And so it happened that a cognate of the word *sclavus*, originally referring to ethnic Slavs, gradually replaced the Latin *servus* or its cognates in virtually all European languages. On account of the Vikings, the slaves were henceforth Slavs.

Novgorod
(Unknown artist in Rambaud's Russia, 1898; source: Wikimedia Commons)

From their base in Novgorod, Swedish Vikings also followed another, more easterly road, which saw them descend the Volga all the way to where the waters of that great river entered the Caspian Sea. The Caspian is not really a sea, but rather a huge lake; we say "sea" because we follow the example of the Ancient Greeks, who believed that they were dealing with an inlet of the (northern) ocean, a kind of distant eastern version of the Mediterranean Sea. The Caspian Sea owed the adjective in its name to the tribes that called its shores home. The Hellenes called it the "Hyrcanian Sea", because to the east of it, in modern Turkmenistan, stretched the homeland of the Hyrcanian people, but it was the Romans who began to speak of the *Mare Caspium*. In doing so, they had in mind the *Caspii*, a people that lived to the west of the Caspian Sea and were neighbors of the more familiar Scythians. However, nothing is known about such a people, and perhaps they simply never existed. Semerano explains the Caspian hydronym in very different terms, and in doing so he relies, as usual, on his thorough knowledge of the most important of ancient Mesopotamian languages, Akkadian. The name *Kaspion* originally referred not to the eponymous sea but to the mountains of the Caucasus. This oronym combined *qas*, 'chain', with *(ap)pu*, '[mountain] peak', and therefore meant simply 'mountain range'. But in the course of time this term started to refer to the sea – or rather, the huge lake – to the east of those mountains, and so the oronym became a hydronym. For the mountains, a new name simultaneously emerged, namely "Caucasus". This term combines *kapu*, 'cliffs' or '[steep] mountains', with *kasu*, 'cold'. The Caucasus are the 'Cold Mountains'.

"Guests from overseas" (Varangian traders far from home)
(Artist: Nicholas Roerich, 1899; source: Wikimedia Commons)

On the banks of the Volga and the Caspian Sea, the Vikings could also trade to their hearts' content with merchants who enjoyed connections with distant China. In other words, the Norsemen were able to exploit the opportunities offered by access to the ancient Silk Road. Was that perhaps the reason why they called that region *Serkland*, a mysterious name believed by some to mean 'silk land'? Another possibility, however, is that this was the Norse version of 'Saracen land', a name that alluded to the fact that the local population consisted primarily of Muslims. In Constantinople, the Vikings may well have co-opted the Byzantine nomenclature *Sarakenos*, itself a derivation from the Arabic *sharqiyin*, 'easterners'. (In Arabic, *sharq* means 'east', 'land of the rising sun'. This root is almost certainly ensconced in the name of the present president of the French Republic, *Sarkozy*, which would therefore mean 'the oriental'. Also, can it be a coincidence that of the Channel Islands the most easterly is called Sark?) When using the term *Saracens*, the Greeks had in mind 'people from the land of the rising sun', more specifically, the Muslim inhabitants of the Levantine coast, Syria, and the rest of the Middle East. It is in this sense that the term would later be used to refer to the opponents of the Crusaders. On their way to the "Holy Land", the latter paused in Constantinople, and there they probably became acquainted – as the Vikings had done before them – with Byzantine names for people that had hitherto been unknown to them. The Crusades were a conflict between the Cross and the Crescent, between denizens of the 'land of the setting sun' and the 'land of the rising sun', between "the west" and "the east".

Between Baghdad and Baltic

The Vikings were eminently familiar with Russia's great river, the Volga, and one of their most important emporia in *Serkland* could be found there, namely, Astrakhan. In Turkish, and also in Iranian, the term *khan* refers to a place where merchants can trade and/or find accommodations; such a place is also known as a caravanserai. The toponym "Astrakhan" denoted a trading post where no duties had to be paid, in other words, a "free trade" market. As for the Volga itself, Semerano claims that its name contains the ancient Usko-Mediterranean root *peleg*, referring to water, and means simply 'the water', or 'the great water'. *Volga*, then, is a cognate of the Greek *pelagos,* 'sea', the Latin terms *Belgae* and *Belgica*, and also of the name of the river that flows through Novgorod, the *Volkhov*. But the name *Volga* is also a cognate of *Bulgarians*, the ethnonym of a people whose ancestors, the so-called "Volga-" or "Proto-Bulgarians", inhabited the Volga Valley approximately 1,500 years ago. The meaning of Bulgarians is therefore 'people living near the [great] water' or, more specifically, 'people living on the banks of the Volga'; the name of their ancient capital, known as Bulgar and situated in the vicinity of modern Kazan, may be interpreted as 'city near the water' or 'city on the Volga'. Around 700 CE, however, the bulk of the Bulgarians migrated from their homeland to a region on the European shores of the Black Sea, just south of the Danube, that bears their name today. In spite of a major migration, then, they continued to honor their name, 'people living near the water'.

A view of Astrakhan
(Unknown artist in Rambaud's Russia, 1898; source: Wikimedia Commons)

By the time the Norsemen made their appearance in the Volga Valley, the Proto-Bulgarians had been replaced there by the Khazars, another Turkic people. The Khazars developed a reputation of being shrewd merchants, who engaged in business with the Christian Byzantines as well as with the Muslim Arabs. Determined to avoid falling under the influence of either of those, they deliberately adopted Judaism as their religion in or around the year 838. When they became trading partners of the Vikings, some Khazars transferred to Eastern Europe in order to do business in Kiev, Minsk, Pskov, and Novgorod. It is claimed by some that this is how the first Jewish communities originated in Russia, in other words, that the Eastern European Jews, the *Ashkenazim*, are descendants of the Khazars. However, this theory is undermined by the fact that genetic tests point to a close affinity between Ashkenazi and Sephardic Jews. According to their own tradition, the Ashkenazi are the descendants of Ashkenaz, a grandchild of Noah, but because during the Middle Ages the Ashkenazi settled mainly in Germany and took to speaking their own version of German, Yiddish ('Jewish'), the term Ashkenazi now means something akin to 'German Jew'. The language of the Sephardic Jews, on the other hand, is Ladino, which is said to resemble Castilian Spanish as it was spoken during the Middle Ages.

Via the Dnieper Route and Constantinople as well as via the Volga Route and Astrakhan, the Vikings also traded with the Arab world, which in the meantime had been united, at least in theory, under the auspices of the Abbasid Caliphate. The Varangians thus also surfaced in the city that functioned as the capital of the Arab world, Baghdad, the fabulous metropolis of the *Thousand and One Nights*. Conversely, Arab merchants undertook occasional voyages to the distant land that was called *Al Rus* in Arabic. Not only the denizens of Baghdad but also those of Andalusian centers such as Cordoba were familiar with the Vikings and had at least some knowledge of their northern homeland. The Arabs called the Baltic Sea *Bahr Warank*, the 'Varangian Sea', much as the Byzantines did, and they were also acquainted with the term Scandinavia, *Sqandiya*. Around 1140, in Palermo, the Arab geographer Al-Idrisi produced a world map for the Norman King of Sicily, Roger II; it revealed distant lands such as *Astalanda,* Estonia, with the capital Tallinn cited as *Qoluwany,* which happened to be the Arab version of the city's Russian name, *Kolivan*.

After the year 1100, the curtain descended rather suddenly on the great Varangian adventure. After a long "Dark Age", Western Europe had finally come to life again economically, politically, and – last but certainly not least – militarily, and its denizens launched the so-called Crusades against the Middle East. This proved an opportunity for Italian seaports, such as Amalfi, Pisa, Genoa, and above all Venice, to develop profitable trade relations with Asia. The main branches of the Silk Road were soon diverted from the Land of the Rus to the partner cities of the Italians; foremost among those were Alexandria, virtually monopolized by Venetian merchants, and Constantinople, where the primacy of the Genoans was externalized by the Galata Tower, an architectural phallic symbol that still dominates the cityscape on the other side of the Golden Horn. Henceforth, fewer and fewer caravans of camels burdened with bags of spices and silk from China headed for the emporia of the once attractive *Austvegr* of the Varangians. In addition, the latter soon found themselves under pressure even in their own Baltic bailiwick. Indeed, from the Germanic heartland a push to the east – the *Drang nach Osten* movement – was gaining momentum, a northern European version of the Crusades. The Teutonic Knights and other German crusaders and colonists penetrated into the Baltic world, conquering land and converting its pagan inhabitants or else exterminating them; they also cut off the road that connected Sweden to the Black and Caspian Seas. The Nordic world was mercilessly marginalized and pushed onto the defensive. Eventually it was to be integrated into the dynamic new Western European system itself, as was signaled by the conversion to Christianity of the once proudly pagan Vikings.

The Galata Tower, constructed in 1348, as it was in the late 19th century
(Photo: J Pascal Sebah, ca. 1870; source: Cornell University Library via Wikimedia Commons)

The Mediterranean Sea – the geographic link between Western Europe, Africa, and the Middle East – was again the center of the world, as it had already been in Antiquity. It would remain that way until approximately 1500, when the great discoveries of Columbus and other Italians, Spaniards, and Portuguese inaugurated the Atlantic Era. By then, however, the Vikings had long retreated from the stage of world history, and in Western and Southern Europe not a soul was aware that brave Nordic adventurers had already alighted on the other side of the Atlantic Ocean five centuries earlier.

CONCLUSION

Archaic Usko-Mediterranean and Indo-European names

This study has focused on the familiar historical heartlands of the Old World, namely, the Middle East, North Africa, India, China, and of course Europe. We have seen that in those areas the names of peoples, countries, mountains, rivers, lakes, and seas constitute a kind of onomastic jetsam that was left behind on the beach of our modern languages by the waves of migrations witnessed in the Old World since the earliest of times. Many of these names – e.g. "Iberia", "Italy", and "Europe" – are extremely ancient and, particularly in the case of Europe, much older than we have been inclined to assume. Furthermore, these names have meanings that we are able to uncover. For that purpose, however, the Greek and Latin etymological dictionaries recommended by the learned champions of Indo-Europeanism are of little or no value. The reason for this is that we are dealing with names that originated long before the arrival – presumably in the course of the second millennium BCE – of the Indo-Europeans, or at least of the emergence of the Indo-European languages. They were already hundreds or even thousands of years old when the Greeks and the Romans, the great heroes of the "Aryan Model" of historiography, alighted on the stage of history.

In order to unveil the secrets of onomastic fossils dating back to the depths of (pre)history, and buried beneath the dust of time, we called upon the so-called Sahara Hypothesis. This new, daring, and even somewhat provocative theory suggests that the oldest names in the Middle East, in North Africa, and even in the far reaches of Asia, including Siberia, as well as in Europe, must be credited to the onomastic account of people who had emerged from the area that is now the Sahara, where they had given rise to one or more of the first Neolithic cultures. Those people spoke some form or other of the pre-Indo-European "substrate language" that has been referred to in this study as "Usko-Mediterranean". They were responsible for the emergence of the great civilizations in the Nile Valley and in Mesopotamia, and they populated Europe and the islands of the Mediterranean Sea long before the rise of the Indo-European languages, an event that is still shrouded in mystery and may or may not have been caused by the arrival, very likely from India, of Indo-European-speaking migrants. With the aid of the "Rosetta Stone" provided by the knowledge of extinct as well as extant Usko-Mediterranean and related Afro-Asiatic languages, for example Sumerian and Akkadian, linguists such as Giovanni Semerano have succeeded in offering *plausible* etymologies for numerous ancient ethno- and toponyms, and their findings were incorporated into this historical study. To be sure, plausibility is not the same as certainty; however, it does imply a considerable degree of explanatory power and persuasiveness, based on linguistic and/or historical arguments. It is up to each individual reader to evaluate the explanatory power of the etymologies that have been offered here.

The Usko-Mediterranean peoples who played leading parts in this tale – Egyptians, Babylonians, Harappans, Phoenicians, Palaeo-Berbers, Etruscans and other "Pelasgians", Iberians, Illyrians, Celts, etc. – were not primitive barbarians, but demonstrated without exception a relatively high level of development, or of civilization. But of course their cultures were "archaic" cultures, and their ways of acting and thinking differed radically from our modern mentality and way of life. That archaic way of thinking and acting was reflected in the names they gave to themselves, to their land, and to rivers, mountains and other prominent features of their environment.

Those names revealed themselves as elementary but meaningful. Each archaic people considered itself, and therefore called itself, *the* people. Sometimes a touch of nuance was added to this elementary nomenclature, for example when a population proudly referred to itself as the "pure", "real", "true", "brave", "wise", or "free" people. So it was in the case of the Usko-Mediterranean nations. We have seen, for example, that the original meaning of "Berbers" was very likely 'humans' or 'people'. And the Basques still call themselves *Euzkadi*, a term that means something like the 'pure' or 'real' (*usko*) people. The same primordial nomenclature was – and continues to be – used by distant relatives of the Berbers and the Basques within the great Dené-Caucasian language family, e.g. by certain native groups in North America, such as the Apaches; these call themselves *Dené*, which also means 'human beings' or 'people'. "People", in the sense of '*the* people' or '*our* people', is likewise the meaning of auto-ethnonyms such as "Huns", "Inuit" (the people we know better as "Eskimos"), and the "Han" of the Chinese.

Archaic people, and not just speakers of Usko-Mediterranean languages, identified humans in general with the earth, and identified their own people with its own piece of the earth, with its own land. The people were children of "Mother Earth", they consisted of "earth" – or "dust", or "clay" – and they were predestined to return upon their death to the earth from which they had sprung, to the earth that had given them life in the first place. It is no coincidence that in many languages the words for "human" and "earth" appear to share the same root. The great expert on ancient myths and religions, Mircea Eliade, for example, has drawn attention to the affinity between the Latin terms *homo* and *humus*, 'human' and 'earth'. Each individual came from "Mother Earth" and consisted of "earth", and in the same manner each (sedentary) archaic people identified with its "earth", that is, with the land it called home. That is why we speak of the "motherland" or, alternatively, the "fatherland". Is it not a wonderful twist of etymology that the name of the continent where humans originated, Africa, from whose "earth" all members of the homo sapiens family have sprung, harbors the same Semitic, Usko-Mediterranean root *afar*, which in the Bible refers to the "earth", "dust", or "clay" God used to create human beings?

The peoples who called themselves "the people" did not have any need to concoct extravagant names for their land. The land where they lived was simply referred to as "the land". This is nicely illustrated by an anecdote from the life of Captain James Cook. When that famous explorer arrived on an isolated island of the Pacific Ocean, he asked the inhabitants what the name of their island was. Cook took down the answer, *tanna*, and that is why "Tanna" is printed next to a little dot on maps of the Pacific. The meaning of *tanna*, however, was nothing other than 'earth' or 'land' (Collingridge 2003: 301). Like the denizens of Tanna, numerous other "primitive" or "archaic" peoples called themselves "the people" and their land "the land", and their contemporary descendants continue to do so, albeit often unconsciously. Few Germans, for instance, realize that *Deutschland* means 'the land of the people', that is, 'the land of *our* people'. 'Land of the/our people' also appears to have been the original meaning of the term used already thousands of years ago by the Usko-Mediterranean inhabitants of Spain to refer to their land; we may not know exactly what this name was, but it has come to us via the Greeks as *Iberia*. The "Iberians" were an Usko-Mediterranean people, close relatives of the inhabitants of North Africa known as Berbers. It is remarkable that the same kind of etymological connection appears to exist between the ethnonym "Berber" and the toponym "Iberia" as between Latin *homo* and *humus*. In this context we recall the case of the auto-ethnonym *Etruscans*, in which the Usko-Mediterranean root *etr* or *atr*, 'land', hides, and which means 'owners of the land'. The Latin name of that people was *Tusci*, as in *Tuscany*, and that ethnonym also denotes a combination of the people and its land: 'inhabitants of the land'. Another variation on the same theme is provided by the name 'rulers/lords of the land', which is the meaning of the auto-ethnonym of the Etruscans, *Rasenna*, and of the ethnonyms Hittites, Scythians, Sarmatians, and Sards. Names denoting ownership of land obviously implied a sedentary lifestyle. Conversely, nomadic people identified themselves, and were also seen by others, as 'lords of the road', which happens to be the meaning of the names of peoples with a nomadic past, if not present, such as the Huns, the Magyars, the Lapps, and the Gypsies.

That a people simply called its land "the land" should not be attributed solely to the archaic *Weltanschauung* with its human-land dialectic. One also has to keep in mind that sedentary archaic people lived in a relatively restricted physical environment and rarely traveled to the lands of other people. Their land was not merely that; it was their world. Consequently, like the inhabitants of Tanna, they had limited onomastic needs. Not only were they themselves *the* people and their land *the* land, but their city – if they had one – was *the* city. We have seen that in the time of the Roman Empire the Basques called their cities *irun* or *ilun*, 'the city', which happens to be the meaning of the names of the town of *Irun* on the Spanish-French border and of *Iruña*, as Pamplona is referred to in the Basque tongue. The city of

Athens was commonly referred to by its citizens as *astu*, undoubtedly a "Pelasgian", that is, Usko-Mediterranean term, and a cognate of the Akkadian *asitu*, 'city'. *Astu* served as the binary alternative to *chora*, the Attic 'countryside' around Athens. As for denizens of the immense Roman Empire, to them Rome was and always remained *urbs*, 'the city', and it was as 'the city', *istanpoli*, that Constantinople was referred to colloquially by the Byzantine Greeks. And let us not forget that the Egyptians also used to call the metropolis of Thebes *Waset*, 'the most important city', or just *Niut*, 'the city'.

In the land of the Celtic, and therefore probably at least partially Usko-Mediterranean Gauls, the much more modest towns were usually situated on top of some hill; such a settlement was known as a *dunum*, and today some towns are still called exactly that, *dunum*, but in an evolved form such as *Dun, Thun,* and *Daun*. When communications improved – probably already before the arrival of the Romans – and people became familiar with more than one *dunum*, it became necessary to introduce some nuance in this nomenclature; in the case of Lyon, for example, the name of the Gallic version of the god Mercury, *Lug*, was added to *dunum*. Sometimes *dunum* similarly received a prefix (or suffix), sometimes a Roman one, as in the case of *Augustodunum*, Autun. As a result, there are today in Europe alone hundreds of names of towns that include *dunum* in some form or another. Finally, it is worth noting that in many countries people often colloquially refer to the nearest city, whatever its official name, simply as "the city" or "town"; when people from the country go shopping, for example, they will typically talk about "going into town," rather than to, say, Chicago.

As it was in the case of cities, so it was with rivers. Archaic peoples felt no need to give the river that crisscrossed their land a more elaborate name than 'the water', the 'river', or perhaps 'the fast-flowing water', 'the mighty river', or 'the river of rivers'. The nineteenth-century onomastician Isaac Taylor offers an interesting remark in this respect:

> At a time when no great intercommunication existed, and when books and maps were unknown, geographical knowledge must have been very slender. Hence whole tribes were acquainted with only one considerable river, and it sufficed, therefore, to call it "The Water", or "The River". Such terms were not at first regarded as proper names; in many cases they only became proper names on the advent of a conquering race (Taylor 1893: 131).

We have seen that in the ancient Usko-Mediterranean languages the key word for "water" was *ayn* or *onna*, originally meaning "liquid," and related to the Greek *oinos*, the Latin *vinum,* and the English *wine*. The names of rivers such as the Indus, the Inn, and the many other European hydronyms in which *ayn* or *onna* are hidden, signify nothing other than 'the water'. If the ancient hydronyms that have been mentioned did in fact often display a little more nuance, it was because the Usko-Mediterranean peoples who had fled the arid Sahara understandably considered water something of vital importance, so that they developed a rainbow of terms to denote it, reflecting sometimes very great but also sometimes very subtle differences. (In analogous fashion, the Arabic language has numerous words meaning "camel".) The Nile attracted Saharan refugees like a magnet, and how could they possibly have referred to that great river by any name other than that of the phenomenon which revealed itself as the *sine qua non* of Pharaonic civilization, namely, its wondrous annual flooding? The "Nile" is indeed "the flood". Of great importance, also, was the difference between fast-flowing and slow rivers. The names of the Rhine and many other Rhins and Renos denoted fast-flowing water. Names such as "Loire" on the other hand, were an onomastic reflection of the slowness, shallowness, and muddiness of certain rivers. There were also many "mighty waters", hence the numerous hydronyms featuring *dan*, for example Jordan and its tributary, the Dan, Danube, Don, Dnieper, as well as *Rhodanus* and *Padanus*, the Latin names of the Rhône and the Po. We have also seen that some rivers were referred to as the "sacred water", which happens to be the meaning of the names of the Seine and the Saône. Finally, rivers might be associated with the mountain or mountain range where their sources were situated; such a combination was denoted by the Usko-Mediterranean root *alb*, the onomastic nucleus of Germany's Elbe River.

And so we have broached the topic of oronyms. In this respect, too, archaic nomenclature was elementary: the mountain situated in the land of the people was called nothing other than "the mountain". The typical Usko-Mediterranean term for such mountains was the very same *alb* that we already encountered in numerous hydronyms; "the Alps" are simply 'the mountains'. Another word for mountain was *wasu*, recognizable in the oronym Vesuvius and in the names of a couple of French towns situated on top of a hill, Vesoul and Vézelay. Mountains or mountain ranges could also be known as "the peaks", and we can recognize cognates of the Akkadian *appu* and the Celtic *penno* – a combination of *appu* plus *onna?* – meaning 'tip' or 'peak', in names such as Pennines, Apennines, and Pennine Alps. Finally, while a river could receive a name that also conjured up the mountain from which it descended, as in the case of the Elbe, mountains were sometimes given names that denoted the waters that flowed, or sprang, from their flanks; an example is the Mont Ventoux, a name in which we recognize the same *vindu*, 'water', as in Venice.

The names of peoples, countries, cities, and rivers were simple, but not trite. They reflected essential, even primordial, elements in the lives of archaic people: the people in the sense of *our* people; the land that was the motherland; the waters of the familiar river, lake, or sea; and the mountains where life-giving waters rose and which often marked the limit of the people's land, its world. The people's language was also of primordial importance. One identified not only with the land, the motherland, but also with the language, the mother tongue, and this found its onomastic reflection in terms such as *Shkupetar* (Albanians) and Arabs, auto-ethnonyms meaning 'those who speak an intelligible language', 'those who speak *our* language'.

Archaic exonyms – names given to other peoples and lands – also tended to refer to elementary things such as language and land. Other peoples spoke other, un-intelligible tongues; such people were 'those who cannot speak', 'those who cannot speak intelligibly', 'the dumb'. We have seen that this is the meaning of the exonym used by the Berbers to refer to the inhabitants of sub-Saharan West Africa, *Iguinawen*, a term from which "Guinea" has descended. The Slavic name for "Germans" – *Nemesti, Nemec* or *Nymiec* – also means 'the dumb'. The ancient Germans themselves used a term with a very similar meaning, *welsch*, when they had in mind their Gallic and, later, their French or Italian neighbors whose idiom came across to them as an unintelligible babble.

Mircea Eliade emphasizes the fact that an archaic people typically considered its land as the center of the world. This view crystallized onomastically in nomenclature such as the Chinese name for China, *Zhong Guo*, 'Middle Kingdom', 'the empire at the center of the world'. It followed that other peoples did not live in the center, but on the periphery, of the world. They lived, for example, in that distant land beyond the eastern horizon where the sun rises, 'the land of the rising sun'. This is what the Chinese called Japan, and their nomenclature was eventually adopted by the Japanese themselves. The same 'land of the rising sun' was also the meaning of toponyms such as *Anatolia, Asia, Levant*, and possibly even of the term *Serica*, used by the Romans to refer to China. An alternative marginal region inhabited by other peoples was the west, 'the land of the setting sun'. This was the meaning of the Mesopotamian term *ereb* from which *Europe* has descended, of the "Pelasgian" root *atalu* that has given us *Italy*, and very likely also of the *Rebu* or *Lebu* – *Libya* – of the ancient Egyptians.

As the sun rises in the morning and sets in the evening, east and west were each associated with "their" time of the day; eastern and western regions thus also became known as 'land of the morning' and 'land of the evening', at least in languages such as German, which uses the nomenclature *Morgenland* and *Abendland*. In analogous fashion, regions to the south, where the sun may be seen at noon, were referred to as "noon". In France the south has always been known as *le Midi*, in Italy they say *il Mezzogiorno*, and in Brussels the railway station in the southern district of the city is called the *Gare du Midi*. The most crucial geographical direction, however, was the east, because this is where the sun rises, the sun that was regarded as the source of all life. The west, on the other hand, where the sun sets and life daily comes to an end, was the region of darkness and death, the locus of the underworld. More particularly, the western waters – those of the Atlantic Ocean – that swallow the sun each evening were associated with darkness and death; the Atlantic Ocean was therefore known to the Romans, the Arabs, and many other peoples as the Sea of Darkness. (The early Christians keenly understood all this and consequently ar-ranged to point churches to the east, i.e., "oriented" them; entering a church from the west and moving eastward to the altar, worshippers symbolically left the darkness and approached the light, the light of the "true faith".)

If they considered the east as the primary direction, then for archaic peoples the south was not only 'noon', it was also 'the right', and this is how Yemen, an Arab toponym meaning exactly that, acquired its name. (Conversely, the north was 'the left'; some etymologists do indeed believe that this is the original meaning of this term.)[102] The south was also the direction where the sun reached its zenith each day – at least in the northern hemisphere – and was consequently "above", while the north was perceived to be "below". The Gulf of Bothnia was called the 'lower gulf' because the Nordic peoples considered it to be the lower part of the Baltic Sea and not the upper, as we now see things.

In order to identify peoples, one could also connect them onomastically with a striking feature of their land, for example, the presence of a large body of water, a great river, a lake, or a sea. Numerous archaic ethnic groups were thus known as 'people of the coast', 'people living near the sea', or 'people of the river bank'. As examples of peoples with this name we can cite the Phoenicians, the Ligurians, the Celtic *Belgae* of the Low Countries as well as those of the south of England, and the many *Veneti* of Antiquity, not only those of the Adriatic Sea but also of Brittany, of Lake Konstanz, and of the shores of the Baltic Sea. Places were likewise onomastically defined in terms of their relation to water, an element of paramount importance in the minds of the migrants who had fled their North African homeland, doomed to be become one of the world's greatest deserts; hence the multiplicity of toponyms containing an Usko-Mediterranean root referring to water or land near water. A prime example is *iber,* meaning 'land surrounded by water', 'peninsula', 'land in contrast to water', 'mainland [as opposed to the sea and/or islands]', or 'town on the meander of a river'. This is the root of Iberia, Epirus, *Iveriu* (Ireland), Britain, Brittany (and its Breton version, *Breizh*), Bern, Brno, Verona, Verdun, and many others. Semerano concludes that "hydrological circumstances tended to define toponyms and ethnonyms as well as hydronyms" (1984: 487).

In the course of the second millennium BCE, Indo-European languages made their apperance in the Old World, as a result of either migrations or, perhaps, of a westward diffusion of the Sanskrit language of ancient India. In any event, those languages were predestined to displace or assimilate the Usko-Mediterranean substrate, at least in the largest part of Europe and in Persia. The speakers of Persian, Greek, Latin etc. were henceforth the lords of the land, and everywhere they distributed new names. However, these names reflected the archaic mentality as much as the existing Usko-Mediterranean topo- and ethnonyms. The land was henceforth "their" land, the land of their people, of the new and supposedly "noble" (because that is widely assumed to be the meaning of "Aryan") *Herrenvolk*. Even the modern versions of the names that were introduced long ago to legitimate the Indo-European conquests speak volumes: *Iran*, for example, is (supposedly) the 'land of the Aryans'; *Deutschland* means 'land of the [i.e., our] people'; and the auto-ethnonym *Slavs* may be translated as 'those who speak our language'. Conversely, the speakers of Usko-Mediterranean languages were robbed, perhaps of their land but certainly of their language. (The Basques, incidentally, managed to retain their language, and now they reclaim their land; the acronym of their independence group ETA stands for *Euzkadi Ta Askatasuna*, 'Basque land and freedom'.) Numerous names of "Pelasgian" peoples and lands were thus irrevocably lost. On the other

---

[102] See *http://www.etymonline.com/index.php?term=north.*

hand, in Egyptian sources, for example, names have been preserved of Usko-Mediterranean peoples whose identities are unknown.

Countless Usko-Mediterranean names have come to us because they were not obliterated by the triumph of the Indo-European languages. *Rome, Italy, Africa, Europe,* and *Asia*, for example, were existing Pelasgian terms that slipped into Greek and Latin and thus managed to survive. Countless Usko-Mediterranean topo- and ethnonyms became immortal because they were "Indo-Europeanized". But his fact also created an etymological problem: in the course of time – and certainly after the obliteration of most of the Usko-Mediterranean languages – those names would become familiar, but people no longer had the slightest idea of their meaning. The Greeks solved this problem, at least to their own satisfaction, by concocting all sort of myths according to which gods and heroes had bequeathed their names to peoples and countries. Famous examples of such "eponymous" characters are Hellen, the alleged ancestor of the Hellenes; Byzas, the legendary founder of Byzantium; the Lydian prince, Tyrsos, to whom the Etruscans owed their Hellenic name ("Tyrsenians" or "Tyrrhenians"); and the Phoenician princess Europa, abducted by Zeus and taken to the land of the setting sun. In much the same way, the Romans convinced themselves that their city bore the name of a heroic founder, Romulus.

Both the Greeks and the Romans believed that they recognized familiar words in enigmatic Usko-Mediterranean names, and so they drew interesting though totally erroneous conclusions. (Of the Greeks, Semerano writes that they were "the most imaginative interpreters of toponyms and ethnonyms" [1984: 551].) The *iver* in the ancient name of Ireland, *Iveriu*, for example, irresistibly evoked the Latin *hibernum*, 'winter', and this is how Ireland was saddled with the hopelessly inappropriate name *Hibernia*, 'winterland'. And in the Berber name of the West-African river Niger, the Romans believed, equally fallaciously, that they recognized the Latin *niger*, 'black'. Ever since the emergence in the nineteenth century of the "Aryan model" of linguistics and history, the champions of Indo-Europeanism have been similarly seeking to identify Indo-European-sounding roots in names that are in reality of Usko-Mediterranean origin. The cases come to mind of the Elbe and the Alps, the supposedly "white" river and "white" mountains.

The speakers of Indo-European languages adopted, or preserved, countless Usko-Mediterranean names. Sometimes they understood their meaning, at least initially, but in many, and possibly most cases, they simply never had a clue what they meant. The Romans took over the "Pelasgian" label for the Hellenes, "Greeks", from the Etruscans, and in Gaul they adopted the exonym used by the local Celts to refer to their eastern neighbors, "Germans". They were very likely unaware that these were pejorative terms, both meaning 'enemies' or 'hostile' or 'unfriendly people'. With very few exceptions, the speakers of Usko-Mediterranean languages have vanished from the stage of history, and even the memory of these peoples was almost entirely lost. However, of their presence and importance in a distant past, untold names of peoples, countries, rivers, and mountains have continued, even in our own time, to bear onomastic witness. It is an irony of history that the rather pejorative names they once gave to the speakers of Indo-European languages have survived in the latters' very own languages.

The undercoat of Usko-Mediterranean ethno-, topo-, hydro-, and oronyms was largely, but not entirely, covered up with an uneven layer of Indo-European onomastic paint as a result of migrations, conquests, infiltrations and cultural/linguistic diffusions that continued for hundreds and even thousands of years. Among the speakers of Indo-European languages, the Greeks played an important onomastic role, not only on account of their colonial activities, whereby numerous new cities such as *Neapolis* were founded, but also due to the conquests of Alexander the Great and the accompanying "Hellenization" of much of the Middle East. It was then, for example, that many "Alexandrias" were founded and that *Kemit* definitively became known, Greek-style, as "Egypt".

After the Greeks, the Romans turned the Mediterranean Sea into a *mare nostrum*, and the creation of their immense empire went hand-in-hand not only with the bestowing of Latin names onto Gallic *dunums* and the Latinization of other Usko-Mediterranean ethno- and toponyms, but also with the foundation of cities whose names were intended to honor Pompey, Caesar, Augustus, and other generals, emperors, and members of the imperial family. After the implosion of the *Imperium Romanum,* migrants and conquerors kept coming and going, leaving behind names throughout the Old World. Most active in this sense were the Germanic "barbarians", who gave us names such as *France, Burgundy*, and *Lombardy*. Then more "outsiders" appeared on the scene, such as the Slavs and the Magyars, who in their own fashion re-baptized the lands and cities, rivers and mountains of Eastern Europe. We should not forget to mention the Vikings, of course. Those Nordic "emigrants" went to work onomastically on the British Isles, in "Normandy", in the "Russian" northeastern reaches of Europe and, if only for a moment, even on the other side of the Atlantic Ocean, but the time was not yet ripe for a full-scale European onomastic adventure overseas. Finally, we must also cite the Arabs, a Semitic people and therefore in some way an Usko-Mediterranean exception to the general rule of the Indo-European onomastic offensive of which the Old World had been a witness since the second millennium BCE. The Arabs went on a name-giving spree all the way to the depths of Central Asia, but within Europe they concentrated on the Iberian southwest, and this resulted in toponyms and hydronyms such as *Gibraltar* and *Guadalquivir.*

Collectively, the names of peoples, countries, cities, rivers, mountains, and seas of the Old World are the result of an original settlement by Usko-Mediterranean peoples, whose *Urheimat* was the Sahara, followed by a couple of millennia of migrations and/or military or cultural conquests by speakers of Indo-European languages, migrations and/or conquests that had probably originated in India. Within the "Old World", then, Europe was for thousands of years the target of demic, military, cultural, and linguistic "offensives" launched from the depths of Africa and Asia. These offensives petered out around the year 1,000 CE, and it is at that moment in history that we have concluded this study. However, it was around the year 1,000 in Western Europe, the westernmost corner of that western peninsula of the great Eurasian land mass, that a socio-economic and political development began which would thoroughly transform not only Europe itself but the entire world. And that development would have major onomastic implications.

Western European feudalism revealed itself to be pregnant with the embryo of capitalism, which was predestined to become the "world system" it so obviously is today. The year 1,000 CE, or thereabouts, turned out to be a dramatic turning point of history. Western Europe ceased to be the scene of the coming and going of outsiders. Instead, the European west – or simply "the West", as one would later say – would begin to export its system, first to the marginal regions of Europe, and then, during the era of the so-called "Great Discoveries", to the other side of the Atlantic, to Asia, Africa, and Oceania. Western Europe would explore, conquer, and recreate the whole world in its own image, to its own advantage, and to the disadvantage of the great majority of the indigenous populations. In order to legitimate all this, and at the same time also to help consolidate its worldwide hegemony, Western Europe would wipe out countless indigenous topo- and ethnonyms, and would distribute (Western-) European names everywhere, or almost everywhere, in the world. That issue will hopefully be the focus of another historico-onomastic study, similar to this one.

BIBLIOGRAPHY

Abalain, Hervé 2000 *Les noms de lieux Bretons*, n.pl.
Allières, Jacques 2003 *Les Basques*, Paris, 7th edition.
Alonso, Jorge [n d] *Tartesos*, Madrid, 4th edition.
Anderson, Perry 1996 *Passages from Antiquity to Feudalism*, London & New York.
Arnáiz-Villena, Antonio (ed.) 2000 *Prehistoric Iberia: Genetics, Anthropology, and Linguistics*, New York.
Arnáiz-Villena, Antonio & Alonso García, Jorge 1999 *Minoicos, Cretenses y Vascos, un studio genético y lingüístico*, Madrid.
—— & —— 2000 *Egipcios, Bereberes, Guanches y Vascos*, Madrid.
—— & —— 2001 *Caucásicos, Turcos, Mesopotámicos y Vascos*, Madrid.
Arnáiz-Villena, A, Gomez-Casado, E & Martinez-Laso, J 2002 Population genetic relationships between Mediterranean populations determined by HLA allele distribution and a historic perspective. *Tissue Antigens* 60 (2): 111-21, August 2002.
Attwood, Bain (ed.) 1996 *In the Age of Mabo: History, Aborigines and Australia*, St Leonards, NSW.
Aubet, Maria Eugenia 1993 *The Phoenicians and the West: Politics, Colonies and Trade*, Cambridge.
Bäbler, Balbina 1998 *Fleissige Thrakerinnen und wehrhafte Skythen: Nichtgriechen im klassischen Athen und ihre archäologische Hinterlassenschaft*, Stuttgart & Leipzig.
Bahlow, Hans 1965 *Deutschlands geographische Namenwelt: Etymologisches Lexikon der Fluß- und Ortsnamen alteuropäischer Herkunft*, Frankfurt am Main.
Baker, Philip 1996 The potential for the development of Arabic-based and other contact languages along the maritime trade routes between the Middle East and China, from the start of the Christian era. Wurm, S A, Mühlhäusler, P & Tryon, D T (eds) *Atlas of languages of intercultural communication in the Pacific, Asia, and the Americas*, Berlin: de Gruyter, pp 637-72 and Maps.
Bendala, Manuel 2000 *Tartesios, iberos y celtas: Pueblos, culturas y colonizadores de la Hispania antigua*, Madrid.
Benecke, Norbert 1994 *Der Mensch und seine Haustiere: Die Geschichte einer jahr-tausendealten Beziehung*, Stuttgart.
Bengtson, John D 1994 Edward Sapir and the 'Sino-Dene' Hypothesis. *Anthropological Science* 102: 207-30; on line at *http://www.nostratic.ru/books/(219)bengtson%20-%20sapir.pdf*.
Berger, Dieter 1993 *Geografische Namen in Deutschland: Herkunft und Bedeutung der Namen von Ländern, Städten, Bergen und Gewässern*, Mannheim.
Bernal, Martin [1987] 1996 *Black Athena: The Afroasiatic Roots of Classical Civilization*, New Brunswick, NJ, 2 vols.
Blackie, C 1887 *A Dictionary of Place-Names Giving Their Derivations*, London, 3rd edition.
Blake, Emma & Knapp, A Bernard (eds) 2005 *The Archaeology of Mediterranean Prehistory*, Malden, MA.
Bottéro, Jean 1998 *La plus vieille religion: en Mésopotamie*, Paris.
Braccesi, Lorenzo 2003 *I Greci delle periferie: Dal Danubio all'Atlantico*, Rome & Bari.
Braudel, Fernand [1949] 1990 *La Méditerranée et le monde méditerranéen à l'époque de Philippe II*, Paris, 3 vols, 9th edition.
—— 1986 *L'identité de la France*, Paris, 3 vols.
Brewer's Dictionary of Phrase & Fable 1996 London, 15th edition.
Briggs, Helen 2006 Ancient humans "followed rains", *BBC News*, July 21, 2006, *http://news.bbc.co.uk/go/pr/fr/-/2/hi/science/nature/5192410.stm*
Burkert, Walter 2004 *Babylon – Memphis – Persepolis: Eastern Contexts of Greek Culture*, Cambridge & London.
Cameron, Kenneth 1996 *English Place Names*, London, new edition.
Carroll, Maureen 2001 *Romans, Celts & Germans: The German Provinces of Rome*, Stroud, UK & Charleston, SC.

Castleden, Rodney 2005 *Mycenaeans*, London & New York.
Catherine, Lucas 2001 *Ik wist niet dat de wereld zo klein was: Reisverslagen van een eerste globalisering*, Berchem [Antwerp].
—— 2002 *Palestina: de laatste kolonie?*, Berchem [Antwerp].
Cavalli-Sforza, Luca & Francesco 1994 *Qui sommes-nous? Une histoire de la diversité humaine*, Paris.
Charton, Edouard (ed.) 1860-61 *Le tour du monde. Nouveau journal des voyages publié sous la direction de M. Edouard Charton et illustré par nos plus célèbres artistes*, Paris, 4 vols.
Choukourov, Charif & Roustam 1994 *Peuples d'Asie centrale*, Paris.
Christian, David 1998 *A History of Russia, Central Asia and Mongolia. Volume I: Inner Eurasia from Prehistory to the Mongol Empire*, Malden, MA.
Collis, John 2003 *The Celts: Origins, Myths & Inventions*, Stroud, UK.
Collingridge, Vanessa [2002] 2003 *Captain Cook: The Life, Death and Legacy of History's Greatest Explorer*, London.
Daniélou, Alain 2003 *A Brief History of India*, Rochester, VT.
Danino, Michel 2006 *L'Inde et l'invasion de nulle part: le dernier repaire du mythe aryen*, Paris.
Daraki, Maria 1994 *Dionysos et la déesse terre*, Paris.
Davis, Kenneth C 1992 *Don't know much about Geography*, New York.
Decret, François 1998 *L'Afrique du Nord dans l'Antiquité: Histoire et civilisations des origines au Ve siècle*, Paris.
Demandt, Alexander [1998] 2005 *Die Kelten*, Munich.
Deroy, Louis & Mulon, Maryanne 1992 *Dictionnaire de noms de lieux*, Paris.
Dihle, Albrecht 1994 *Die Griechen und die Fremden*, Munich.
Ekwall, Eilert 1928 *English River-Names*, Oxford.
Eliade, Mircea [1952] 1980 *Images et Symboles: Essais sur le symbolisme magico-religieux*, Paris.
—— 1965 *Le sacré et le profane*, Paris.
Eridanos, the River of Ancient Athens 2000 Athens.
Etienne, R, Müller, C & Prost, F 2000 *Archéologie historique de la Grèce antique*, Paris.
Evans, Arthur 1921 *The Palace at Minos*. London.
Fage, J D 1995 *A History of Africa*, London & New York, 3rd edition.
Feo, Giovann 2001 *Prima degli Etruschi: I Miti della Grande Dea e dei Giganti alle origini della civiltà in Italia*, Viterbo.
Finkelstein, Israel & Silberman, Neil Asher 2005 *Keine Posaunen vor Jericho: Die archäolog-ische Wahrheit über die Bibel*, Munich, 2nd edition.
Finley, M I [1954] 2002 *The World of Odysseus*, New York.
Frau, Sergio 2002 *Le Colonne d'Ercole: Come, quando e perché la Frontiera di Herakles/Milqart dell'Occidente slittò per sempre a Gibilterra*, Rome.
Frisk, Hjalmar 1960 *Griechisches Etymologisches Wörterbuch*, Heidelberg.
Gates, Charles 2003 *Ancient Cities. The Archaeology of Urban Life in the Ancient Near East and Egypt, Greece, and Rome*, London & New York.
Giebel, Marion 2006 *Reisen in der Antike*, Düsseldorf & Zurich.
Glover, T R 1959 *De Antieke Wereld*, Utrecht & Antwerp.
Gomez Espelosin, F Javier, Perez Largacha, A & Vallejo Girves, M 1995 *La Imagen de España en la Antigüedad Clasica*, Madrid.
Graf, David F 1996 The Roman East from the Chinese Perspective. *Les Annales Archéologiques Arabes Syriennes: Revue d'Archéologie et d'Histoire*, vol. XLII, 199-216.
Grant, Michael 1988 *The Ancient Mediterranean*, New York.
Graves, Robert 1999 *The White Goddess: A Historical Grammar of Poetic Myth*, Manchester.
Griffith, Brian 2001 *The Gardens of Their Dreams: Desertification and Culture in World History*, London & New York.
Guerber, Hélène Adeline 1909 *Myths of the Norsemen from the Eddas and Sagas*. London: Harrap.
Guide Vert: Provence 2002.
Guilaine, Jean 2000 *Premiers paysans du monde: Naissance des agricultures*, Paris.
—— 2003 *De la vague à la tombe: La conquête néolithique de la Méditerranée (8000-2000 avant J.-C.)*, Paris.
Gwin, Peter 2008 Lost Tribes of the Green Sahara: How a dinosaur hunter uncovered the Sahara's strangest Stone Age graveyard. *National Geographic*, September 2008, 126-43.
Haarmann, Harald 2002 *Lexikon der untergegangenen Sprachen*, Munich.

Hagan, Helene E. 2000 *The Shining Ones: An etymological essay on the Amazigh roots of Egyptian civilization.* n.pl.: self-published.

Hoyland, Robert G 2001 *Arabia and the Arabs: From the Bronze Age to the coming of Islam*, London & New York.

Hugoniot, Christophe 2000 *Rome en Afrique: de la chute de Carthage aux débuts de la conquête arabe*, Paris.

Jacques, Edwin 1995 *The Albanians: An Ethnic History from Prehistoric Times to the Present*, Jefferson, NC.

Jobling, M A, Hurles, M, & Tyler-Smith, C 2004 *Human Evolutionary Genetics: Origins, Peoples & Disease*, New York.

Kazanas, Nicholas 2005 Anatolian Bull and Vedic Horse, *http://www.omilosmeleton.gr/pdf/en/indology/AbVh.pdf.*

Khazanov, Anatoly M 1994 *Nomads and the Outside World*, Madison, WI, 2nd edition.

Kiernan, V G 1972 *The Lords of Human Kind: European Attitudes to the Outside World in the Imperial Age*, Harmondsworth.

Kirsch, Jonathan 2004 *God against the Gods: The History of the War Between Monotheism and Polytheism*, New York.

Klinger, Jörg 2007 *Die Hethiter*, Munich.

Knobloch, Johann 1995 Zum Geheimnamen Roms, Ofisch, M & Zinko, C (eds), *Studia Onomastica et Indogermanica: Festschrift für Fritz Lochner von Hüttenbach zum 65. Geburtstag,* Graz.

Kohlmeyer, Kay, *et al.* 1991 *Wiederentstehendes Babylon. Eine antike Weltstadt im Blick des Forschung.* Berlin

Krahe, Hans 1964 *Unsere ältesten Flussnahmen*, Wiesbaden.

Kuhn, Thomas 1962 *The Structure of Scientific Revolutions*, Chicago.

Kunstmann, Heinrich 1996 *Die Slaven: Ihr Name, ihre Wanderung nach Europa und die Anfänge der russischen Geschichte in historisch-onomastischer Sicht*, Stuttgart.

Kuper, Rudolph & Kröpelin, Stefan 2006 Climate-Controlled Holocene Occupation in the Sahara: Motor of Africa's Evolution, *Science*, vol. 313, August 11, 2006, 803-07.

Lal, B B 2005 Some thoughts on the home of the Indo-European languages and culture, Tripathi, D N (ed.), pp 54-61.

Lanfranchi, Pierluigi 2004 *I barbari: Da invasori a padri d'Europa*, Florence & Milan.

Le Bon, Auguste 1884 *La civilisation des Arabes.* Paris.

Leeming, David 2004 *Jealous Gods and Chosen People: The Mythology of the Middle East*, Oxford.

Lhote, Henri 1973 *The Search for the Tassili Frescoes: The story of the prehistoric rock-paintings of the Sahara,* London, 2nd edition.

Locquin, Marcel, with Zartarian, Vahé 2002 *Quelle langue parlaient nos ancêtres préhistoriques?*, Paris.

Lombard, Pierre 1991 Du rythme naturel au rythme humain: vie et mort d'une technique traditionelle, le *qanat*. Cauvin, M-C (ed.) *Rites et rythmes agraires*, Lyon & Paris, pp. 119-26.

Losique, Serge 1971 *Dictionnaire Etymologique des Noms de Pays et de Peuples*, Paris.

Lot, Ferdinand 1961 *The End of the Ancient World and the Beginnings of the Middle Ages*, New York.

MacDonald, R. (ed.) 2001 *The Encyclopedia of Mammals*, Oxford.

Magnani, Stefano 2003 *Geografia storica del mondo antico*, Bologna.

Maier, Bernhard 2004 *Kleines Lexikon der Namen und Wörter keltischen Ursprungs*, Munich, 2nd edition.

Mallory, J P 1991 *In Search of the Indo-Europeans: Language, Archaeology and Myth*, New York.

Man, John 1999 *Atlas of the Year 1000*, Glasgow.

Markale, Jean 1993 *The Celts: Uncovering the Mythic and Historic Origins of Western Culture*, Rochester, VT.

Markey, Sean 2006 Exodus From Drying Sahara Gave Rise to Pharaohs, Study Says, *National Geographic News,* July 20, 2006.

Matvejević, Predrag [1993] 2000 *Mediterraneano: Un nuovo breviario*, n.pl. 5th edition.

—— 1998 *Il Mediterraneano e l'Europe: Lezioni al Collège de France*, Milan.

McEvedy, Colin 1967 *The Penguin Atlas of Ancient History*, London.

McKenna, Terence 1992 *Food of the Gods: The Search for the Original Tree of Knowledge. A Radical History of Plants, Drugs and Human Evolution*, London.

Melnikova, E A 1996 *The Eastern World of the Vikings: Eight Essays about Scandinavia and Eastern Europe in the early Middle Ages*, Gothenburg.

Menghin, Wilfried (ed.) 1997 *Die Franken: Wegbereiter Europes, 5.-8. Jahrhundert – Les Francs: précurseurs de l'Europe, Ve – VIIIe siècle*, Berlin.
Miserey, Yves 2008 Comment le Sahara est devenu un désert, *Le Figaro*, le 14 mai 2008.
Morgan, David 1990 *The Mongols*, Cambridge, MA & Oxford.
Morvan, Michel 1996 *Les origines linguistiques du basque,* Bordeaux.
Moscati, Sabatino 1997 *Les Phéniciens*, Paris.
Murger, Henri 1851 *Scènes de la vie bohème,* Paris.
Nagaswamy, R 1993 The Dravidian Problem: Epigraphic Sources, Deo, S B & Kamath, Suryanath (eds.), *The Aryan Problem*, Pune, pp. 84-85.
Nagy, Sandor 1973 *The Forgotten Cradle of the Hungarian Culture.* Toronto.
Nantet, Bernard 1998 *L'invention du désert: Archéologie au Sahara*, Paris.
Nissen, Hans J 1999 *Geschichte Alt-Vorderasiens*, Munich.
Otero, Edgardo D 2004 *El origen de los nombres de los países del mundo (y de muchas de las islas que éstos poseen)*, Buenos Aires, 3rd edition.
Pajarola, Jano Felice 1997 *Raeti Incogniti: Vergangenheit, Gegenwart und Zukunft der Räterforschung*, www.jfp.ch/inhalt/bw/infos/raeti/raeter_inhalt.htm.
Pardo Mata, Pilar 2002 *Mediterráneo: Fenicia, Grecia y Roma*, Madrid.
Pausanias 1971 *Guide to Greece*, London, 2 vols.
Pauwels, Jacques 2006 *Een geschiedenis van de namen van landen en volkeren.* Berchem.
Pei, Mario. *The Story of Language*, New York, 1960.
Petracca, Francesco. *Antichità italiche ed etrusche*, Catania, 1985.
Philippa, M, Debrabandere, F, & Quak, A 2003, 2005 *Etymologisch Woordenboek van het Nederlands,* vols 1(A- E) and 2 (F – Ka), Amsterdam.
Postel, Verena 2004 *Die Ursprünge Europas: Migration und Integration im frühen Mittelalter*, Stuttgart.
Prayon, Friedhelm 1996 *Die Etrusker: Geschichte – Religion – Kunst*, Munich.
Prezzo, Rosella & Redaelli, Paola 2002 *America e Medio Oriente: luoghi del nostro immaginario*, Milan.
Renfrew, Colin 1990 *Arqueología y lenguaje: La cuestion de los orígines indoeuropeos*, Barcelona. (First published in 1987 as *Archaeology and Language: The Puzzle of Indo-European Origins*, London.)
—— 1996 *L'Europa della preistoria*, Rome and Bari. (First published in 1979 as *Before Civilization: The Radiocarbon Revolution and Prehistoric Europe,* Cambridge.)
Roberts, David 1842 *The Holy Land: Syria, Idomea, Arabia, Egypt & Nubia.* London.
Roberts, J M 2004 *Ancient History: From the First Civilizations to the Renaissance*, London.
Rodinson, Maxime [1968] 1994 *Mahomet*, Paris.
Room, Adrian 1994 *African Placenames: Origins and Meanings of the Names for Over 2000 Natural Features, Towns, Cities, Provinces and Countries*, Jefferson, NC & London.
—— 1996 *Placenames of Russia and the Former Soviet Union: Origins and Meanings of the Names for over 2000 Natural Features, Towns, Regions and Countries,* Jefferson, NC & London.
—— 2006 *Placenames of the World: Origins and Meanings of the Names for 6,600 Countries, Cities, Territories, Natural Features and Historic Sites*, Jefferson, NC & London, 2nd edition.
Rübekeil, Ludwig 1992 *Suebica: Völkernamen und Ethnos*, Innsbruck.
Ruhlen, Merritt 1994 *The Origin of Language: Tracing the Evolution of the Mother Tongue*, New York.
Ruiz-Gálvez Priego, Marisa 1998 *La Europe Atlántica en la Edad del Bronce: Un viaje a las raíces de la Europe occidental,* Barcelona.
Russo, Lucio 2003 *La rivoluzione dimenticata: Il pensiero scientifico greco e la scienza moderna,* Milan, 3rd edition.
Schirokauer, Conrad 1991 *A Brief History of Chinese Civilization*, New York.
Schmid, Wolfgang P 1994 *Linguisticae Scientiae Collectanea: Ausgewählte Schriften von Wolfgang P Schmid anlässlich seines 65. Geburtstages*, Berlin & New York.
Schmidt, Alexander 1992 *Geschichte des Baltikums: Von den alten Göttern bis zur Gegenwart*, Munich & Zürich.
Schuller, Wolfgang 2002 *Griechische Geschichte*, Munich, 5th edition.
Schwertheim, Elmar 2005 *Kleinasien in der Antike*, Munich.
Semerano, Giovanni 1984 *Le origini della cultura Europea: Rivelazioni della linguistica storica*, Florence.
—— 1994a *Le origini della cultura Europea. Vol. II. Dizionari Etimologici : Basi semitiche delle lingue indeuropee. Dizionario della lingua greca,* Florence.
—— 1994b *Le origini della cultura Europea. Vol. II. Dizionari Etimologici : Basi semitiche delle lingue indeuropee. Dizionario della lingua latina e di voci moderne*, Florence.

—— 2001 *L'infinito: un equivoco millenario. Le antiche civiltà del Vicino Oriente e le origini del pensiero Greco*, Milan.
—— 2003 *Il popolo che sconfisse la morte: Gli etruschi e la loro lingua*, Milan.
—— 2005 *La favola dell'indoeuropeo*, Milan.
Sergent, Bernard 1995 *Les Indo-Européens: Histoire, langues, myths*, Paris.
Shastri, Ajay Mitra 2005 Indo-European original home and language are myths. Tripathi, D N (ed.) pp. 97-109.
Shipley, Graham 2000 *The Greek World after Alexander 323-30 BC*, London & New York.
Slifkin, Nosson 2004 *The Camel, the Hare, and the Hyrax: A Study of the Laws of Animals with One Kosher Sign in Light of Modern Zoology*, Southfield, MI.
Smith, William 1910 *A Smaller Classical Dictionary of Biography, Mythology, and Geology,* London.
Snowden, Frank M jr 1970 *Blacks in Antiquity: Ethiopians in the Greco-Roman Experience*, Cambridge, MA.
Taylor, Isaac [1863] 1893 *Words and Places or Etymological Illustrations of History, Ethnology and Geography*, London & New York.
Thapar, Romila 2003 *The Penguin History of Early India: From the origins to AD 1300*, New Delhi.
Thoraval, Yves 1999 *Lexikon der islamischen Kultur*, Darmstadt.
Tripathi, D N 2005 The Indo-European homeland: an Indian perspective. Tripathi, D N (ed.), pp. 21-41.
Tripathi, D N (ed.) 2005 *A discourse on Indo-European languages and culture.* New Delhi.
Udolph, Jürgen 1994 *Namenkundige Studien zum Germanenproblem*, Berlin & New York.
Unesco 1986 *Reports and papers of the symposium organized by Unesco in Paris 16 to 18 January 1984.* Paris.
Urmes, Dietmar 2003 *Handbuch der geographischen Namen: Ihre Herkunft, Entwicklung und Bedeutung*, Wiesbaden.
van Berchem, Denis 1967 Sanctuaires d'Hercule-Melqart: Contribution à l'Etude de l'expansion phénicienne en Méditerranée, *Syria*, XLIV, p. 73 ff.
van der Ben, Dick 2000 *La forêt de Soignes: Passé – Présent – Avenir*, Brussels, 2nd edition.
van Istendael, Geert 1989 *Het Belgisch labyrint : De schoonheid der wanstaltigheid*, Amsterdam.
van Loon, Jozef 2006 Een etymologie en haar historische implicaties: De stamnaam Caerosi (De bello gallico 2.4), *Verslagen en Mededelingen van de Koninklijke Academie voor Nederlandse Taal- en Letterkunde,* vol. 116, pp. 375-400.
—— [forthcoming] Neue Erkenntnisse und Hypothesen über die Germanenstellen bei Caesar und Tacitus, *Beiträge zur Geschichte der deutschen Sprache und Literatur.*
Vennemann, Theo 2003 *Europa Vasconica – Europa Semitica*, Berlin & New York.
Vurpas, Anne-Marie & Claude Michel 1997 *Noms de lieux de la Loire et du Rhône*, Paris.
Weber, Daniela 2006 Völkernamen, Ländernamen, Landschaftsnamen. http://idw-online.de/public/pmid-69648/zeige_pm.html
Wells, H G [1919] 1971 *The outline of history: being a plain history of life and mankind.* Garden City, New York, revised and updated edition.
Wells, Spencer 2002 *The Journey of Man: A Genetic Odyssey*, New York.
Werngeland, Oscar 1909 *Myths of the Norsemen from the Eddas and Sagas.* London: Harrap.
Whitelam, Keith W 1997 The *Invention of Ancient Israel: the Silencing of Palestinian History*, London & New York. [First published in 1996.]
Wiederentstehendes Babylon: Eine antike Weltstadt im Blick der Forschung 1991 Berlin.
Wolfram, Herwig [1995] 2002 *Die Germanen*, Munich, [seventh edition].
Woodhead, A G 1964 *Kunst en beschaving der West-Grieken*, Zeist.
Zehnacker, Hubert (ed.) 1999 *Pline l'Ancien: Histoire Naturelle*, Paris.
Zucca, Raimondo 2005 *Les peuples italiques et les origines de Rome*, Aix-en-Provence.

The abduction of Europa
(Artist: Antonio Carracci [1583-1618]; source: Wikimedia Commons)

INDEX
of names of people(s), places, and languages

Aa 124
Aberdeen 112, 123
Abila 59
Aborigines 107
Abraham 19, 32, 95
Abyssinia 101
Achaean 96
Acropolis 40
Adam 17
Adige 90
Adria 90, 98, 106
Adrianople 135
Adriatic 49, 87-88, 90-91, 96, 98, 106, 127-28, 139, 203
Aegean 49, 70-72, 78, 90, 94, 98-99-100, 125
Aegeus 98
Aemillus Lepidus 106
Aeolic 58
Afghan(istan) 40, 101, 172
Africa(n) 4-5, 10-11, 25, 27, 29, 40-41, 48-49, 59, 61-63, 65-67, 83, 97, 100-02, 136-37, 141, 153, 156, 160, 163-64, 166, 170, 186, 196-97, 199, 202-04, 206
Afro-Asiatic languages 10, 27, 30-31, 53, 62, 198
Agadir 63
Agrigento 94-95, 98
Agrippina 117
Ain 121
Ainu 8, 172
Aisne 121-22
Aix-en-Provence 109
Akhenaton 31-33
Akkadia(n) 10, 20, 22, 24, 31, 35, 38-40, 42, 44, 47, 51-52, 54, 57, 59, 62, 71-72, 76-78, 80, 83, 86-87, 89-90, 93-94, 97-99, 103-04, 106-08, 111, 113, 115, 118-20, 123-25, 129, 135-36, 141, 145, 146-47, 150, 159, 172, 182, 188-92, 198, 200-01

Alalia 81-82
Alamanni(c) 146
Albania(n) [Balkans] 87-89, 120, 126, 170, 201
Albania [Caucasus] 89, 170
Alba(n)(ia) [Scotland] 89
Albany, NY 89
Albi 121
Albion 126-27, 144
Alborz/Elburz 170
Aleppo 121
Alesia 108
Alexander the Great 24, 58, 64, 101-02, 136, 167, 171, 205
Alexandretta 102
Alexandria 101-02, 134, 136, 159, 163, 195, 205
Algarve 164
Algeria(n) 16, 62, 136, 160
Algiers 166
Alhambra 166
Alicante 131
Almoravids 162
Alpheios 121
Alps 6, 87, 90, 105-07, 110, 113, 120, 170, 201, 204
Al Qusr 23; see Luxor
Alsace, Alsatian 130, 146
Altai(c) 140, 171
Altamira 5, 15
Amalfi 195
Amazons 78, 98
Amber Road 106, 139, 188-89
America 1, 107, 147, 172, 185
Amharic 101
Ampurias 79-80
Amu-Darya 171
Anatolia(n) 8, 17-18, 35, 37, 46, 50, 71-72, 75, 82, 100, 202
Andalusia 54, 132, 164, 166, 169, 195
Angle, Anglia 144, 149
Ankara 36, 107
Antibes 80
Antwerp 105

Aosta 110
Apache 7, 172, 198
Apennines 87, 105-06, 201
Apollonia 187
Aquileia 106, 118, 139
Aquitania(n), aquitaine 111
Arab, Arabia, Arabic 3, 10, 12, 20, 24, 26, 28, 30, 38, 48, 53, 56-57, 59, 61-63, 64, 66, 78, 111, 120, 136-37, 142, 153-55, 157-71, 173, 176, 179, 188, 193, 195, 201-02, 205
Arabia Felix 153, 155-56
Aragon 165
Aral Sea 171, 173
Aramaic 31, 35, 39, 61, 85, 157, 159
Ararat 37
Arcadia 9
Armenia(n) 37, 90, 168-69
Armorica 127
Arne 120
Arno 105, 120
Artemis 18
Aryan 11-12, 30, 38-41, 46-46, 84, 197, 203-04
Ashkenazi 195
Asia(n) 7-8, 10-11, 48-49, 65-67, 72-73, 79, 100-01, 136-37, 140, 150, 153, 167-68, 171-74, 177-78, 186, 195, 197, 202, 204-06
Asia Minor 70, 72, 83, 98, 107, 122, 124, 157
Assos 72-73
Assyria(n) 19-20, 30, 35, 60, 64, 67, 72, 74, 100, 134, 153, 159
Astrakhan 194-95
Asturia 165
Athena 11
Athens 9, 98, 123, 200
Atlantic 26-28, 49, 52, 54-55, 58-60, 62-63, 66, 69-70, 79-80, 101, 111, 128-29, 131, 133-34, 163-64, 182-84, 196, 202, 205-06

213

Atlantis 70
Atlas 68-69, 101
Attic(an) 82, 200
Attila 106, 139-40, 143, 150
Aude 120
Aue 124
Augsburg 118, 128, 150
Augustus 46, 110, 113, 118, 125, 132-134, 205
Aurelian 157
Australia 107
Austria(n) 88, 113, 116, 118, 122, 134, 137, 148, 150, 152
Autun 113, 200
Auvergne 90
Avestan 38
Avignon 121
Avon 122
Ayer's Rock 16
Azania 160
Azerbaijan, Azeris 169

Babylon(ian) front cover, ii, 20, 22, 30, 35, 38, 43, 47, 52, 60, 64, 67-68, 71, 73-74, 100, 107, 119, 155, 157, 159, 167, 190, 198
Baden-Württemberg 117
Bad Pyrmont 130
Baffin Island 185-86
Baghdad 3, 167-68, 175, 194-95
Balearic, Baleri 27, 60, 86
Balkan(s) 5, 24, 88, 96, 142, 148
Ballon d'Alsace 130
Baltic 6, 118-19, 141, 186-88, 190-91, 194-96, 203
Bantu 160
Barbarian 28, 139, 151
Barbary 28, 166
Barcelona 60, 80
Basque 7, 10, 19, 23-24, 29, 46, 83, 97, 111, 129, 132, 165, 198-200, 203
Bastia 81
Bavaria(n) 122, 145, 150, 152
Bayonne 129
Bayuwar 145-46
Bedouins 153
Beijing 175, 179
Beirut 48
Belchen 130
Belgian, Belgic(a), Belgium 112, 115-16, 124, 127, 147-48
Belgrade 112, 124, 135
Ben (first element in name of many Scottish mountains) 87

Benghazi 101
Beothuk 186
Berber(s) 10, 12, 25-27, 29, 50, 63, 97, 101, 136-37, 151, 161, 163-64, 166, 198-99, 202, 204
Bering Strait 172
Berlin 107, 122
Bern 122-23, 152, 203
Bharat ('India') 43
Biarritz 129
Bilbao 129
Biscay 50, 54, 80, 111, 129, 131
Black Forest 130, 146
Black Sea 37, 49, 72, 75-78, 90, 100, 124, 177, 188, 190, 194, 196
Bohemia(n) 145, 152
Bokhara 172
Bologna 106, 120
Bonn 106
Bordeaux 111
Bosnia 106, 120
Bosporos 76-77, 190
Bothnia(n) 189-90, 203
Boyar 145
Boulogne 106
Braunau 152
Brazil 156
Bregenz 122
Brennus 105
Breton 127-28, 203
Britain, Britannia, British 5-6, 41, 43, 54, 80, 87. 89, 112, 115, 124-28, 144-45, 149, 171, 182, 203, 205
Britannic, Brittany 6, 54, 63, 80, 113, 127-28, 135, 203
Brno 122, 152, 203
Bruges 183
Brussels 122
Buddha, Buddhism, Buddhist 98, 173
Bulgaria(n) 194-95
Burgundian, Burgundy 80, 112-13, 120, 143, 145, 205
Byblos 31, 48-49, 57
Byzanteum, Byzantine 24, 64, 77, 125, 135, 142-44, 152, 158-59, 162, 188, 190-91, 193-95, 200, 204

Cabo Fisterra 134
Cadiz 55, 59, 102, 111, 164
Cadmos 74
Caesar, J 24, 108-09, 111, 114-17, 123, 125, 127, 132-34

Cairo 159-60
Calais 133
Caledonia 127, 145
Calpe 59, 164
Campania 92, 95
Canaan(ite) 31, 33-35, 47-48, 50-51-54, 57-60, 62, 64, 69, 75, 79, 94
Canada, Canadian 185-86
Canary Islands 27-29
Candia 131
Cannes 131
Cantabria(n) 129, 131, 134, 165, 176
Cantal 131
Canterbury 131
Canton(ese) 168, 179
Cape of Good Hope 137
Carcassonne 121
Caria 122
Carinthia 122
Carnac 6
Carpathian 121, 151
Carpentras 121
Carrara 122
Carthage(na), Carthaginian 30, 49, 51, 58, 60-63, 68, 80-82, 85-86, 93-95, 132, 136-37, 141, 162-63
Casablanca 161-62
Caspian Sea 37-38, 171, 188, 192, 196
Castile, Castilian 129, 165, 195
Catalan 79
Çatal Hüyük 17
Cathay 176, 178-79
Catalonia 86
Caucasian, Caucasus 5, 7, 9, 19, 37-38, 83, 90, 168-69, 193
Celtiberians 107, 126, 128
Celt(ic) 8-9, 13, 46, 87, 105-09, 111, 113-18, 120-22,125-28, 133, 144-45, 148-49, 152, 183, 198, 200-01, 203-04
Cerdagne 86
Cervin(o) 122
Ceuta 164
Chalkedon 77
Changan 3, 136, 168, 178
Channel Islands 193
Chantilly 132
Chatillon-sur-Seine 80
Chechens 9, 37
Chersonesos 75-76
China, Chinese 3, 7, 45, 58, 73, 136, 140, 153-55, 157, 168,

171, 173-79, 193, 197-98, 202
Christ 61, 155
Christendom 3, 176
Christian(ity) 18, 24, 59, 94, 107, 112, 114, 136, 152-53, 158-59, 162, 165-66, 168-69, 174, 176, 188, 195-96, 202
Chur 122
Ciane River 94
Cleopatra 24
Clovis 142-43, 145
Colli Albani 121
Colmar 146
Cologne 117-18
Colombia 156
Columbus, C 1, 68, 102, 129, 185, 196
Compostela 110
Constantine 77, 135-36
Constantinople 23-24, 56, 76, 135-36, 152, 188, 190-91, 193, 195, 200
Cook, J 199
Copt(ic) 24, 159
Cordoba 56, 165-66, 195
Corfu 97, 122
Corinth 122, 129-30
Cornwall 54, 80, 149
Corsica 80-81
Cossack 174
Costa Brava 79
Covadonga 165
Crassus 134
Cretan, Crete 5, 19, 49, 70, 83, 86, 98, 122, 131
Crimea 177
Croat(ia)(n) 64, 88, 102, 135, 151-52
Crusade(r) 193-96
Cumae 96
Cumberland 149
Cyclades, Cycladian 99-100
Cypriot, Cyprus 49-50, 60, 64
Cyrenaica, Cyrene 49, 101-02, 136-37
Cyrus 64
Czech 145, 148, 152

Dalmatia(n) 88, 102, 187
Damascus 30, 145, 155, 158, 166
Damavand 131, 170
Dan 123, 201
Danaean 96
Dane, Danish 118, 182, 190
Danube 78, 88, 116-17, 123-24, 128-29, 135, 140, 145, 150, 194, 201
Dar es Salaam 160
Dardanelles 72, 75-76
Daun 112
Dead Sea 48, 123
Delos 99
Delphi 77, 99
Demeter 18
Dené-(Sino-)Caucasian 7-8, 19, 172, 198
Denmark 118, 181, 190
Deutsch(land) 1, 146, 203
Diana 18
Dinan 112
Dinant 112
Dnieper 78, 123, 190, 195, 201
Dniester 123
Dol-en-Bretagne 142
Don (Russia) 123, 201
Don (Scotland) 123
Donegall 112
Dordogne 111
Dorian, Doric 71, 94, 96
Dover 126, 131, 133
Dravidian(s) 19, 41, 43-44, 74
Druid 44
Dublin 183
Dubrovnik 187
Dumbarton 112
Dumfries 112
Dun 112
Dunbar 112
Dundee 112
Dunedin 112
Dunfermline 112
Dungall 112
Dunhill 112
Dunlop 112
Duoro 133
Durrës 88
Dutch 9, 14, 24, 46, 51, 124, 147-48, 182-83

East Anglia 144
Eberbach 123
Ebersberg 123
Ebro 79, 132, 165
Eden, Garden of 17, 40
Edinburgh 112
Edirne 135
Egypt(ian) 3, 5, 10-13, 16, 20-26, 30-34, 36, 44, 47-50, 53, 62-63, 67-68, 70-71, 83, 85, 98, 100-02, 136-37, 154-57, 159-60, 162, 198, 200, 202, 204-05
Elam(ite) 19, 44

Elba 81, 86, 91-92
Elbe 120, 126, 201, 204
Elche 54
Emilia 106
England, English 51, 72-73, 80, 85, 87, 89, 108, 111, 115-16, 122-27, 129, 131, 134, 137, 142, 144, 146-47, 161, 169, 182-83, 186, 200, 203
Ephesus 18, 100
Epirus 96-97, 203
Erik the Red 184-85
Erin 125
Eritrea(n) 156
Erzgebirge 81
Eskimo 172, 186, 198
Essex 144
Estonia(n) 46, 120, 150, 187, 190, 195
Ethiopia 25, 63, 101, 156
Etna 93, 95
Etruria, Etruscan, Etruscoid 3, 9, 13, 46, 51, 81-85, 87-88, 90-91, 96, 103-06, 140, 150, 172, 198-99, 204
Euphrates 16, 20-21, 32, 37, 48
Europa 74, 77, 204, 212
Europe(an) 3, 5-6, 8-12, 26-27, 29-31, 45-50, 54-56, 59, 65-66, 71, 74-78, 83, 86, 90, 112, 115, 119-20, 124, 131, 134-35, 137, 142, 147, 150, 152-53, 157, 160, 162, 164, 166, 171, 174, 177-79, 181, 186-88, 190-92, 194-97, 200, 202-06
Eve 17
Everest 173

Faro 102
Faroes 183
Farsi 167
Fiesole 105
Finland, Finn(ic), Finnish 5, 46, 150, 171, 187, 189-90
Finno-Ugric 150, 171, 187-89
Flanders, Fleming, Flemish 105, 123, 131, 148, 183
Florence 82, 105, 114, 120
Foglia 106
Forêt de Soignes 122
France 1, 72, 80, 108, 111, 120, 122, 127, 129, 131-32, 141, 143, 145, 166, 177, 182, 205
Franconia, Frank(ish) 3, 8, 42, 64, 142-43, 145-46, 165
Fréjus 109

French 1, 8, 24, 28, 41, 50-51, 53, 64, 72-73, 75, 81, 86-87, 89, 92, 97, 100, 102, 106-10, 112-15, 118-24, 129-31, 146-48, 152, 164, 183, 186, 193, 199, 201-02
Friuli 110

Gabes 101
Gadir 53, 55, 58-60, 63, 79-80, 111, 133, 169
Gaelic 89
Galatian 107-08
Galicia 54, 79, 111, 133-34
Gallia Belgica 115
Gallia Cisalpina 105, 107
Gallia Transalpina 107
Gallic 80, 109, 111, 113-16, 127, 145, 148, 200, 202, 205
Gallipoli 75-76
Garamants 97
Garda 122
Garonne 80, 111, 121, 142
Gascon(y) 129, 132
Gaul 1, 8, 42, 44, 80, 87, 105, 107-11, 113-17, 122, 124-25, 127-28, 139, 141-43, 145-46, 148, 200, 204
Gdansk 188
Geneva 86, 115, 148
Genghis Khan 174-75, 177
Genoa(n) 29, 70, 76, 81, 86, 195
Georgia(n) 37-38, 168-69
German, Germanic, Germany 1, 9, 19, 24, 36, 39, 41, 51, 72, 81, 83-84, 87, 96-97, 107, 112, 115-20, 122-24, 128, 130-31, 140-52, 164, 177-78, 182-83, 187-88, 191, 195-96, 199, 201-02, 204-05
Germanicus 117
Ghent 131, 176
Gibraltar 5, 52, 59-60, 69, 94, 164, 205
Gironde 80, 111
Giza 23
Golden Fleece 75, 78
Golden Horde 177
Golden Horn 77, 195
Goth(ic), Gotland 119, 140-43, 145, 164, 186
Graia 96
Granada 165-66
Great Wall of China 175, 178-80
Greece, Greek 1-2, 8, 10-13, 16, 18, 20, 22-25, 28, 31, 34, 37, 40, 43, 45, 47-50, 54-55, 57-62, 64-86, 88-104, 107-08, 110-13, 115-16, 118, 121-22, 125, 127, 132-33, 135-37, 150, 152, 155-57, 159-60, 163, 170-71, 176-77, 181, 183-84, 188, 190, 192-94, 197, 199-200, 203-05
Greenland 184-86
Greenwich 182
Guadalquivir 53-55, 132, 205
Guanches 28-29
Guangdong 168
Guangzhou 168, 179
Guinea 29, 63, 202
Guyenne 111
Gypsies 24-25, 45, 152, 199

Hadrian 52, 132, 138
Ham, Hamite, Hamitic 10, 19, 22, 25-26, 30, 53, 83, 101
Hamilcar 60-61
Han 8, 136, 155, 178, 198
Hannibal 60-61, 132
Hanno 63
Harappa(n) 12, 40-45, 198
Harun Al-Rashid 167
Hattusas 36
Hay(astan) 37
Hebrew 10, 18, 25, 31-35, 39, 52, 57, 59, 62, 71, 83, 87, 97-98, 106, 115, 119, 123, 141, 153, 159, 189
Hebrides 183
Hellas, Hellenes, Hellen(ist)ic 1, 9, 11, 24, 55, 59, 67-69, 71, 75, 78-81, 84, 91-99, 101-04, 107, 113, 136-37, 156, 184, 192, 204
Helle 75, 95
Hellespont 75-76
Helsinki 190
Helvetia(n) 113
Hercules 53, 59, 66, 69, 110, 134
Hermes 111-12
Hesperia 79-80
Hibernia 125, 204
Himalayas 40-41, 173
Himilco 63
Hindi 41, 98
Hindu 171
Hiram 57
Hispania 49, 52, 78, 132, 166
Hitler 39, 152
Hittite 30, 35, 45-46, 71-72, 159, 199
Homer 16, 71, 75, 96
Huelva 52, 54

Hun 106, 139-40, 142-43, 150, 172, 198-99
Hungarian, Hungary 24, 88, 135, 150-51, 171
Hvar 102
Hyrcanian 192

Iberia(n) [Spain/Portugal] 3, 5-6, 25, 27, 29, 37, 49-54, 56, 60, 79-80, 83, 86, 97, 102, 107, 111, 125-27, 129, 131-34, 142, 164-66, 197-99, 203, 205
Iberia [Georgia] 37
Iberos 79
Ibiza 86
Iceland 119, 183-84
Idrisi 195
Ilion 72
Ill 146
Illyria(n) 3, 87-88, 90, 96, 112, 187, 198
Ilm 115
Ilmen 115
Imazighen 28
India(n) 5, 10-13, 19, 24-25, 38, 40, 43-46, 101, 153, 168, 171-73, 176, 203, 205
Indian Ocean 137
Indo-Aryan 38
Indo-European 1, 3, 8-13, 35, 38-41, 44, 46, 49, 71, 83-85, 91, 96, 103-04, 106, 111, 115-16, 119-20, 123, 126, 142, 147-48, 150, 167, 170, 173, 197, 203-05
Indus 12, 16, 20-21, 40-45, 101, 170-71, 200
Inn 122, 200
Inuit 172, 186, 198
Invernia 125
Ionia(n) 67, 75, 96, 98, 100
Iran(ian) 11, 38-40, 45-46, 84, 151, 154, 167-68, 170-72, 194, 203
Iraq(i) 16, 19, 48, 167
Ireland, Irish 125-26, 183, 189, 203-04
Irun 132, 199
Isaac 32-34
Ischia 91
Iskenderun 102
Islam(ic) 26, 61, 153-54, 158-59, 162-63, 166-69, 171, 173-74, 176
Isphahan 170
Israel(ite) 30-35
Issoudun 112

Istanbul 135-36, 191
Italian, Italy 10, 24, 28, 39, 46, 51, 71-72, 75, 80-87, 90-96, 98, 100, 103, 105-06, 108-10, 117, 120, 122-24, 136-37, 139, 141-43, 147-48, 166, 195-97, 202, 204

Jacob 32
James I 127
Japan 73, 136, 172, 175, 179, 202
Jerez 164, 169
Jerusalem 35, 52, 57, 158
Jew(ish) 30, 34-35, 49, 52, 158, 166, 195
Jordan 30-32, 34, 123, 155, 201
Juda(ism) 35, 153, 195
Jute, Jutland 145

Kabul 40
Kabylians 28
Kahlu 134
Kairwan 58, 162-63
Kale 133-34
Kalymnos 127
Kandahar 102
Kantharos 131
Kara Kum 171
Karakorum 175
Karpathos 122
Kashgar, Kashi 172-73
Kashmir 171
Kassiterides 69
Kazakh(stan) 172-74
Kazan 194
Kemit(e) 3, 21-23, 26, 43, 74, 205
Kent 131, 176
Kerkyra 122
Khartoum 21
Khatan, Khitan 176
Khazar 195
Kiev 190, 195
Kirghistan, Kirghizia(n) 172-73
Kizil Kum 171
Koblenz 118
Konstanz 128, 203
Korea 175
Koressos 100
Kublai Khan 175-76, 178
Kurds 36, 64
Kyoto 175

Labrador 185-86
La Coruña 134
Ladino 195
La Napoule 80

Langobards 143
Languedoc 112, 120
L'Anse aux Meadows 185-86
Lanzarote 29
Laon 113
Lapp 190, 199
Lascaux 5-6, 15
Las Medulas 54, 132
Latin 23, 27-28, 30, 42-43, 46, 50-51-52, 55-56, 61-62, 66, 77, 85, 87-88, 90-93, 95, 97, 101, 103-04, 106-07, 109, 111-27, 129-31, 133, 136-37, 142, 144-47, 149-51, 164, 166, 178, 182, 188, 191-92, 194, 197, 199-200, 203-05
Latium 103, 106
La Turbie 110
Lausanne 148
Lazio 103
Lebanese, Lebanon 30-31, 48, 64, 72, 90, 123, 155
Lech 128, 150
Le Creusot 81
Leiden 113
Leie 115, 131
Leiff Ericson 184-85
Leman 115
Léon 54, 132, 165
Leptis (Magna) 49, 137
Le Puy-en-Velay 112-13
Les Maures 166
Levant(ine) 31, 47, 59-60, 64, 71, 157, 193, 202
Libya(n) 4, 16, 25-26, 60, 63, 70, 74, 86, 97, 101, 136-37, 160, 202
Liffey 183
Liguria(n) 80, 86-87, 91-92, 107, 110, 115, 203
Lisbon 133, 166
Lithuania(n) 120, 188
Liverdun 112
Loire 112, 115, 120, 201
Lombard, Lombardy 143, 205
London 124, 164
Lothal 43
Loudun 113, 124
Louis IX (St. Louis) 177
Louis XVI 114
Lucca 111
Lugo 111
Lusitania 133
Lutetia 114
Luxeuil 111
Luther 35, 147

Luxor 23
Lydia(n) 82-84, 204
Lyon 111-13, 200
Lys (river) 115

Macedonia(n) 64, 87-88, 101
Madrid 54
Maghreb 160-62, 167
Magna Graecia 91, 95-96, 103-04
Magyar(s) 3, 149-50, 176, 189, 199, 205
Malacca 60
Malaga 59-60
Malay 179
Mallorca 64, 86
Malta 6, 60, 64
Mandarin 175, 177, 179-80
Marcomanni 145
Marco Polo 176, 178-80
Marmara 75-76, 124
Marne 122
Marrakech 161
Mars 110
Marseilles 80-81, 86, 108
Martel, C 165
Massachusetts 185
Masurian 185
Matapan 97
Matterhorn 87, 122
Mauritania 62, 137, 166
Mecca 153, 155, 158
Medes 38-39
Medina 158
Mediterranean 1, 5, 19, 27, 33, 37, 48-50, 55, 58-62, 64-66, 68-71, 75, 78-84, 94, 101, 103, 109-10, 118, 122, 132-34, 137, 141, 159-60, 192, 196-97, 199, 205
Médoc 111
Megara 77
Mehmet the Conqueror 136
Melkart 55, 57, 59, 61, 69, 110
Memphis 22, 24, 35, 49, 159
Merida 132-33
Mesopotamia(n) 3, 5, 10-11, 16-17, 20, 30-32, 37-42, 44-45, 47-48-49, 67, 72-73, 90, 96, 123, 127, 153-54, 157, 159, 167-68, 171, 175, 192, 197, 202
Messena 94
Messina 94
Metz 112
Meuse 112, 124
Mezzogiorno 202
Middlesex 144
Midi 202

Milan 106, 143
Minoan 5, 70-71, 83, 86, 99
Minorca 86
Minsk 195
Misr (Egypt) 159
Mocha 156
Moesia 124
Mogador 63
Mohammed(an) 153-54, 158-59, 167-69, 172, 174
Mohenjo-Daro 40
Monaco 110
Mongol(ia)(n) 19, 171-80
Monti Metalliferi 81
Montmartre 114
Mont Saint-Michel 112
Moor(ish) 137, 166
Moravia 152
Morbihan 54, 128
Morrocan, Morocco 26, 28, 52, 55, 62-64, 68, 137, 153, 161-62, 164, 166
Moscow 124
Moselle 118, 124, 135
Moses 33-34
Moskva 124
Mostar 120
Mughulistan 174
Musbury 124
Musgrave 124
Muslim 38, 137, 153-54, 158, 162, 166-67, 169, 171, 173, 176, 193, 195
Mycenae(an) 45, 70-72, 75, 78, 97
Mysia 124

Nabataean 155
Nanking 175
Naples 80, 91-92
Napoleon 81
Narbonne 80, 106, 110
Narva 120
Naukratis 100
Navajo 7
Navarra 165
Naxos (Capo Schiso) 94
Nebuchadnezzar 52, 60, 64
Nepal(ese) 173
Neretva 106, 120
Neris 120
Nero 117
Nerva 120
Netherlandic, Netherlands 14, 109, 113, 147-48
Newfoundland 129, 185-86
Nice 80

Niiemen 188
Niger 17, 30, 204
Nigeria 30
Nile 3, 11, 13, 16, 20-22, 26, 30, 43, 48, 63, 100-02, 136, 159, 197, 201
Nimrud 134
Niniveh 43
Nordic 118, 182, 188, 196, 203, 205
Norman(dy) 95, 112, 126, 182, 195, 205
Norse(men) 181-88, 191, 193, 195
North Sea 118, 120, 131, 144, 183-84
Norway 119, 181, 183, 186
Nova Scotia 185
Novgorod 188-90, 192, 194-95
Nubia 25, 101
Numidia(n) 62, 136
Nuremberg 145

Odenathus 157
Olympia 121
Oman 155
Omar Khayyam 167
Ophir 63, 156
Oqba 163
Omsk 172
Orange 109
Orkneys 184
Ortygia 94
Ostrogoth 142
Oxus 171

Padua 90
Paestum 66, 92-93, 95
Pakistan 25, 170-71
Palatine Hill 104
Palaeo-Berber 26-28, 53, 59, 62, 198
Palermo 56, 93-94, 195
Palestine 34-36, 49, 155, 158
Palmyra 157
Pamirs 40, 171, 173
Pamplona 132, 200
Pannone, Pannonia 87-88, 134, 150
Paris 113-15, 132, 182
Parthian 38, 102, 136
Pelasgian 8, 28, 73, 77, 81, 83-84, 86-88, 92-93, 95-97, 99, 116, 198, 200, 202, 204
Pelops 97
Peloponnese, Peloponnesus 75, 94, 97, 121

Pennine Alps, Pennines 87, 201
Pennsylvania 147
Péronne 122
Persepolis 38, 43; see also Persian
Persia(n) 8, 13, 16, 37-39, 43, 64, 67, 78, 100-01, 136, 153, 157-58, 167, 169-72, 179, 188, 203
Pesaro 1-6
Petra 153-55, 157
Pharaohs, Pharaonic 3, 13, 20-22, 26, 31-33, 36, 48-49, 63, 68, 100, 159, 201
Pharos 102, 134
Philistines 33-35
Phocaca 80
Phoenicia(n) 1, 12, 31, 47, 49-65, 68, 70, 74-75, 78-86, 93-94, 104, 113, 132-33, 136-37, 157, 159-60, 163, 166, 169, 188, 198, 203-04
Pict 127
Piedmont 92
Pillars of Hercules/Melkart 58-59, 63, 66-70, 75, 79, 94, 133-34, 163,
Piombino 81
Piraeus 131
Pisa 105-06, 195
Pithecusa 91-92
Plato 70
Po 87, 90, 106, 123, 143, 201
Poitiers 165
Poland, Pole, Polish 187-88, 191
Pompei 92
Pompey 132, 205
Pontic 78, 142, 191
Populonia 81
Port-aux-Basques 129
Porto 133
Portoferraio 81
Portugal, Portuguese 54, 102, 133, 137, 161-62, 164, 168, 196
Poseidon 97-98
Provence 80, 108-09, 111, 131, 166
Prussia(n) 152
Pskov 195
Puni(c) 60-61, 69, 80-82, 95, 107-08, 132
Punjab 43, 171
Punt 156
Pygmy 16
Pyrene 129-30
Pyrenees 5, 50, 86, 110, 120-21, 129, 131, 142, 165, 172

218

Qin-Shihuang 178
Queen of Sheba 156

Rabat 162
Raeti(a)(n), Raeto-Roman(sh) 86-88, 121
Rasenna 84, 140, 172, 199
Ravenna 142-43
Red Sea 62-63, 156-57
Regensburg 106
Reggio di Calabria 94
Reims 115
Remus 82, 103-04, 204
Renne Rive 120
Reno 120, 201
Reykjavik 184
Reza Shah 39
Rhine 6, 115-20, 124, 140, 143, 145-46. 201
Rhodes 122
Rhone 80, 109-11, 113, 121, 123, 201
Rialto 139-40
Richelieu 132
Rio Tinto 53-55
Riviera 86, 110, 131
Roger II 195
Roma (Gypsies) 25, 45
Romagna 144
Roman 3, 8, 22-25, 28, 30, 42, 46, 50-52, 54, 56-57, 59, 61-64, 66, 77, 79-82, 84-88, 90-91, 94-96, 101-20, 122-23, 125, 127-29, 131-39, 141, 143-46, 149-50, 152, 155-58, 163-66, 168, 170, 178, 183-84, 191-92, 197, 199-200, 202, 204-05
Romance 92, 147-49, 151
Romania(n) 25, 148
Rome 23, 25, 61, 103-05, 108, 118-19, 121, 132, 136, 140, 142, 155, 157, 200, 203
Romulus 82, 103-04, 204
Rouen 182
Runic 191
Rus(sia)(n) 6, 8, 38, 115, 120, 142, 152, 172, 174, 176-78, 187-88, 190-91, 194-95, 205

Saar 135
Saba 156
Sabine 85, 117
Sagunto 30
Sahara(n) 4-7, 9-13, 16-22, 27-28, 30, 35, 39-42, 44-46, 53, 62-64, 83-84, 86, 88, 101, 117, 119, 129, 137, 160, 172, 197, 200-02, 205
Saint Denis 114
Saint Petersburg 120, 189
Salé 166
Salerno 92
Salian 145
Samar[i]a 19
Samarkand 172
Samnite 85, 104
San Miniato al Monte 114
Sanskrit 12, 25, 41-46, 131, 173, 203
Santiago de Compostela 134
Santorini 70
Saône 80, 111, 113, 122, 201
Saracen 160, 193
Saragossa 132
Saraswati 40
Sard, Sardic, Sardinia, 49, 60, 64, 71, 85-88, 199
Sark 193
Sarkozy 193
Samarkand 176
Sarmatia(n) 78, 187, 190, 199
Sassanian 136, 157-58, 167, 169-70
Satan 18
Saxon(y) 118, 144, 146, 149
Scandinavia(n) 119, 125, 141, 182-84, 186, 188, 190, 195
Scheldt 123, 131
Scilly Isles 54, 93
Scipio Africanus 132
Scot(land), Scottish 30, 87, 89, 126-27, 145, 183-84
Scythia(n) 78, 107, 142, 187, 190-92, 199
Segesta 95
"Sea Peoples" 33-34, 36, 71, 85
Seine 80, 113, 122, 182, 201
Selinunte, Selinus 94-95
Semite(s), Semitic 8, 10-12, 26, 30-31, 35, 38-43, 47-53, 57, 61, 67, 70, 72, 74, 78, 83, 115, 118, 120-21, 153-55, 157, 160, 171, 189, 191, 205
Senne 122
Seoul 175
Sephardic Jews 52, 195
Serb(ia)(n) 88, 151-52
Serkland 193-94
Seuil de Naurouze 80
Seville 54-55, 107, 132, 166
Sextius Calvinus 109

Shandong 173
Shanxi 173
Sheba 156
Shiite 160
Shiraz 169
Siberia(n) 7-8, 140, 172, 197
Sicilian, Sicily 49, 60, 64, 71, 91, 93-95, 195
Siculi, Sikeloi 93
Sidon 31, 48-49, 57
Sierra Morena 53, 55, 81
Silk Road 3, 155, 168, 178, 193, 195
Sinai 35, 48
Sindh 25, 170-71
Sinis 35
Sinti 25
Sion 35
Skraeling 186
Slav(ic) 88-89, 135, 145, 149-52, 174, 176, 187-92, 202-03, 205
Slovenia 150
Soloman 34, 52, 56-58, 63, 156
Somalia 156
Somport 110
Sorrento 92
Spain, Spaniard, Spanish 19, 24, 29, 37, 39, 50-55, 57, 60-61, 64, 79-81, 86, 111, 120, 128-29, 131-33, 137, 141-42, 161-62, 164-65, 169, 171, 195-96, 198-99
Sporades 100
Stonehenge 6
Strasbourg 146
Sudan 21, 26, 62, 101, 155, 160
Sumer(ian) 10, 13, 16-20, 24, 31, 41, 43-44, 51, 68, 81, 83, 85, 87, 90, 103, 106, 111, 115, 136, 150, 198
Sussex 144
Swabian 117
Swahili 160
Swede(n), Swedish 181, 186-90, 192
Swiss, Switzerland 86-87, 112-13, 120-22, 130, 146-48
Syracuse 94-95
Syria(n) 30, 48, 121, 154-55, 157-58, 193
Syrte, Syrtis 101

Tabor 35
Tagus 133, 142
Taj Mahal 172
Tajik(istan) 172

Taklamakan 173
Talas 173
Tallinn 190, 195
Tamerlane 176
Tamil 41, 44
Tangiers 49
Tanna 199
Tanzania 160
Tarim 45, 173
Tariq 164, 166, 171
Tarn 121
Tarquinia 84
Tarshish 63
Tartar 177
Tartessian, Tartessos 53-55, 58, 60, 69, 79, 82, 94, 133, 166
Taunus 112
Teheran/Tehran 170
Teide (volcano) 28
Temse 123-24
Tenerife 28
Teutonic 147
Thames 73, 123-24, 131, 135, 183
Thebes 23, 73, 200
Theodoric 123
Thera 70-71
Theseus 98
Thessalonika 152
Thrace, Thracian 76, 192
Thuin 112
Thule 119, 125, 184
Thun 112
Thuringia(n) 146
Tiber 60, 92, 103-04, 120-21
Tibet 173
Tien-Shan 173
Tigris 16, 20-21, 32, 37, 134
Tin Islands 69, 80
Tocharian 45
Tokyo 175
Toledo 142, 144, 162, 164, 166
Toul 142
Toulouse 111, 142
Tours 115, 165
Trafalgar 164
Trajan 132
Trapani 93
Trèves 118
Trier 118
Tripoli(tania) 137
Troy 72, 75
Tuaregs 28
Tunis(ia) 60-62, 64, 101, 137, 160, 163
Turin 106
Turk, Turkey, Turkic, Turkish 8, 36, 60, 64, 76, 78, 98, 120, 134-36, 150, 154, 169, 171-74, 188, 194-95
Turkestan 171-73
Turkmenistan 172, 183
Tuscany 82, 103, 122, 199
Tut Ankh Amun 25, 49
Tyre 30, 48-49, 57-60, 74, 93
Tyrrhenian, Tyrrhenol, Tyrsenol 82-84, 91, 106, 204

Ugaritic 85
Uighur 173
Uluru 16
Umbrian 85
Ur 19, 32
Urartu 37
Urdu 171
Urusalim 35
Usko-Mediterranean 7-10, 12, 18-20, 23-24, 27, 30, 32, 35, 37, 39-40, 44-47, 50-51, 57, 59, 71-73, 77-79, 81, 83-90, 92-97, 99-100, 103-07, 110-13, 115-16, 118-31, 133-36, 140, 142, 145, 150, 160, 163, 165, 170-72, 176, 182, 184, 188-91, 194, 197-201, 203-05
Uzbekistan 172, 176

Valencia 166
Vandal(ia) 139-41, 164, 166
Vannes 128
Varangian 190-91, 193, 195-96
Vedas, Vedic 40-42, 46
Veneti(c) 87, 90, 106, 127-28, 130, 139, 150, 189
Venetians, Venice 70, 75-76, 88, 90, 106, 131, 139, 189, 195, 201, 203
Ventoux 130, 201
Vercingetorix 108-09
Verdun 112, 203
Verona 122-23, 152, 203
Vesoul 92, 201
Vesuvius 73, 92, 201
Vézelay 92, 201
Vienna 135, 150
Viking 3, 181-83, 185, 187-88, 190-96, 205
Vinča 135
Vindelici 116, 128
Vindu 127, 130
Vinland 185-87
Virginia 185
Visigoth 142-43, 145, 164

Viso 92
Volga 177, 192-95
Volkhov 188, 194
Volterra 81
Vosges 130

Wales 126-27, 149
Wallachia 148
Wallonia, Walloon 148
Waset 23
Wasserkuppe 131
Welschland 148-49
Wertach 128
Weser 145
Wessex 144
Wien 135
Wimbledon 112
Windsor 135
Wutan 155

Xanadu 178
Xian 3, 136, 168, 178
Xinjiang 45, 173-74

Yadz 169
Yemen(ite) 155-57, 202
Yiddish 195
Yonne 122
Yverdun 112

Zagora [Morocco] 88
Zagora Dalmata 88
Zagoria 88
Zagros 40, 88
Zakros 88
Zakynthos 30
Zama 62
Zankle 94
Zanzibar 160
Zenobia 157
Zeus 11, 74-75, 77, 97, 184, 204
Zion 35
Zoroastrian 167, 169

Made in the USA
Charleston, SC
23 April 2011